Pragmatism as
Anti-Authoritarianism

Pragmatism as Anti-Authoritarianism

Richard Rorty

Edited by Eduardo Mendieta

Foreword by Robert B. Brandom

THE BELKNAP PRESS OF
HARVARD UNIVERSITY PRESS

Cambridge, Massachusetts, and London, England

First Harvard University Press paperback edition, 2024
First printing

Library of Congress Cataloging-in-Publication Data

Names: Rorty, Richard, author. | Mendieta, Eduardo, editor. | Brandom, Robert,
    writer of foreword.
Title: Pragmatism as anti-authoritarianism / Richard Rorty ; edited by Eduardo Mendieta;
    foreword by Robert B. Brandom.
Description: Cambridge, Massachusetts : The Belknap Press of Harvard University Press,
    2021. | Includes bibliographical references and index.
Identifiers: LCCN 2021007200 | ISBN 9780674248915 (cloth) | ISBN 9780674295476 (pbk.)
Subjects: LCSH: Pragmatism. | Authoritarianism. | Ethics.
Classification: LCC B832 .R584 2021 | DDC 144/.3—dc23
LC record available at https://lccn.loc.gov/2021007200

Contents

FOREWORD

Achieving the Enlightenment

ROBERT B. BRANDOM

Pragmatism as Anti-Authoritarianism is Richard Rorty's long-lost, last book.[1]
Its first English-language publication is an epoch-making event. Written ten
years before his death, this volume presents Rorty's final, mature version and
vision of his path-breaking pragmatism. Further, it announces a substantially
new phase in the development of that view. At its core is a commitment to
human self-determination. The principal animating and orienting impulse of
pragmatism is now identified as its anti-authoritarianism. Its ultimate goal is
our emancipation, both in practice and in theory, from subjection to non-
human authority. Pragmatism points us at the sort of freedom that consists in
humans taking full rational responsibility for our own doings and claimings.

On this conception, pragmatism is an intellectual movement of world-
historical significance. Rorty construes pragmatism as aiming at nothing
less than a second Enlightenment—as offering what is needed properly to
complete the task begun in early modern times by the first Enlightenment.
The key to the conceptual division of labor he envisages between the two historical phases of the Enlightenment is the "anti-authoritarianism" of the
title—a theoretical and a practical attitude. It is the rejection in both spheres
of the traditional understanding of authority and responsibility in terms of
subordination and obedience. It is to be replaced by a conception of judging
and acting as exercising the authority to undertake commitments that come
with a correlative responsibility to justify them, to offer reasons for them that
can be assessed by our fellow discursive practitioners.

As Rorty is thinking of it, the great achievement of the original Enlightenment is on the side of ethics. In broadest terms, it is substituting the secular for the sacred in our understanding of the source and nature of our most

fundamental obligations. The tradition that the Enlightenment reacted against and recoiled from took normative statuses of authority and responsibility to be independent of the attitudes of those whose statuses they were. Norms were understood as ontologically determined by the objective structure of things, epitomized by the *scala natura,* the Great Chain of Being. That is a hierarchical ontological structure of superiority and subordination, in which superiors have the authority to command and subordinates the responsibility to obey. (It is what determines "My station and its duties," as the title of F. H. Bradley's essay has it.) It is a natural structure with intrinsically normative significance. In its later Christianized form, it is taken to have been instituted by the supernatural fiat of the ultimate superior and authority, God. Thence derives the "divine right of kings," devolved through the various feudal ranks, bottoming out in the righteousness of man's dominion over the beasts. In both forms, those that take the norms to be read off of the natures of things and those that also take those normatively significant natures to be supernaturally ordained, the ultimate source of our responsibilities and obligations lies outside of us, in something non-human, in the way things anyway are, apart from and independently of our practical activities and attitudes. Our job is to conform our attitudes and practices to these normative statuses of superiority and subordination, authority and responsibility, about which we don't have a say.

From the pragmatist point of view that Rorty sees as prefigured by the Enlightenment, both the natural and the supernatural versions of this traditional picture are *fetishistic,* in Marx's technical sense. They reify what are in fact the products of human practices and project them into the non-human, merely natural or supernatural, world. By contrast, in its finest flowering in social contract theories of political obligation such as those of Hobbes, Locke, and Rousseau, Enlightenment thought grounds normative statuses of authority and responsibility instead in human attitudes and practices of consent, negotiation, and agreement. In seeing this humanizing of the norms governing our practical activity as the core Enlightenment insight, Rorty is at one with Kant's account in his popular essay "Was Ist Aufklärung?" For there Kant construes the Enlightenment as announcing the emancipation and coming to maturity of humanity, our casting off our juvenile need for and dependence on normative tutelage from without, in favor of the adult dignity that consists in ourselves taking responsibility for our ultimate commitments.

In the background of this understanding of the message of the Enlightenment is Kant's account of positive freedom: the freedom *to* do something one could not otherwise do, as opposed to the negative freedom that consists in freedom *from* some constraint. Kant understands freedom as autonomy: the authority to bind ourselves (*autos*) by norms (*nomos*), to acknowledge and undertake commitments, *making* ourselves responsible by *taking* ourselves to be responsible. The resulting constraint of commitments is intelligible as distinctively *normative* constraint (as opposed to the matter-of-factual constraint of compulsion by greater power) just insofar as it is the result of *self*-binding. This conception radicalizes what Kant learned from Rousseau's dictum that "obedience to a law one has prescribed for oneself is freedom."[2] For Kant turns Rousseau's definition of freedom into a criterion of demarcation of the genuinely normative. By analyzing normativity in terms of autonomy—a distinctive kind of positive freedom—Kant moves decisively beyond the traditional understanding of normativity in terms of subordination and obedience. Here the central inspiration of the Enlightenment achieves its most explicit self-conscious expression. This articulation of the intimate and ineluctable connection between freedom and genuinely *normative* bindingness underwrites a distinctive liberal, democratic approach to politics. It shows up as having as its implicit *telos* that everyone who is *bound* by a law should have a say in *imposing* that law: the ideal of universal suffrage, in the sense of according all those bound by (responsible to) laws the authority to make them.

The edifying lesson Rorty sees the Enlightenment as teaching is that fear of God and fealty to His authority are to be replaced by human freedom, self-reliance, and solidarity in the form of individual autonomy on the side of ethics, and social commitment to and participation in liberal political practices and institutions, on the side of politics. Our practices are the real source of our commitments and responsibilities, and those practices should be understood as involving no authority beyond what we institute and exercise by engaging in them. Instead of looking outside of human practice for our ultimate commitments, we are to look to what emerges in conducting the human conversation. Liberal political institutions are to structure that conversation procedurally—in effect, to provide the *language* in which that conversation takes place. This is anti-authoritarianism on the side of our practical activity. The theme of *Pragmatism as Anti-Authoritarianism* is that pragmatism should be understood as defined by its commitment to bringing about a *second* Enlightenment. Its task is to broaden the anti-authoritarian lesson of the first Enlightenment beyond the practical sphere, applying it to the theoretical sphere. It is to be applied not only to ethics and politics, but to epistemology.

Rorty admits that the extension he proposes is not one the philosophers of the original Enlightenment envisaged or endorsed. Early in Lecture 2 of this book he tells us

> The anti-authoritarianism which was central to the Enlightenment . . . finds its ultimate expression in the substitution of the kind of fraternal cooperation characteristic of an ideal democratic society for the ideal of redemption from sin. The Enlightenment rationalists substituted the idea of redemption from ignorance by Science for this theological idea, but Dewey and James wanted to get rid of that notion too. They wanted to substitute the contrast between a less useful set of beliefs and a more useful set of beliefs for the contrast between ignorance and knowledge. For them, there was no goal called Truth to be aimed at; the only goal was the ever-receding goal of still greater human happiness.

The Enlightenment's critical rejection of religious obedience was complemented by its constructive endorsement of scientific knowledge. But Rorty sees a crucial analogy between the idea of the authority of a non-human God over proprieties of practical conduct (what it is good to do) and the idea of the authority of a non-human Reality over proprieties of theoretical belief (what it is good to think and say). As he says in a different version of the lecture given here as Lecture 1:

> There is a useful analogy to be drawn between the pragmatists' criticism of the idea that truth is a matter of correspondence to the intrinsic nature of reality and the Enlightenment's criticism of the idea that morality is a matter of correspondence to the will of a Divine Being. The pragmatists' anti-representationalist account of belief is, among other

things, a protest against the idea that human beings must humble themselves before something non-human, whether the Will of God or the
Intrinsic Nature of Reality.

Rorty's idea is that the concept of Reality plays the same invidious role for
the pragmatist Enlightenment on the cognitive side that God played for the
original Enlightenment on the practical side.

He finds this thought already in the classical American pragmatists. On
this conception, their thought is rooted in that of the British Utilitarians of
the nineteenth century: Jeremy Bentham, James and John Stuart Mill, and
Alexander Bain. The American pragmatists show up as extending their
thought from the practical realm, to apply also to the cognitive realm. What
is extended is the idea of the relativity of values to human interests—the
thought that practical norms are ultimately to be derived from the needs and
wants of the desiring beings understood to be subject to those norms. The
pragmatists assimilate doxastic, cognitive, theoretical conduct oriented to
reality and truth to practical, intentional, value-reflecting conduct oriented
to the right and the good, viewing them as different species of a common
genus. A bit later in Lecture 1 Rorty tells us that

> what Dewey most disliked about both traditional "realist" epistemology
> and about traditional religious beliefs is that they discourage us by telling
> us that somebody or something has authority over us. Both tell us that
> there is Something Inscrutable, something which claims precedence
> over our cooperative attempts to avoid pain and obtain pleasure.

At the center of the version of pragmatism Rorty announces in this book is
the thought that just as we should be anti-authoritarian in ethics in rejecting
the authority of God over the correctness of what we do, we should be anti-
authoritarian in epistemology by rejecting the authority of objective reality
over the correctness of what we believe. Construed as the non-human locus
of this sort of authority, Reality no more exists than God does.

This is a radical idea. It is one thing to emancipate ourselves from practical domination by the patriarchal dictates of what William Blake called
"Old Nobodaddy." That is in a certain sense something we can do by coming
to suitably redescribe and reconceive ourselves. For what we are freeing

ourselves from is a snare powered by a delusion. (Here we can still think of
the truth as setting us free.) We have a pretty good idea both of what it is to
understand ourselves to live in a God-less world, and even what it is like
actually to live in such a world. The same cannot evidently be said about
emancipating ourselves from constraint by objective reality.

The ideal of autonomy that sees us as ultimately bound by no moral facts
or moral laws we do not ourselves set, or at least acknowledge, is an intelligible and in many ways attractive one. But don't we have to think of ourselves
as bound by objective facts and laws of nature whose constraint does not depend at all on our acknowledgment of them? (For Kant, that is the fundamental distinction between constraint by laws, "natural necessity," and constraint by *conceptions* of laws "practical necessity.") The idea that we could
emancipate ourselves from *that* sort of constraint by any kind of redescription or reconceptualization seems to depend on a kind of magical thinking
located somewhere between extremely implausible and just plain crazy.

Of course, that is not the sort of position Rorty is urging on us. Traditionally, the concept of objective reality is called on to play a dual role. As Rorty
often says, it is understood to be at once both the *cause of sense* and the *goal
of intellect*. The first concerns causal relations, the second, normative ones.
This fundamental Kantian distinction between norms and causes shapes
Rorty's thought throughout his life. He wholeheartedly endorses the idea of
reality as *causally* constraining us. In this regard, his pragmatism is wholly
naturalistic. Like classical American pragmatism, it is essentially a Darwinian
naturalism rather than a Newtonian naturalism. It construes us as at base
animals coping with our environment. Objective reality forces itself upon us
by its recalcitrant resistance to our wants and the sometimes surprising and
disappointing consequences of our actions, forcing us both to adapt it to our
ends and to adapt to it ourselves. It is the physical arena we act in and deal
with, setting Deweyan "problems" and framing Deweyan "inquiries" with
which creatures like us respond.

Rorty's issue is with how we conceive the other, normative, dimension: the
sense in which reality also functions as the "goal of intellect." He is concerned
to deny a particular picture of that epistemic goal. He often marks the conception that is his target by using an uppercase "R" in referring to the target
of his objections. The capital letter does not just indicate derision—though
of course, it does that, too. Rorty uses it to demarcate a specifically *represen-*

tational understanding of the cognitive relation to what causally conditions and constrains us that we are aiming at. Reality with the invidious "R" is reality as the nondiscursive end of a representational relation: reality as what cognition aims to represent. Rorty wants to teach us how to live without that representationalist idea of Reality, as we have learned to live without the idea of God.

Representation is the core concept of Enlightenment epistemology. In many ways, it has dominated philosophical thinking about the relations between mind and world ever since. As its title indicates, this conception is the target of Rorty's criticism in his first monograph, *Philosophy and the Mirror of Nature* (hereafter *PMN*)—the book that made him famous. The paradigmatic expression of the representationalist picture of mind as the mirror of nature is Spinoza's. Because "the order and connection of things is the same as the order and connection of ideas," nature and God's mind are two modes of one substance, two aspects of what there is, "Deus sive natura" (God or Nature). Spinoza concludes that any cognitive progress our finite minds make in better mirroring nature, eliminating the flaws of our errors and the gaps of our ignorance, is also progress in making our finite minds more identical with the infinite mind of God.

The premodern philosophical tradition understood the relations between mind and world, appearance and reality, in terms of *resemblance*. Resemblance is a matter of sharing some properties, as a good picture shares properties of color and shape with what it is a picture of. The correspondence of thought with thing that makes a thought true and so a candidate for knowledge is their sharing something: an Aristotelian form, or participation in the same Platonic Form. Error occurs when the appearance in the mind and the reality it seeks to know do not resemble one another by sharing a form.

Descartes saw that the new science of his day made this picture untenable. Copernicus taught that the reality of which the stationary Earth and the moving Sun were appearances was a rotating Earth and a stationary Sun. No shared properties there. Galileo taught that the best, most veridical appearance of periods of time was lengths of geometrical lines, and further—and from the point of the resemblance model, worse—that the most veridical appearance of accelerations was the areas of triangles. At this point, resemblance has been left wholly behind. Descartes invents the new, more abstract philosophical notion of *representation* to help in the understanding of these

new, vastly more successful theoretical guises in which the reality of the
natural world could appear to us in science. The paradigm of representational
relations is the correspondence Descartes worked out between algebraic for-
mulae and geometrical figures, in his analytic geometry. The equations
"$x^2+y^2=1$" and "$x+y=1$" do not at all resemble the circle and the line they
determine. But correspondences such as that between the two simultaneous
solutions of those equations and the two points of intersection of those figures show that the algebraic representings are veridical appearances that give
us a hitherto unparalleled grip on the geometrical reality they represent. (Spinoza saw that this worked because the *local* isomorphism required by the
resemblance model had been replaced by a *global* isomorphism of equations
and figures—the "order and connection" of algebraic ideas that was the same
as the "order and connection" of geometrical things—and drew deep *holist*
semantic and metaphysical conclusions that would be of central significance
for later German Idealism.)

The new Enlightenment representational paradigm was immensely productive in epistemology and the philosophy of mind. Exploiting this metacon-
ceptual resource is one of the common philosophical strategies that binds together Descartes's British Empiricist and Continental Rationalist successors.
The rationalists were less willing than the empiricists to treat representational
relations as unexplained explainers: primitives from which to elaborate their
philosophical theories. But both Spinoza and Leibniz accepted the need to
explain representation as a principal criterion of adequacy of their epistemological theories. They sought to do so in terms of the relation of being a reason
for, paradigmatically the relation of premise and conclusion of an inference,
which was for them more basic in the order of philosophical explanation.

But the advance to the more abstract model of representation came with a
cost. Giving up the requirement that representing appearances share properties with, and so resemble the reality represented by them drives a wedge
between appearance and reality. It makes possible a wholly new, substantially
more corrosive sort of skepticism than that available on the old resemblance
picture. For it raises a worry about whether the whole realm of mental representings might swing entirely free of any represented reality, and how, epistemically confined as we seem to be to our representings, we could know
whether or not things are as they are represented to be, whether they really
are as they appear.

In *PMN* Rorty argued that representationalist understandings of mind and meaning originally developed by early modern philosophers and still dominant in updated-form twentieth-century analytic philosophy doomed their advocates to an unfruitful oscillation between skepticism and foundationalism. Foundationalism shows up as the only alternative to skepticism when one considers the practices of reasoning that might justify knowledge-claims. Conceptions of justification that lead either to an infinite regress or to circularity seem themselves to be in the end themselves forms of skepticism. The only non-skeptical alternative (within what is sometimes called the "Agrippan trilemma" in epistemology) is then foundationalism. Rorty characterizes its strategy as the postulation of "epistemically privileged representations" that function as regress-stoppers. Regresses on the side of premises—justifying p by appeal to q, and then q by appeal to r, and so on—terminate in representings given in sensation, paradigmatically something looking (appearing) red. Regresses on the side of inferences—where the skeptical challenge is not to premise q offered as a reason for the conclusion p but for the implication of p by q—terminate in the subject's grasp of the meanings of the terms or the contents of the concepts deployed in the knowledge-claims p and q. Both kinds of representations are understood as characterized by the distinctive kind of epistemic privilege Descartes used to demarcate minds from bodies, as Rorty identified it in his classic 1970 paper "Incorrigibility as the Mark of the Mental."

For it is a structural requirement of the representational picture of the mind and its knowledge of reality that if anything is to be known representationally, something must be known *non*-representationally. If the reality I know is known by being represented by my representings of it, then I must know my representings themselves in some other way than just by representing them in turn. For the alternative would launch a *semantic* regress, of representings of representings of representings . . . in which no terminal knowledge is ever finally achieved. If representational knowledge (or even awareness) is to be possible, at some point, there must be representings of which I am aware simply by *having* them, rather than by representing them. Their occurrence must be self-intimating. The idea of knowledge mediated by representings presupposes the idea of immediate knowledge of representings. That is the Cartesian idea of the mind as the locus of representing events (sensings and thinkings) whose very existence already guarantees the subject's knowledge of their existence. Their contents must be immediately, non-representationally available. Since error is understood as *mis*-representation, that immediate knowledge of the appearings that are representings must be immune to error: incorrigible.

Rorty takes it that the great achievement of mid-century analytic philosophy was the thoroughgoing critique of Cartesian regress-stopping privileged representings. It had the effect, he thought, of driving a stake through the heart of foundationalism, and thereby the representational paradigm itself. He saw one aspect of it as carried through by Wilfrid Sellars against the idea of judgments to which we are epistemically entitled in virtue solely of what is given to us in sensation, in his masterwork "Empiricism and the Philosophy of Mind." He saw a complementary aspect of it as worked out by W. V. O. Quine against the idea of judgments justified wholly by our grasp of their meanings, in his critique of analyticity in his classic "Two Dogmas of Empiricism." That these two landmark philosophical works, though in many ways quite different, can be seen as illuminating two sides of one coin, as ways of working out one unified line of criticism, is one of Rorty's deepest and most original insights. It is a paradigm of how a way forward philosophically can be opened up by redescribing how we got to where we are.

It was by thinking hard about how Sellars's and Quine's arguments worked, and what they had in common, that Rorty worked out his own view, as presented in his 1982 book, *Consequences of Pragmatism*. He found in classical American pragmatism, especially as articulated by James and Dewey, the basis of an alternative to the representationalist tradition that he had argued was doomed to find itself forced to choose between an untenable foundationalism and an unpalatable skepticism. At the center of his version of pragmatism is a social practice theory of normativity in general. *Normative* statuses, he claims, are always and everywhere *social* statuses. That we should understand norms not as features of the natural or even supernatural world, but as instituted by the practical attitudes we adopt to one another was, for him, one of the principal orienting lessons of the Enlightenment, epitomized by social contract theories of political obligation.

Without calling it "pragmatism," Rorty had called upon understanding normative statuses in terms of social practices already in his early papers on eliminative materialism. He begins there by understanding Cartesian minds in terms of the epistemic status of incorrigibility. As we've seen, where error is explained as consisting in misrepresentation, some representings must be taken to be immune to the possibility of error. Otherwise, not only knowledge but the possibility of error itself is unintelligible. That thought is what led Descartes to his unprecedented assimilation of thoughts, images, and pains as species of a genus. Rorty goes on to understand incorrigibility in normative terms: as a distinctive kind of *authority*. The authority of sincere, contemporaneous first-person reports of whether one is in pain or of what one is currently thinking have a distinctive kind of authority: they cannot be overridden by any evidence available to other subjects. In the decisive third step of his argument, Rorty then analyzes that authority as a matter of the role such sincere, contemporaneous first-person reports play in the practices of a community. That authority, he claims deflatingly, should be understood as consisting just in how such reports are taken or treated by other practitioners. That social status of unoverridability need not be understood as grounded in or reflecting any independent ontological fact. It is *just* a distinctive status conferred by a contingent constellation of social practices and attitudes.

He had begun this line of thought by trying to answer Wallace Matson's question "Why isn't the mind-body problem ancient?" Rorty concludes by observing that the practices that institute the distinctive kind of authority that is Cartesian incorrigibility are historically variable. Our practices did not always have this shape, and they might change again to a different one. Progress in neurophysiology might lead us to treat scientists' claims about what is going on in a subject's brain as potentially overriding their sincere first-person reports of being in pain, imagining a triangle, or thinking of a fish on a dish. The social normative status of incorrigibility of such reports would then no longer exist—and so, Rorty argues, neither would the Cartesian minds that we had genuinely had so long as our practices instituted the right sort of authority. The result of the telling redescription of incorrigibility as a normative status instituted by social practices of taking or treating some reports *as* incorrigible is eliminative materialism about Cartesian mindedness.

On this way of understanding it, Rorty's argument for eliminative materialism is the origin story of his pragmatism. If one understands knowledge, or truth, or being the goal of intellect or inquiry, as normative statuses, then a social practice account of normative statuses in general will entail a kind of *pragmatism* about those statuses. It will consist in understanding those normative statuses in terms of their role in our practices, and understanding how playing that role can institute that sort of normative significance and confer it on some of our doings. What then comes to the fore is not *relations* of representation or truth to something external that grounds those normative statuses, but our *practices* of giving, asking for, and assessing reasons, of justifying our commitments (both theoretical and practical) to our fellows. To call something a *reason* is to offer a *normative* characterization of it: to attribute to it the capacity to confer on a commitment a distinctive kind of *entitlement* or *authority*. Pragmatist epistemology focuses to begin with on our social practices of reasoning and justifying—things we *do*. The relation of truth that some of our doings, thought of as representings, might have to bits of our environment, thought of as represented by them, would be brought into the story only later, and only if and insofar as postulating such representational relations is needed or at least helpful to explain some feature of the practices of intelligent coping in which justifying and the giving and assessing of reasons plays a starring role.

Rorty sees both Sellars and Quine, each in his own way, as offering critiques—of the Myth of the Given (Sellars) and the Myth of the Museum (Quine), immediate sensuous and semantic knowledge, respectively—that are at base pragmatist arguments in this sense. Sellars offers a social-practical deflation of the incorrigibility of claims about how things merely look or appear. He analyzes that normative status reflecting the fact that such claims have the significance of overtly *withholding* the endorsement that would be made by the corresponding claim about how things really are. "The coin *looks* elliptical" is noncommittal, having something like the force of "I am tempted to say that the coin *is* elliptical, but I suspect my responsive dispositions might not be reliable under these conditions, so I'm not willing to commit myself to that." Such a claim is incorrigible because no substantive commitment is being undertaken by such a manifestation of a disposition. Further, one can only withhold endorsements one is capable of making, so the incorrigibility-through-virtual emptiness of "looks" claims makes sense only in an environment where one can already make risky claims about how things are. So the latter accordingly cannot be understood in terms of the former. Quine points out the fragility of the unfalsifiability of statements such as "Bachelors are unmarried males" that are supposed to be true in virtue of the meanings of their terms alone, and the practical functional indistinguishability of claims like this from platitudinous general truths such as "There have been black dogs." In this way he queries whether any feature of our actual practices of holding on to some claims "come what may" in the way of challenges is actually explained by postulating a distinction between those made true by what we mean and those made true by what we believe. In each case, the normative status of claims that possess the epistemic privilege invoked to terminate potential regresses of justification is exhibited to be the fragile, contingent product of optional features of our discursive social practices. So Rorty could see the pragmatism he was articulating as arising implicitly already within the immanent critiques to which the latest, logical empiricist incarnation of the representationalist tradition had given rise in the 1950s.

However, as he elaborated the pragmatism that he intended to provide a constructive alternative to the semantic and epistemological representationalism that had structured the philosophical tradition from Descartes through Kant, and then from Wittgenstein's *Tractatus* through Carnap, Tarski, and Quine down to his colleague David Lewis, Rorty came to be dissatisfied with *PMN*'s criticism of that model as skewering us on the fork of skepticism and foundationalism. Looking back, in the intellectual autobiography he wrote just before his death in 2007, Rorty says, "I still believe most of what I wrote in *Philosophy and the Mirror of Nature*. But that book is now out of date."[3] Already by the 1980s it seemed that nobody cared about the epistemological issues of skepticism and foundationalism anymore.[4] Those issues just didn't loom large enough or seem threatening enough in the philosophical landscape of the last decades of the twentieth century to rest the critique of the representational paradigm and so the recommendation of pragmatism on the need to evade those alternatives. Even so, representationalism remained rampant and reigned supreme in contemporary philosophical thought about mind, meaning, and knowledge. Rorty continued to believe that the representationalist paradigm was fatally flawed, and that pragmatism was its situationally appropriate successor conception. In addition to the Deweyan original, he now saw the later Wittgenstein's dethroning of concern with meaning in favor of concern with use (semantics in favor of pragmatics, in a broad sense) and the early Heidegger's critical grounding of the representationalist presence-at-hand expressed by explicit theoretical principles in the social-practical readiness-to-hand of equipment deployed in skillful practical coping as arguing for pragmatism about discursive norms. His greatest recent philosophical heroes were all aligned with his pragmatism. But he needed a new anti-representationalist argument.

Pragmatism as Anti-Authoritarianism announces his discovery of that sought-after alternative, and elaborates his new, *anti-authoritarian* critique of representationalism. As such, it marks a major new stage in the development of Rorty's thought. It can be thought of as based on redescribing representation in normative terms—in much the same way that his argument for eliminative materialism was based on redescribing Cartesian mindedness in normative terms. That is what allows pragmatism in the form of a social practice account of normativity to get a grip. In this case, the insight can be found already in Kant (Rorty's arch-representationalist foe in *PMN*). For one of Kant's axial ideas is his normative construal of intentionality. For him, what distinguishes the judgments and intentional actions of discursive beings from the responses of merely natural ones is that they are subject to distinctively *normative* assessment—both of the subject's reasons for them and for their correctness. Judgments and actions express the subject's *commitments*. They are something the subject is *responsible* for. They are exercises of the subject's *authority* (specifically: the authority to undertake commitments, to make oneself responsible, the form of positive freedom that is autonomy). All of these are normative notions. In this way, Kant moves decisively beyond Descartes's *ontological* distinction between minded creatures and everything else, to redescribe it rather as a *deontological* distinction.

As a consequence of this normative turn, Kant breaks with the tradition and takes the minimal units of awareness to be judgments, rather than concepts or sense-impressions ("ideas"). For judgments are the smallest unit for which one can take responsibility, to which one can commit oneself. (Frege puts the same point by saying that judgeable contents are the smallest logical unit to which pragmatic, paradigmatically assertoric, force can attach. The later Wittgenstein identifies sentences as the smallest linguistic unit that can be used to make a move in a language game.) For Kant the "objective form of the judgment" is "the object $= X$" because the object one is thinking about is what one becomes responsible *to* in judging. In effect, he is pointing out the normative dimension of representation. What is represent*ed* exercises *authority* over what count as represent*ings* of it just in virtue of being *responsible* to it, in the sense that what is represented provides the standard for assessments of the correctness of representings of it. There is, of course, also a dimension of matter-of-factual (and even subjunctively robust *counter*factual) isomorphism between representeds and representings: what Sellars called "picturing." It is what Spinoza invokes with his slogan about the identity of the order and connection of things and the order and connection of ideas. But Spinoza not only failed to appreciate the essentially normative character of the "order and connection of ideas," he failed to appreciate the essential normative dimension of the representational relation between them. Kant fully appreciates both.

I think that the thought that animates Rorty's extension of Enlightenment anti-authoritarianism from ethics to epistemology in *Pragmatism as Anti-Authoritarianism* is precisely this insight into the essentially normative character of representational relations: the sense in which in order to do their appointed semantic job they must be understood as normative relations of *authority* of representeds over representings, and correlative *responsibility* of representings to representeds. It is this idea that brings into relief and makes visible the special, distinctively normative understanding of our causally conditioning environment that Rorty denominates "Reality" and, boldly, puts in a box with "God," denying whose normative authority over human conduct he takes to be the crowning achievement of Enlightenment. For Reality is reality conceived of specifically as what is represented, in the normative sense of exercising authority over human doxastic commitments—that is, as providing normative standards for assessment of their correctness. It is reality understood as a non-human authority to which human cognitive practices are subject.

This idea is the basis for Rorty's anti-authoritarian protest against the conception of reality-as-represented. The objection is that this idea endorses a kind of semantic *tyranny*. Tyranny is authority without correlative responsibility. (It is what Hegel calls "Mastery.") The missing responsibility in question is answerability to demands for *reasons* legitimating that authority. As Kant makes clear, one of the central motivating ideas and commitments of the Enlightenment is that liability to *criticism*—assessment of reasons—and genuine authority are inseparable. Only what can be queried and challenged to justify itself by providing reasons is properly authoritative. For Rorty, this is where God and Reality alike fail the test of critical reason. They are not participants in practices of giving, asking for, and assessing reasons, in justifying and demanding justifications. The lesson he thinks we should learn from the first Enlightenment is that we answer only to each other, that we are beholden to no authority outside our practices. What is authoritative are the reasons we give to each other, the justifications we can offer and assess. Those justificatory and critical practices determine the meanings of the vocabularies we use and the contents of our commitments. We conduct those reasoning practices, deploy our vocabularies, in a natural environment that causally constrains us in many ways. But *normative* constraint is wholly our creature, a historically sedimented accumulation that is instituted by our own social practices and the practical attitudes we adopt while engaging in those practices. That is the conclusion Rorty draws by conjoining his pragmatist social-practical analysis of normativity with an appreciation of representation as a relation of authority and responsibility between representeds and representings. The route from a pragmatist understanding of norms as instituted by social practices to anti-authoritarianism in *epistemology*—the theme of the second, pragmatist Enlightenment that Rorty envisages—goes through a *semantic* understanding of representation in *normative* terms.

I have been telling a story, offering a version in my terms, of the conceptual background, both in the history of philosophy and in the development of Rorty's own thought, that I see as framing the arguments he presents, in his own, characteristically vivid vocabulary in the body of this book (indeed, beginning already in his helpful Preface). I want to register briefly that at this point in the discussion of the concept of *representation* at least, I part company with Rorty. It seems to me that one can both adopt a social-practical approach to normativity and appreciate the essentially normative character of the relations between representeds and representings without concluding— as I think Rorty goes on to do—that *because* normative statuses are always and everywhere *instituted by* social practices, *therefore* authority and responsibility can only be *vested in* or *exercised by* participants in such practices: the ones who can give reasons and so take rational responsibility for the authority they exercise. I take it that the best response to all these considerations is not to adopt global anti-representationalism in semantics. Rather, social pragmatists about normativity should take on the hard work of crafting a pragmatically acceptable account of the sort of authority and responsibility involved in the representational dimension of conceptual contentfulness, and explain how it is instituted and administered by the discursive practices we engage in. I think Hegel already tried to do that, and I have taken some steps along the path he indicates.

Rorty was well aware of this strategic disagreement, and reveled in exploring it. When he originally presented this material in 1996 as the Ferrata Mora lectures at the University of Girona he generously invited me, John McDowell, and Bjørn Ramberg to accompany him as discussants. Our week in that magical Catalan city was filled with lively, extended debates. Rorty addressed some of these controversies in his two final lectures. In Lecture 9 of this book he offers this summary:

> Brandom is, in this respect, to Davidson as McDowell is to Sellars. Each thinks that a distinguished precursor was unfortunately tempted to throw the baby out with the bath. Brandom wants to recuperate "representation" and McDowell wants to recuperate "perceptual experience." It is natural, therefore, that both Brandom and McDowell have doubts about my own version of pragmatism—a version which delights in throwing out as much of the philosophical tradition as possible, and urges that philosophers perform their social function only when they change intuitions, as opposed to reconciling them.

Reflecting on this disagreement with my beloved *Doktorvater* is at the heart of my own philosophical work. Here I want only to acknowledge it, not to pursue it.

For the important point, as I see it, is that in announcing, adopting, and developing in this work his new anti-authoritarian pragmatist argument against the representationalist semantic and epistemological paradigm that has dominated the Western philosophical tradition since Descartes's brilliant and momentous introduction of that framework, Rorty diagnoses a fundamental, but hitherto unremarked, tension in the most basic commitments of Enlightenment philosophy. It is a tension between its critical, humanistic, anti-authoritarian reclamation of ethical and political authority and responsibility from non-human usurpers, on the one hand, and on the other the core strategy of its epistemology: understanding mindedness and meaning in terms of *representation*. Rorty sharpens this tension into a contradiction by redescribing the first as rejection of any picture of creatures who can give and assess reasons but are nonetheless subject to the overriding authority of something non-human that provides a normative standard for assessments of the ultimate correctness of those practices, and redescribing the second as the acceptance of a particular instance of just such a picture. For Rorty, the collision between these ideas is "the little rift within the lute, that by and by will make the music mute, and ever widening slowly silence all." For the proper Enlightenment teaching, he argues, is that we should give up (as pragmatically unintelligible) the normative notion of "ultimate correctness" that is correlated with that concept of "overriding nonhuman authority," in both the practical and the cognitive domains. Whether or not one accepts that conclusion, the redescription Rorty offers in this volume, which makes that tension visible, should be acknowledged as a major contribution to our philosophical thinking about the Enlightenment. It is one of Rorty's Big Ideas.

I want to conclude by pointing out that we are now in a position to appreciate properly the magnitude and significance of the late development in Rorty's thought effected by his adoption of practically progressive Enlightenment anti-authoritarianism as the new basis for his rejection of the whole representationalist tradition in the philosophy of mind and epistemology. For this *Kehre* reveals a popular caricature of that development as not only simplistic, unnuanced, and flat-footed, but as fundamentally wrong-headed. According to this pastiche, after a brief flirtation with analytic philosophy, culminating in his articulation and defense of eliminative materialism, in *PMN* Rorty offered a thoroughgoing criticism of Enlightenment philosophy, and decisively and emphatically condemned and rejected both its rationalism and its empiricism. He dismissed every aspect of Kant's synthesis of these strands of thought, as the culmination of the failed project of Enlightenment philosophy. And Rorty further scorned the whole subsequent tradition downstream for simply continuing to do philosophy, in the sense of "the sort of thing that Kant did." In *Consequences of Pragmatism* he announced and elaborated his constructive alternative: a pragmatism inspired by James and Dewey, but expanded so as to encompass also the early Heidegger and the later Wittgenstein. *Contingency, Irony, and Solidarity* then confirmed Rorty's disdain for Enlightenment philosophy and Kant, and ceases to pretend that his pragmatist alternative is anything other than a contemporary form of Romanticism, and (so) irrationalism. Mimicking the Romantic recoil from the Enlightenment, Rorty displaces natural science in favor of art and politics in assessing the high culture. The role of reason is minimized, and replaced by passion and power in the understanding of human beings. Rorty then confirms his turn away from philosophy toward politics by writing *Achieving Our Country*.

In fact, what Rorty criticized and rejected in *PMN*, and continued to criticize and reject ever after, is only the *epistemology* of the Enlightenment, specifically its placing of its master-concept of *representation* at the center of our philosophical understanding of our discursive practice, reason, and mindedness in general. He wholly applauds the Enlightenment's secular, humanistic, critical, and emancipatory commitments and accomplishments, as theoretically articulating the progressive transformation of traditional institutions and forms of life into distinctively modern ones. As *Pragmatism as Anti-Authoritarianism* makes abundantly clear, Rorty sees the task of pragmatism (as the way forward for philosophy that he recommends) as being the *completion* of the project of Enlightenment. According to his diagnosis, doing that requires correcting its epistemology, so as to repair the deformations wrought by its reliance on the representational model.[5] For, properly understood, that model turns out to be incompatible with essential progressive insights and impulses of the Enlightenment: the distinctive fusion of freedom and responsibility it began to make visible, if at first only dimly. It is in the service of that reformed Enlightenment project that Rorty's pragmatism seeks to frame a broader conception of *experience,* as the ecologically situated socially and historically articulated process of Hegelian *Erfahrung,* rather than as individual self-intimating immediate episodes of Cartesian *Erlebnis.*

As to the charge of irrationalism, I hope my remarks here make clear just how point-missing such a characterization would be. Far from rejecting the notion of *reason,* Rorty seeks a broader, deeper conception of it. To that end, his pragmatism follows Peirce in focusing to begin with on the kind of selectional process common to evolution and learning, and follows Dewey in thematizing the radical transformation wrought by engaging in specifically *discursive* social practices: practices of giving, seeking, and assessing reasons. Rather than jettisoning reason, Rorty argues that the Enlightenment needs to be brought to completion by rejecting the semantic representationalism at the core of its epistemology precisely because that strand of its thought is not compatible with the critical, anti-authoritarian conception of reason and the role of reasoning in the normative life of human beings that he takes to be the principal glory of that movement of thought. Indeed, like his hero Hegel before him, Rorty is, *inter alia,* the prophet of a particular kind of emancipatory reflective reason. For he practices, preaches, and theorizes about the sort of self-consciousness that consists in redescription: in deploying new vocabularies that alter what we take to be a reason for what, and so what we can mean and think. What is on display in this volume is Rorty's pragmatism as his final synthesis of Enlightenment naturalism (the mirror, image of scientific fidelity to nature) and Romantic creativity (the lamp, image of artistic creative genius) precisely as an inspiring new conception of reason.

Preface

The lectures in this volume attempt to envisage what philosophy would be like if our culture became secularized through and through—if the idea of obedience to a non-human authority were to disappear completely. One way of putting the contrast between an incompletely and a completely secularized culture is to say that the former retains a sense of the sublime. Complete secularization would mean general agreement on the sufficiency of the beautiful.

The sublime is unrepresentable, undescribable, ineffable. By contrast, a merely beautiful object or state of affairs unifies a manifold in an especially satisfying way. The beautiful harmonizes finite things with other finite things. The sublime escapes finitude, and therefore both unity and plurality. To contemplate the beautiful is to contemplate something manageable, something which consists of recognizable parts put together in recognizable ways. To be swept away by the sublime is to be carried beyond both recognition and description.

Unlike beauty, sublimity is morally ambiguous. Plato's Idea of the Good is of something sublimely admirable. The Christian Idea of Sin is of something sublimely evil. The romance of Platonism, and of the Beatific Vision, is of something unspeakably precious—something which even Homer or Dante can never hope to capture. The romance of Radical Evil is the romance of something unspeakably depraved, something utterly different from mere failure to make the right choice. It is the deliberate willingness to turn away from God. It is inconceivable how one could make that turn—how Satan could have rebelled. But it is also inconceivable how one could look on the face of God and live.

Not all religions require sublimity, but orthodox Christian theology—the religious discourse which has dominated the West—has always brushed aside the finitely beautiful and the finitely ugly, the finitely benevolent and the finitely vicious, in favor of the infinite distance between us and the non-human being whom we vainly attempt to imitate. This theology borrowed its imagery from Greek philosophy's attempt to abstract from finite human purposes. Carpenters and painters, politicians and merchants, calculate finite means to finite ends. Philosophy, the Greeks said, must transcend such ends.

The metaphors of pure luminosity and abyssal darkness in Plato's *Republic*, and the idea of an unmoved mover in Book Lambda of Aristotle's *Metaphysics* provide the materials for a surrogate religion—one designed to meet the needs of a certain kind of intellectual, the kind obsessed with purity. Such intellectuals have no use for the religions of the people, for their sense of the sublime is too intense to be satisfied by the merely beautiful, their need for purity too great to be satisfied by stories about highly sexed Olympians. The chaste Fathers of the Christian Church inherited from these intellectuals the idea that the first causes of things must be immaterial and infinite— that the beauties of the material world were at best symbols of the immaterial sublime.

After Galileo and Newton, philosophy turned over cosmology, and the question of first causes, to natural science. But the epistemological, subjectivist twist which Descartes gave philosophy produced a new version of the Sublime. This was the infinite, abyssal, unbridgeable gap between our pragmatic minds or jerry-built languages and Reality as It Is in Itself. The problematic of modern philosophy has, I argued in *Philosophy and the Mirror of Nature*, centered around the impossible attempt to cross this gap. The pathos of epistemology is the pathos created by setting ourselves an unreachable goal—defining the point of inquiry as the attainment of a description of reality which would swing free of human needs and interests. Epistemology restages the orthodox Christian narrative of the impossible attempt of a soul burdened by Original Sin to imitate God—the impossible attempt of a conditioned being to live up to the unconditioned.

This pathos is reworked yet again when Kant denies knowledge in order to make room for moral faith—when he tells us that we can give up on the impossible attempt to know things as they are in themselves, but only if we are then willing to take on an equally impossible task. This new task is that of bringing an empirical self under the control of an unconditional moral demand—the demand that none of the components of that self shall serve as a motive for action. "Duty, thou sublime and awful name!," Kant says, reducing both the beautiful and the ugly things of this spatio-temporal world to what Fichte called "the sensible material of our duty." Still later this moralistic version of the sublime was to take the form of the infinite distance that separates us from the Other.

Nietzsche's account of "How the 'True World' Became a Fable" lies in the background of these lectures, as in that of much of twentieth-century philosophy. Nietzsche tells a story of how we got from Plato to Kant, and of how we then awoke from a gradually fading nightmare to "breakfast, and the return of cheerfulness." John Dewey told a complementary story of a post-Kantian awakening by showing how the French Revolution enlarged our sense of the politically possible and how industrial technology has enlarged our sense of other mundane possibilities. These changes, Dewey says, made us realize that we may be able to make the human future very different from the human past: they help us get over the philosophical idea that we can know our own nature and limits. In the last two centuries, it has become possible to describe the human situation not by describing our relation to something ineffably different from ourselves, but by drawing a contrast between our ugly past and present and the more beautiful future in which our descendants may live.

The philosophical views sketched in these lectures offer a way of thinking about the human situation which abjures both eternity and sublimity, and is finitistic through and through. The lectures try to sketch the result of putting aside the cosmological, epistemological, and moral versions of the sublime: God as immaterial first cause, Reality as utterly alien to our epistemic subjectivity, and moral purity as unreachable by our inherently sinful empirical selves. I follow Dewey in suggesting that we build our philosophical reflections around our political hopes: around the project of fashioning institutions and customs which will make human life, finite and mortal life, more beautiful.

Simultaneously with Nietzsche, Dewey urged that we turn our backs on the very idea of Reality as It Is in Itself. Nietzsche saw this idea as an expression of the same weakness, the same masochistic desire to bow down before the non-human, as had permeated Christian "slave-morality." Dewey saw it as a survival of the ancient world's organization of society into artisans and priests. Nietzsche said that if we can get rid of the idea of the True World, we shall also get rid of the idea of a World of Appearance. Dewey added that it would help to get rid of the appearance-reality contrast if we viewed the beliefs we call "true" pragmatically, as tools for adjusting means to ends, rather than as representations of the intrinsic nature of reality.

For Nietzsche and Dewey, the idea that Reality has an intrinsic nature which common sense and science may never know—that our knowledge may be only of Appearance—is a relic of the idea that there is something non-human which has authority over us. The idea of a non-human authority and the quest for sublimity are both products of self-abasement. Pragmatism says that the conditioned is all there is: that human beings have nothing to know save their relations to each other and to other finite beings. To be satisfied with the conditioned, to give up the quest for the infinite, would be to rest content with beauty. Those who have achieved such contentment will see the pursuit of truth as the pursuit of human happiness, rather than as the fulfillment of a desire which transcends mere happiness.

Nietzsche's hostility to the ascetic priests was, unfortunately, combined with a contempt for democracy. He was sickened by the thought of "the last men"—the people who were content with ordinary human happiness. Dewey agreed with Nietzsche that we should set aside ascetic ideals, but he disagreed with him about greatness. Nietzsche feared that human greatness would be impossible if we all became happy citizens of a democratic utopia. Dewey was not interested in greatness except as a means to the greater happiness of the greatest number. For him, great human beings (great poets, great scientists, great thinkers) were finite means to further finite ends. They helped make new, richer, more complex, and more joyful forms of human life available to the rest of us.

Throughout the twentieth century, there has been a struggle between secularists who follow Nietzsche in hankering for a kind of greatness which cannot be viewed as a means to a larger end, and secularists who are pragmatic and finitistic in the manner of Dewey. Heidegger is an example of the former. The early Heidegger found a release from the merely beautiful in the sublime, abyssal thought of death, and also in the contrast between the merely ontic and the sublimely ontological. The later Heidegger contrasted the mere happiness of the inhabitants of a peaceful and prosperous utopia, living with a technologically controlled environment, with the spiritual greatness which would result from a sense of the Truth of Being.

Had Dewey read the later Heidegger, he would have seen nothing wrong with *Die Zeit des Weltbildes*, nor with the technological utopia described and dismissed in *Die Frage nach der Technik*. He would have welcomed a world of beautiful *Gestelle*, beautiful rearrangements of the human and natural world, rearrangements made in order to make possible richer and fuller human lives. Habermas, who did read the later Heidegger, is equally unconcerned with the need for something more than happiness. For those two thinkers, there is nothing higher or deeper to be yearned for than a utopian democratic society—nothing more to be desired than the peace and prosperity which would make possible social justice.

For thinkers of this sort—those who are content with beauty—the proper place for sublimity is in the private consciousness of individuals. The sense of the Presence of God, like the sense of Radical Evil, may survive in the interior space of certain minds. Those minds are likely to be responsible for the production of the great works of the human imagination—for astonishing works of art, for example. But for thinkers like Dewey, Rawls, and Habermas these works are not the proper concern of philosophical reflection. Such reflection should instead be concerned with creating a society in which there will be room for many different forms of private consciousness—for both those who have, and those who lack, a sense of the sublime.

The Heideggerian sense that justice and happiness are not enough persists among post-Heideggerian intellectuals. Sometimes this sense appears in the form of the belief that justice and happiness are "as impossible as they are necessary." The latter phrase appears frequently in the work of Derrida, a great imaginative writer who takes sublimity and ineffability as his principal themes. Similar notions appear in the work of writers influenced by Lacan's notion of "the sublime object of desire"—notably Slavoj Žižek. Lacan and Žižek see both art and politics as centering around an unachievable but unforgettable sublimity, for which the mere beauty of peace, prosperity, and happiness can never substitute.

From the point of view taken in these lectures, the attempt to make sublimity central to reflection on the human future is as dangerous as making God, or Sin, or Truth central to such reflection. As I see it, philosophy should treat the quest for the unconditioned, the infinite, the transcendent and the sublime as a natural human tendency—one which Freud has helped us understand. We should see it, as Freud saw the sublimation of sexual desire, as a precondition for certain striking individual achievements. But we should not see it as relevant to our public, socio-political, cultural prospects.

This means that we should separate the quest for greatness and sublimity from the quest for justice and happiness. The former is optional, the latter is not. The former may be required of us by our duties to ourselves. The latter is required of us by our duties to other human beings. In religious cultures, it was believed that besides these two sets of duties, we also had duties to God. In the completely secularized culture I envisage, there will be no duties of this last sort: our only obligations will be to our fellows and to our own fantasies. So the only place for the sublime will be in the realm of the individual imagination—in the fantasy lives of certain people, those whose idiosyncrasies make them capable of feats which the rest of us find both awesome and inexplicable.

Since I initially broached this suggestion of the need to split the private from the public (in my *Contingency, Irony, and Solidarity*) I have been criticized for trying to put the two in watertight compartments. I have no wish to do that. The utility of imaginative feats, bound by no social norms, for the public discourse of later ages is undeniable. Had thinkers like Plato, Augustine, and Kant, and artists like Dante, El Greco, and Dostoevsky, not aspired to sublimity, the rest of us would not possess the beautiful residues of these aspirations. Our lives would be far less varied, and the forms of happiness for which we are able to strive would be much poorer. But this does not mean that we should arrange our public institutions to suit the quest for greatness or for sublimity.

We have learned from the history of theocratic cultures, and of the quasi-theocratic state religions of the twentieth century, not to think of public institutions as vehicles of greatness. We should think of them as attempts to maximize justice and happiness by whatever makeshift devices (proportional representation, constitutional courts, the random patchwork of associations we call "civil society") give promise of doing the job. We should not expect or want our public institutions to have a firm philosophical foundation—a connection with the nature of Reality or of Truth.

In the spirit of Dewey, we should see these institutions as tools to be justified by their success in getting certain finite jobs done, rather than as instantiations of eternal truths. Moral and political principles should be viewed as abbreviations for narratives of successful use of tools, summaries of the results of successful experiments, rather than as insights into the nature of anything large (Society, or History, or Humanity). We should be as suspicious of attempts to ground political proposals on large theories of the Nature of Modernity as we are of attempts to ground them on the Will of God.

I hope that the contrast I have been developing between beauty and sublimity has given the reader some sense of what to expect from these lectures. I shall end this preface by being a bit more specific about the topics which the lectures cover.

The ten lectures break into five groups of two each. The first two focus on the philosophy of religion. I offer an account of American pragmatism as an attempt to mediate the so-called "warfare between science and theology" which dominated so much of the high culture of the nineteenth century. More particularly, I treat pragmatism as an attempt to let a sense of democratic citizenship take the place of a sense of obligation to a non-human power. My account of Dewey's thought is of an attempt to let participation in democratic politics play the spiritual role which used to be played, in less hopeful ages of the world, by participation in religious worship.

This theme of substituting time and beauty for eternity and sublimity is continued in the second pair of lectures, but in a quite different key. I criticize Jürgen Habermas's idea that assertions are universal validity claims as a last, and unnecessary, attempt to preserve something of the older, pre-pragmatist, Kantian philosophical tradition. I see Habermas's account of "the moment of unconditionality" built into all validity claims as a last echo of Kant's and Husserl's attempt to make philosophy transcendental. I offer an alternative account of linguistic practice, one which eschews reference to both universality and unconditionality, and in which assertions have no aim beyond conversational utility.

The third pair of lectures turns from philosophy of language to what might, somewhat misleadingly, be called metaphysics. In "Pan-relationalism" I argue that a lot of the best recent philosophy can be summed up as an attempt to get rid of the substance-accident and essence-accident distinctions by claiming that nothing can have a self-identity, a nature, apart from its relations to other things. I argue that a thing has as many identities as there are relational contexts into which it can be put. This suggestion chimes with my suggestion (in an essay called "Inquiry as Recontextualization" which I published some years ago) that there is no such thing as "the correct context" in which to read a text, place a person, or explain an event. Rather, there are as many such contexts as there are human purposes. For the same reason, there is no such thing as *the* correct description of anything: there are only the descriptions which, by relating it to other things, put it in contexts which serve our current, varied, needs.

The second lecture in this pair—"Against Depth"—says that if we are pan-relationalists we shall see everything on, so to speak, a single horizontal plane. We shall not search for the sublime either high above, or deep beneath, this plane. We shall instead move things about, rearrange them so as to highlight their relations to other things, in the hope of finding ever more useful, and therefore ever more beautiful, patterns. From this point of view, great intellectual achievements (Newton's laws, Hegel's system) are not categorically different from small technical achievements (getting the pieces to fit together neatly in a piece of cabinetry, getting the colors of the landscape to harmonize in a watercolor, finding a reasonable political compromise between conflicting interests).

The fourth pair of lectures turns to ethics and politics, and is, once again, anti-Kantian in its message. It relies upon John Dewey's attempt to see morality in finitistic terms—as a matter of solving problems rather than of living up to something with a sublime and awful name. I try to weave Dewey's views together with the neo-Humean account of morality offered by Annette Baier, as well as with the political philosophy of Michael Walzer. These three philosophers seem to me to complement each other beautifully, and to help us see our moral task as the enlargement of our moral community—the inclusion of more and more different sorts of people in our use of the term "we." From this perspective, moral progress is not a matter of greater obedience to law but of wider ranging sympathy. It is less a matter of reason than of feeling—less a matter of principle than, as Baier puts it, of trust.

The final two lectures are somewhat more narrow-gauged and less ambitious than those that precede. They concern the work of two contemporary analytic philosophers who have been influenced by many of the same figures (notably Wilfrid Sellars and Donald Davidson) as I have: Robert Brandom and John McDowell. Both men are the authors of books published quite recently (in 1994) which are being widely discussed among anglophone philosophers. I discuss my agreements with Brandom and my disagreements with McDowell in order to place my Deweyan, pragmatist views within the current anglophone philosophical scene.

I regard Brandom's *Making It Explicit* and McDowell's *Mind and World* as analytic philosophy at its best: that is to say, analytic philosophy permeated with historical consciousness, with awareness of the continuities and discontinuities between Greek philosophy, pre-Kantian modern philosophy, and recent reactions against Kant. Both books are extremely ambitious and exceptionally accomplished. So they seemed good dialectical foils to use in clarifying my own position.

Since these lectures cover quite a wide variety of topics and philosophical debates, it may be tempting to think of them as offering a philosophical system. But pragmatists should not offer systems.

To be consistent with our own account of philosophical progress, we pragmatists must be content to offer suggestions about how to patch things up, how to adjust things to each other, how to rearrange them into slightly more useful patterns. That is what I hope to have done in these lectures. I see myself as having shifted a few pieces around on the philosophical chess-board, rather than as having answered any deep questions or produced any elevating thoughts.

Professor Josep-Maria Terricabras, who is responsible for the Ferrater Mora Chair at the University of Girona, not only did me the great honor of inviting me to give these lectures, but kindly invited both Brandom and McDowell—as well as two other philosophers from whom I have learned much, David Hoy and Bjørn Ramberg—to form part of my audience. I am most grateful to Professor Terricabras and his colleagues for their invitation. I am also grateful to the audience in Girona for their penetrating and stimulating questions, and for the generous spirit in which they received my attempts to advance the cause of pragmatism.*

---

* It is important to note when Richard Rorty completed this manuscript of the Ferrater Mora Lectures, or at least this Preface, which he signed "Bellagio, July 22, 1997."

1

Pragmatism and Religion

1. Sin and Truth

The title of this series of lectures perhaps should have been "pragmatism as anti-authoritarianism."* I shall be interpreting the pragmatists' objection to the view that truth is a matter of correspondence to the intrinsic nature of reality on the analogy of the Enlightenment's criticism of the view that morality is a matter of correspondence to the will of a Divine Being. I see the pragmatists' account of truth, and more generally their anti-representationalist account of belief, as a protest against the idea that human beings must humble themselves before something non-human, whether the Will of God or the Intrinsic Nature of Reality. So I shall begin by developing an analogy which I think was central to John Dewey's thought: the analogy between ceasing to believe in Sin and ceasing to believe that Reality has an intrinsic nature.

All footnotes in this volume are the editor's, and Rorty's footnotes are included here as endnotes. The first lecture was published as "Pragmatism as Anti-Authoritarianism" in "Le Pragmatisme / Pragmatism," special issue, *Revue Internationale de Philosophie* 53, no. 207 / 1 (1999): 7–20 (hereafter *RI*). There, the first paragraph reads: "There is a useful analogy to be drawn between the pragmatists' criticism of the idea that truth is a matter of correspondence to the intrinsic nature of reality and the Enlightenment's criticism of the idea that morality is a matter of correspondence to the will of a Divine Being. The pragmatists' anti-representationalist account of belief is, among other things, a protest against the idea that human beings must humble themselves before something non-human, whether the Will of God or the Intrinsic Nature of Reality. Seeing anti-representationalism is a version of anti-authoritarianism permits one to appreciate an analogy which was central to John Dewey's thought: the analogy between ceasing to believe in Sin and ceasing to accept the distinction between Reality and Appearance" (7).
* The first sentence is missing from the Spanish translation.

Dewey was convinced that the romance of democracy—that is, taking the point of human life to be free cooperation with our fellow humans in order to improve our situation—required a more thorough-going version of secularism than either Enlightenment rationalism or nineteenth-century positivism had achieved. It requires us to set aside *any* authority save that of a consensus of our fellow humans. The paradigm of subjection to such authority is believing oneself to be in a state of Sin. When the sense of Sin goes, Dewey thought, so should the duty to seek for correspondence to the way things are. In its place a democratic culture will put the duty to seek unforced agreement with other human beings about what beliefs will sustain and facilitate projects of social cooperation.

To have a sense of Sin, it is not enough for you to be appalled by the way human beings treat each other, and by your own capacity for malice. You have to believe that there is a Being before whom we ought to humble ourselves. This Being issues commands which, even if they seem arbitrary and unlikely to increase human happiness, must be obeyed. When trying to acquire a sense of Sin, it helps a lot if you can manage to think of a specific sexual or dietary practice as forbidden, even though it does not seem to be doing anybody any harm. It also helps to anguish about whether you are calling the divine Being by the name he or she prefers.

To take the traditional correspondentist notion of Truth with full seriousness, you must agree with Clough, that "It fortifies my soul to know / That, though I perish, Truth is so." You must feel uneasy when you read William James saying that "ideas . . . become true just in so far as they help us to get into satisfactory relations with other parts of our experience." Those who resonate to Clough's lines think of Truth—or, more precisely, Reality as it is in itself, the object accurately represented by true sentences—as an authority we must respect.

To respect Truth and Reality in the proper way,* it is not enough to adjust one's behavior to changes in the environment: to come in when it rains, or to shun bears. You must also think of Reality not just as an assortment of such things as rain and bears, but as something which, so to speak, looms behind such things—something august and remote. The best way to get into this way of thinking is become an epistemological skeptic—to start

* Rorty corrected the manuscript, crossing out "relevant" and changing it to "proper way."

worrying about whether human language is capable of representing the way Reality is in itself, whether we are calling Reality by the right names. To worry in this way, you need to take seriously the question of whether our descriptions of Reality may not be all too human—whether Reality (and therefore Truth as well) may not stand aloof, beyond the reach of the sentences in which we formulate our beliefs. You must be prepared to distinguish, at least in principle, between the sort of belief which embodies Truth and beliefs which are merely tools, beliefs which merely increase your chances of happiness.

Dewey was quite willing to say of a vicious act that it was sinful, and of "$2+2=5$" or "Elizabeth the First's reign ended in 1623" that these sentences were absolutely, unconditionally, eternally, false. But he was unwilling to say that a power not ourselves had forbidden cruelty, or that these false sentences fail to accurately represent the way Reality is in itself. He thought it much clearer that we should not be cruel than that there was a God who had forbidden us to be cruel, and much clearer that $2+2=4$ than that there is any way things are "in themselves." He viewed the theory that truth is correspondence to Reality, and the theory that moral goodness is correspondence to the Divine Will, as equally dispensable.

For Dewey, both theories add nothing to our ordinary, workaday, fallible ways of telling the good from the bad and the true from the false. But their pointlessness is not the real problem. What Dewey most disliked about both traditional "realist" epistemology and about traditional religious beliefs is that they discourage us by telling us that somebody or something has authority over us. Both tell us that there is Something Inscrutable, something which claims precedence over our cooperative attempts to avoid pain and obtain pleasure.

Dewey, like James, was a utilitarian: he thought that in the end the only moral or epistemological criteria we have or need is whether performing an action, or holding a belief, will, in the long run, make for greater human happiness. He saw progress as produced by increasing willingness to experiment, to get out from under the past. So he hoped we should learn to view current scientific, religious, philosophical, and moral beliefs with the skepticism with which Bentham viewed the laws of England: he hoped each new generation would try to cobble together some more useful beliefs—beliefs which would help them make human life richer, fuller, and happier.

2. Classical Pragmatism*

So much for an introductory statement of the theme which I shall be developing. Shortly I shall rehearse this theme in another key by bringing in Freud. But it may be useful if I first say something about the similarities and differences, particularly in regard to their views about religion, between Dewey and the other two classical pragmatists: Charles Sanders Peirce and William James.

Peirce kicked pragmatism off by starting from Alexander Bain's definition of belief as a rule or habit of action. Starting from this definition, Peirce argued that the function of inquiry is not to represent reality, but rather to enable us to act more effectively. This means getting rid of the "copy theory" of knowledge which had dominated philosophy since the time of Descartes—and especially of the idea of intuitive self-knowledge, knowledge unmediated by signs. As one of the first philosophers to say that the ability to use signs is essential to thought, Peirce was a prophet of what Gustav Bergman called "the linguistic turn in philosophy."

Like nineteenth-century idealists such as T. H. Green and Josiah Royce, Peirce was anti-foundationalist, coherentist, and holist in his view of the nature of inquiry. But he did not, as most of Hegel's Anglophone followers did, think of God as an all-inclusive, atemporal experience which is identical with Reality. Rather, as a good Darwinian, Peirce thought of the universe as evolving. His God was a finite deity who is somehow identical with an evolutionary process which he called "the growth of Thirdness." This quaint term signifies the gradual linking of everything up with everything else through triadic relationships. Rather strangely, and without much in the way of argument, Peirce took all triadic relationships to be sign-relations, and vice versa. His philosophy of language was intertwined with a quasi-idealistic metaphysics.

James and Dewey both admired Peirce, and shared his sense that philosophy must come to terms with Darwin. But they sensibly paid little atten-

---

* In *RI* this section heading reads: "Classical Pragmatism and the Need to Reconcile Science with Religion (1)." The (1) is a footnote: "This section incorporates material from my article 'Pragmatism' in the forthcoming *Routledge Encyclopedia of Philosophy*, edited by Edward Craig" (9), which was published in 1998. Rorty's contribution is still present in the online edition at www.rep.routledge.com.

tion to his metaphysics of Thirdness. Instead they focused on the profound anti-Cartesian implications of Peirce's development of Bain's initial anti-representationalist insight. They developed a non-representationalist theory of belief acquisition and testing which culminates in James's claim that "'The true'... is only the expedient in our way of thinking." James and Dewey both wanted to reconcile philosophy with Darwin by making human beings' pursuit of the true and the good continuous with the activities of the lower animals—cultural evolution with biological evolution.

All three of the founding pragmatists combined a naturalistic, Darwinian view of human beings with a distrust of the problems which philosophy had inherited from Descartes, Hume, and Kant. All three hoped also to save moral and religious ideals from empiricist or positivist skepticism. It is important, however, not to be blinded by these similarities, and by the fact that the three men are always treated as members of a single "movement," to the fact that they had very different philosophical concerns. It is probably only the chauvinistic need to have a distinctively American philosophy which has engendered the idea of a pragmatic movement. It is best, I think, to view these three men simply as three interesting philosophers who happened to be American, and had a perceptible influence on each other's work—but as no more closely allied with one another than, say, Brentano, Husserl, and Russell.

Although the three knew and respected the other two, the motives that drove them to philosophy were very different. Peirce thought of himself as a disciple of Kant, improving on Kant's doctrine of categories and his conception of logic. A practicing mathematician and laboratory scientist, he was more interested in these areas of culture than were James or Dewey. James took neither Kant nor Hegel very seriously, but was far more interested in religion than either Peirce or Dewey. Dewey, deeply influenced by Hegel, was fiercely anti-Kantian. Education and politics, rather than science or religion, were at the center of his thought.

Peirce was a brilliant, cryptic, and prolific polymath, whose writings are very difficult to piece together into a coherent system. Peirce protested James's appropriation of his ideas, for complex reasons having to do with his obscure and idiosyncratic metaphysics, and in particular with his doctrine of "Scotistic realism"—the reality of universals, sometimes considered as triadic relations, sometimes as sign-relationships, sometimes as potentialities, and sometimes as dispositions. Peirce was more sympathetic to idealism than

James, and found James's version of pragmatism simplistic and reductionist. James himself, however, thought of pragmatism as a way of avoiding reductionism of all kinds, and as a counsel of tolerance.*

Although he viewed many metaphysical and theological disputes as, at best, exhibitions of the diversity of human temperament, James hoped to construct an alternative to the anti-religious, science-worshipping, positivism of his day. He approvingly cited Giovanni Papini's description of pragmatism as "like a corridor in a hotel. Innumerable chambers open out of it. In one you may find a man writing an atheistic volume; in the next someone on his knees praying for faith; in a third a chemist investigating a body's properties . . . they all own the corridor, and all must pass through it." His point was that attention to the implications of beliefs for practice offered the only way to communicate across divisions between temperaments, academic disciplines, and philosophical schools. In particular, such attention offered the only way to mediate between the claims of religion and those of science.

Dewey, in his early period, tried to bring Hegel together with evangelical Christianity. Although references to Christianity almost disappear from his writings around 1900, in a 1903 essay on Emerson he still looked forward to the development of "a philosophy which religion has no call to chide, and which knows its friendship with science and with art." The anti-positivist strain in classical pragmatism was at least as strong as its anti-metaphysical strain.

Dewey urged that we make no sharp distinction between moral deliberation and proposals for change in socio-political institutions, or in education. He saw changes in individual attitudes, in public policies, and in strategies of acculturation as three interlinked aspects of the gradual development of freer and more democratic communities, and of the better sort of human being who would be developed within such communities. All of Dewey's books are permeated by the typically nineteenth-century conviction that human history is the story of expanding human freedom, and by the hope of substituting a less professionalized, more politically oriented, conception of the philosopher's task for the Platonic conception of the philosopher as "spectator of time and eternity." He thought that Kant, especially in his moral philosophy, had preserved that Platonic conception.

---

* This entire paragraph was deleted from *RI*.

In *Reconstruction in Philosophy* (1920) Dewey wrote that "under disguise of dealing with ultimate reality, philosophy has been occupied with the precious values embedded in social traditions . . . has sprung from a clash of social ends and from a conflict of inherited institutions with incompatible contemporary tendencies." For him, the task of future philosophy was not to achieve new solutions to traditional problems, but to clarify "men's ideas as to the social and moral strifes of their own day." This historicist conception of philosophy, which developed out of Hegel's and resembled Marx's, has made Dewey less popular among analytic philosophers than Peirce or James. His intense concern with parochially American political and social issues has also served to limit interest in his work. Yet precisely because of his self-conscious historicism Dewey was, I shall be arguing in these lectures, the classical pragmatist whose work may have the greatest utility in the long term.

Whether or not Dewey is the most useful of the three classical pragmatists, Peirce seems to me the least useful.* Although he wrote more than either of the other two, and was perhaps the most "professional" of the three, his thought lacked focus and direction. Contemporary philosophers who call themselves pragmatists typically take over only one thing from Peirce: his substitution of talk of "signs" for talk of "experience." Instead of "signs," however, they speak of "language," which means excluding what Peirce called "icons" and "indices" from the realm of signs, and including only what Peirce called "symbols." It seems safe to say that if Peirce had never lived, that would have made no great difference to the history of philosophy. For Frege would have made the linguistic turn single-handedly.

Some contemporary philosophers, such as Hilary Putnam and Jürgen Habermas, give Peirce an importance that I would not. That is because these two philosophers take over Peirce's definition of "truth" as that to which opinion is fated to converge at the end of inquiry, of "reality" as what is believed to exist at that convergence point. I do not find this notion of convergence clear or helpful, for reasons that I shall be giving in later lectures.

My main reason for thinking Peirce relatively unimportant, however, is that he does not become engaged, in the way in which James and Dewey did become engaged, with the problem which dominated Kant's thought and which was at the center of nineteenth-century thought in every Western

---

* The remainder of this paragraph and the next paragraph have been deleted from *RI*, p. 12.

country: the problem of how to reconcile science and religion, how to be faithful both to Newton and Darwin* and to the spirit of Christ. That problem is the paradigm of the sort of conflict between old ways of speaking and new cultural developments which Dewey took it to be the philosopher's task to resolve.

The need to reconcile science and religion was all-important for Dewey during his first thirty years, and for James throughout his life. By contrast, Peirce's discussion of it consists of rather banal remarks—remarks which were the commonplaces of nineteenth-century thought. We find him saying, for example, that the apparent clash between these two areas of culture is the result of "the unphilosophical narrowness of those who guard the mysteries of worship." He rejects the suggestion that he is "to be prevented from joining in that common joy at the revelation of enlightened principles of religion which we celebrate at Christmas and Easter because I think that certain scientific, logical and metaphysical ideas which have been mixed up with these principles are untenable" (6.427).† He says that the only distinctive thing about Christianity is the idea that love is the only law (6.440–1), and that Christianity's ideal "is that the whole world shall be united in the bond of a common love of God accomplished by each man's loving his neighbor" (6.443). This is a pretty standard nineteenth-century Anglophone way of following up on Kant's *Religion Within the Limits of Reason Alone*. It amounts to saying that you can [have] Christian ethics without Christian theology, and therefore without interfering with Newtonian cosmology or Darwinian accounts of human origins.

This easy compromise struck James and Dewey, as it struck Nietzsche, as *too* easy. This is because these men took religion a lot more seriously than Peirce ever did. Peirce was raised an Episcopalian, claimed that that was the only religion for a gentleman, and experienced, as far as we know, no great spiritual crises which expressed themselves in religious terms.

---

* In the lecture manuscript, Rorty crossed out "Newton and Darwin" and wrote "the scientific enterprise." *RI* retained "Newton and Darwin" (12).

† Charles S. Peirce, *Collected Papers of Charles Sanders Peirce*, vol. 6, ed. Charles Hartshorne and Paul Weiss (Cambridge: Cambridge University Press, 1958). The convention when citing Peirce's *Collected Papers* is to list the volume number followed by the section number. Thus 6.427 refers to volume 6, section 427.

James* was raised by his eccentric father on a kind of idiosyncratic blend of Swedenborg and Emerson. Though he and his siblings had the good sense not to take their father's idiosyncratic theological *ideas* with any great seriousness, William took his father's religious *experiences* very seriously indeed. He suffered the same sort of spiritual crises as had afflicted Henry James, Sr., and was never sure whether to describe them in psychological or religious language.

Dewey was the only one of the three classical pragmatists to have had a really strenuous religious upbringing—the only one to have encountered religion, so to speak, in its full fury. He was also the only one [who] ever swallowed it full strength. His mother continually asked him "Are you right with Jesus?" and his biographers agree that belated resentment at his mother's meddling piety was central to the formation of Dewey's mature thought.

Despite the fact that James never had to cast off an orthodoxy imposed in his youth, the need to bring his father into the same intellectual universe as that inhabited by his scientifically oriented friends (such as Peirce and Chauncey Wright) was very important in shaping his thought. I suspect that we owe the pragmatist theory of truth to this need. For the underlying motive of that theory is to give us a way to reconcile science and religion by viewing them not as two competing ways of representing reality, but rather two non-competing ways of producing happiness. I take the anti-representationalist view of thought and language to have been motivated, in James's case, by the realization that the need for choice between competing representations can be replaced by tolerance for a plurality of non-competing descriptions, descriptions which serve different purposes and which are to be evaluated by reference to their utility in fulfilling these purposes rather than by their "fit" with the objects being described.

If James's watchword was tolerance, then Dewey's was, as I have said, anti-authoritarianism. His revulsion from the sense of sinfulness which his religious upbringing had produced led Dewey to campaign, throughout his life, against the view that human beings needed to measure themselves against something non-human. As I shall be saying in more detail later, Dewey used the term "democracy" to mean something like what Habermas means by the term "communicative reason": for him, this word sums up the idea that human beings should regulate their actions and beliefs by the need to join

* "by contrast," is added in *RI*, 13.

with other human beings in cooperative projects, rather than by the need to stand in the correct relation to something non-human. This is why he grabbed hold of James's pragmatic theory of truth.

Although James will always be the most sympathetic and most readable of the three classical pragmatists, Dewey was, I think, the most imaginative. This is because he was the most historically minded: the one who learned from Hegel how to tell great sweeping stories about the relation of the human present to the human past. Dewey's stories are always stories of the progress from the need of human communities to rely on a non-human power to their realization that all they need is faith in themselves; they are stories about the substitution of fraternity for authority. His stories about history as the story of increasing freedom are stories about how we lost our sense of sin, and also our hope of another world, and gradually acquired the ability to find the same spiritual significance in cooperation between finite mortals that our ancestors had found in their relation to an immortal being. His way of clarifying "men's ideas as to the social and moral strifes of their own day" was to ask his contemporaries to consider the possibility that weekday cooperation in building democratic communities could provide everything "higher"— everything which had once been reserved for weekends.*

3. Pragmatism as Liberation from the Primal Father

Before saying more about the pragmatists' way of reconciling religion and science, I want to make an excursus into Freud. Freud's account of the origin of conscience, of the superego, seems to me another version of the anti-authoritarian strain which motivated Dewey. The dialectical standoff in contemporary analytic philosophy between pragmatists and their "realist" opponents is best understood as the reciprocal unintelligibility to one another of two types of people. The first are those whose highest hopes are for union with something beyond the human—something which is the source of one's superego, and which has the authority to free one of guilt and shame. The second are those whose highest hopes are for a better human

---

* In *RI*, Rorty added at the end of this paragraph: "His way of making practice prior to theory was to say that both philosophy and religion were of value only insofar as they put the traditionally 'higher' to everyday use" (15).

future, to be attained by more fraternal cooperation between human beings. These two types of people are conveniently describable in Freudian
terms: they are the people who are still subject to the need to ally themselves
with an authority-figure and those who are untroubled by this need.*

Hans Blumenberg has argued that the Renaissance was a period in which
people turned from eternity to futurity. This turn is the one which, in my
view, is fully accomplished, in the area of philosophy, only by pragmatism.
The de-eternalization of human hope had to wait four hundred years to become philosophically explicit. The representationalist tradition in philosophy

---

* This paragraph reads differently in *RI*. There Rorty wrote:

Freud's account of the origin of conscience provides a good handle by which to grasp Dewey's
motives. For the dialectical standoff in contemporary analytic philosophy between pragmatists and their "realist" opponents (Nagel, Dworkin, Searle, et al.) is usefully thought of
as reciprocal unintelligibility to one another of two very different types of people. The first
are those whose highest hopes are for union with something beyond the human—something
which is the source of one's superego, and which has the authority to free one of guilt and
shame. The second are those whose highest hopes are for a better human future, to be attained
by more fraternal cooperation between human beings. These two types of people are conveniently describable in Freudian terms: they are the people who think subjection to an authority-
figure is necessary to lead a properly human life and those who see such a life as requiring
freedom from any such subjection (2).

The (2) is a footnote that reads:

For a good example of this contrast within recent Anglophone moral philosophy, see some
remarks of Thomas Nagel at pp. 206–207 of his "Reply" to Christine Korsgaard, included in
Korsgaard's *The sources of normativity* (Cambridge: Cambridge University Press, 1996)
[200–209]. There Nagel says that a self-description, a sense of one's own moral identity—a
sense that one could not live with oneself if one performed a certain action—is not a sufficient account of the reason why one should not perform that action. "The real reason,"
Nagel says, "is whatever would *make* it impossible for him to live with himself. . . ." Nagel
goes on to say that unless there is some non-empirical Kant-style, universalistic, account of
what moral identity one *should* have, then "morality is an illusion." Dewey, early in his
career, rejected Kantian in favor of Hegelian ethics. After he read Darwin, he abandoned
Hegelianism in favor of a naturalistic account of the rise of democratic societies and of the
emergence of the Enlightenment ideals which Hegel and Kant shared. Eventually his bête
noir became the doctrine which Nagel makes explicit: that something less contingent and
more universal than the empirical, environmental conditions which shape a human being's
moral identity is necessary if morality is not to be an illusion" (15–16).

which was dominant in those four hundred years hoped that inquiry would put us in touch, if not with the eternal, at least with something which, in Bernard Williams's phrase, "is there anyway"—something non-perspectival, something which is what it is apart from human needs and interests. Pragmatists do not think inquiry can put us more in touch with non-human reality than we have always been, so in their view the only question is: will human life be better in the future if we adopt this belief, this practice, this institution?

Freud, in his last and wackiest book, *Moses and Monotheism,* offers us an account of human progress which complements Blumenberg's. There he tells the story of how social cooperation emerges from parricide, from the murder of the primal father by the primal band of brothers:

> It must be supposed that after the parricide a considerable time elapsed during which the brothers disputed with one another for their father's heritage, which each of them wanted for himself alone. A realization of the dangers and uselessness of these struggles, a recollection of the act of liberation which they had accomplished together, and the emotional ties with one another which had arisen during the period of their expulsion, led at last to an agreement among them, a sort of social contract.
>
> [But] recollection of their father persisted at this period of the 'fraternal alliance'. A powerful animal—at first, perhaps, always one that was feared as well—was chosen as a substitute for the father . . . On the one hand the totem was regarded as the clan's blood ancestor and protective spirit, who must be worshipped and protected, and on the other hand a festival was appointed at which the same fate was prepared for him that the primal father had met with. He was killed and devoured by all the tribesmen in common. (S. E., v. 23, 82–3)*

Freud goes on to argue that totemism was "the first form in which religion was manifested in history," and to claim that "the first step away from totemism

* Sigmund Freud, *The Standard Edition of the Complete Psychological Works of Sigmund Freud,* ed. James Strachey in collaboration with Anna Freud, vol. 23: (1937–1939), *Moses and Monotheism, An Outline of Psycho-Analysis and Other Works* (London: Hogarth Press, 1964; New York: Norton, 1986), 82–83. Rorty is following the citation convention of listing the volume, followed by the page number.

was the humanizing of the being who was worshipped." This humanization produced first a mother-goddess, and then polytheism of mixed genders. Polytheism was succeeded by the great patriarchal monotheisms, through a process which phallogocentrists call "purification" and which Freud regarded as a recapturing of psycho-historical truth. In these religions, the murdered father was restored to his rightful role as one who demanded unconditional obedience, although he was now banished from the earth to the sky.

Platonism, one can imagine Freud saying, was a depersonalized version of this sort of monotheism—a further attempt at so-called purification. In this depersonalized form, proper respect for a de-humanized father-figure is shown not by obedience to him but by an attempt to become identical with him. We do this by surrendering everything in us which separates us from him (such as space, time, and the body). We good sons aim at becoming identical, so to speak, with good, kind, loving, generous aspects of father, while ignoring the violent and willful aspects. Platonism gives us a way of imitating, so to speak, all that was great and good and admirable in our fathers without having to imitate their unpleasant idiosyncrasies. We wish, by purifying ourselves, to become identical with what father *would* have been like if he had ever managed to behave decently. The Idea of the God is Father stripped of parts and passions.*

In the broad sense of the word "metaphysics," which Heidegger employs when he says that metaphysics is Platonism and Platonism metaphysics, metaphysics looks to pragmatists like an attempt to snuggle up to something so pure and good as to be not really human, while still being enough like a loving parent so that it can be loved with all one's heart and soul and strength. Plato's infatuation with mathematics—the paradigm of something neither willful nor arbitrary nor violent, something which embodied *anagke* with no trace of *bia*—gave him the model for this being: the outline of the father-figure, so to speak, without any distracting detail.

Freud's interest in Plato was in fact restricted almost entirely to the discussions of Eros and of androgyny in the *Symposium,* but suppose that he

---

* In the manuscript Rorty has crossed out: "The idea of the," leaving only "God is Father Stripped of parts and passions." The Spanish translation reads: "La Idea del Bien es el Padre despojado de partes vergonzosas y pasiones" (35). *RI* reads: "The Idea of the Good is the idea of Father, stripped of his more terrifying parts and passions" (17).

had turned his eyes on the Theory of Ideas. Had he done so, I think that he would seen worship of the bare Idea of Father as the origin of the conviction that it is *knowledge,* rather than love, which is the most distinctively human achievement. For Plato arranged things so that we could please Father best by doing mathematics, or, at a second best, mathematical physics.

This conviction of the importance of knowledge runs through the history of what Derrida calls "the metaphysics of presence"—the history of the Western search for a still point in the turning world, something one can always rely on, always come home to, something, as Derrida says, "beyond the reach of play." The quest for such a reassuring presence is, for all those who resonate to Aristotle's claim that "all men by nature desire to know," the proper way of life for the good son. To devote oneself to getting knowledge as opposed to opinion—to grasping unchanging structure as opposed to awareness of mutable and colorful content—one has to believe that one will be cleansed, purified of guilt and shame, by getting closer to something like Truth or Reality. When opponents of pragmatism say that pragmatists do not believe in truth, they are saying that pragmatists do not grasp the need for such closeness, and therefore do not see the need for purification. They are, their metaphysically inclined opponents suggest, *shameless* in their willingness to revel in the mutable and impermanent. Like women and children, they seem to have no superego, no conscience, no spirit of seriousness.*

As Blumenberg sees it, the repersonalization of God which occurred when Christianity took over eventually turned itself inside out. It did so when Occam drew the voluntaristic consequences of Divine Otherness, and thereby helped reduce monotheism, if not to absurdity, at least to unusability by the intellectuals. Occamism made the will of our Father in Heaven so inscrutable that all connection snapped between his will and our desires, between us and Him. He became less like somebody to get close to than somebody who could tolerate no relation save sheer obedience. He ceased to be a possible object of contemplation and rapport. So the rediscovery of Plato by the Renaissance

---

* In *RI* Rorty added footnote 3, which reads: "See Kant's hilarious section on the differences between the sexes in his *Observations on the feeling of the sublime and the beautiful* [*sic*]. Women, according to Kant, cannot act from principle, cannot act morally, because they don't have any sense for the sublime—they cannot feel the awe which is appropriate before patriarchal authority" (18). See Immanuel Kant, *Observations on the Feeling of the Beautiful and the Sublime,* trans. John T. Goldthwait (Berkeley: University of California Press, 1960).

humanists repeated the move toward depersonalization, and the turn from theology to metaphysics, which had been made when the Idea of the Good offered a purified form of worship to pagan intellectuals.

Dewey never read any Freud to speak of, but if he had I think that he would have accepted Freud's account of the maturation of humanity, and he could have used it to strengthen and supplement his own story of how the West overcame Greek dualisms in the course of inventing modern technology and modern liberal societies—two inventions which he took to be part of the same anti-authoritarian movement. He would have seen the successive de-centerings performed by Copernicus, Darwin, and Freud himself as helpful in forcing us to stop looking outside the human community for salvation, and making us instead explore the possibilities offered by social cooperation. In particular, I think that he might have seen modern democratic societies as founded on, as it were, fraternity alone—that is to say, fraternity freed from memory of paternal authority. Only pragmatism reaps the full advantages of parricide.*

Only in a democratic society which describes itself in pragmatist terms, one can imagine Dewey saying, is the refusal to countenance any authority save that of consensus reached by free inquiry complete. Only then can the fraternity which was first glimpsed when the primal father was killed by the band of brothers be achieved. This achievement had been deferred by the many attempts, made over many millennia, to come to terms with the specter of the murdered father: the attempts which make up the history of monotheism and of metaphysics. It will no longer be deferred, Dewey thought, once we come to treat our collective superego, our collective sense of what counts as a moral abomination, as having no authority separate from that of tradition, and when we treat tradition itself as endlessly malleable and revisable by its inheritors.†

---

* In *RI*, this last sentence reads: "Only pragmatism, he might have remarked, reaps the full advantage of that primal parricide" (19).

† *RI* closes with a subheading "4. Conclusion" which reads:

   I have discussed elsewhere James' and Dewey's solutions to the problem of reconciling science with theology, and have argued that Dewey was more successful than James in purifying religion of the appeal to authority (4). This was, I think, because James got a kick out of sublimity—out of the sense of limitlessness—whereas Dewey did not. James, in his *Varieties of*

I hope that it is clear by now why I chose the title "Anti-Authoritarianism in Epistemology and Ethics" for this series of lectures.* By anti-authoritarianism in ethics I mean the development of the attitude I just described—the attitude that makes our sense of what counts as a moral abomination not an insight produced by a part of ourselves that is linked to something non-human and good, but simply a revisable cultural inheritance. By anti-authoritarianism in epistemology I mean the substitution of intersubjectivity, in the form of free consensus among the members of those curious enough to inquire, for objectivity, where objectivity is understood as a privileged relation to a non-human being, such as God or Reality or Truth.

Religious Experience, is a connoisseur of unusual experiences. His reaction to report of the rapture of the soul is like his reaction to the experience of the San Francisco earthquake of 1907: he wanted the earthquake to become more intense, to show what it could *really* do. Dewey seems to have been incapable of such connoisseurship, and of any Bataille-like fascination with the extreme. His taste is for the beautiful. His only acknowledgment of the sublime consists in his hope that the contingently produced series of better and better societies will continue indefinitely into an unimaginably better future. This was the hope that that democracy would produce ever more beautiful forms of human cooperation and mutual enjoyment, ever more complex ways of satisfying novel human needs. Dewey relished the imagined spectacle of ever richer, ever more diverse, forms of human fraternity. But he was devoid both of the need to abase himself before authority, and of sympathy with those who find such abasement thrilling. As he saw it, his anti-authoritarianism was a stage in the gradual replacement of a morality of obligation by a morality of love. This is the replacement which, in the West, is thought to have been initiated by certain passages in the New Testament (5) (19–20).

Footnote (4) reads: "See my 'Religious Faith, Intellectual Responsibility, and Romance' in Ruth-Anna Putnam, ed., *The Cambridge Companion to William James* (Cambridge: Cambridge University Press, 1997), 84–102, and also my 'Pragmatism as Romantic Polytheism' in Morris Dickstein, ed., *The New Pragmatism* (forthcoming in 1998 from Duke University Press)." This last essay is reprinted as Richard Rorty, "Pragmatism as Romantic Polytheism," in *Philosophical Papers*, vol. 4: *Philosophy as Cultural Politics*, 27–41 (Cambridge: Cambridge University Press, 2007). Footnote (5) reads: "On Dewey's relationship to Christianity, see the magisterial study of his religious thought: Steven Rockefeller, *John Dewey: Religious Faith and Democratic Humanism* (New York: Columbia University Press, 1991)."
* This is the title Rorty gave to the series of his Girona lectures, and this is the subtitle of the Spanish edition of the book. In light of Rorty's later publications, the title of the book has been abbreviated and the subtitle dropped.

4. James's Way of Reconciling Religion and Science

I turn now, in this final section of my lecture, to one of the least popular and most criticized portions of William James's work: this essay "The Will to Believe." This essay argues that we do not need to reconcile science and religion, since we can, so to speak, keep them in separate compartments by viewing them as tools to satisfy non-competing needs. I shall try to put this argument in the context of James's overall anti-representationalism.

In thinking about James, it helps to remember that James not only dedicated *Pragmatism* to John Stuart Mill, but reiterated some of Mill's most controversial claims. In "The Moral Philosopher and the Moral Life," James says that "The only possible reason there can be why any phenomenon ought to exist is that such a phenomenon actually is desired" (*WB*, 149).* This echo of the most ridiculed sentence in Mill's *Utilitarianism* is, I suspect, deliberate. One of James's most heartfelt convictions was that to know whether a claim should be met, we need *only* ask which other claims—"claims actually made by some concrete person"—it runs athwart. We need not also ask whether it is a "valid" claim. He deplored the fact that philosophers still followed Kant rather than Mill, still thought of validity as raining down upon a claim "from some sublime dimension of being, which the moral law inhabits, much as upon the steel of the compass-needle the influence of the Pole rains down from out of the starry heavens" (*WB*, 148).

The view that there is no source of obligation save the claims of individual sentient beings entails that we have no responsibility to anything other than such beings. Most of the relevant sentient individuals are our fellow humans. So talk about our responsibility to Truth, or to Reason, must be replaced by talk about our responsibility to our fellow human beings. James's account of truth and knowledge is a utilitarian ethics of belief, designed to facilitate such replacement. Its point of departure is, once again, Peirce's treatment of a belief as a habit of action, rather than as a representation. A utilitarian philosophy of religion need not ask whether religious belief gets something right. It need only ask how the actions of religious believers interfere with the lives

---

* William James, *The Will to Believe and Other Essays in Popular Philosophy* (Cambridge, MA: Harvard University Press, 1979) (hereafter *WB* in Rorty's text), 149.

of other human beings, and how the needs filled by religious belief might be filled without creating such interference.

Our responsibility to Truth is not, for James, a responsibility to get things right. Rather, our obligation to be rational is exhausted by our obligation to take account of other people's doubts and objections to our beliefs. This view of rationality makes it natural to say, as James does, that the true is "what would be better for us to believe" (42).*

But of course what is good for one person or group to believe will not be good for another person or group. James never was sure how to avoid the counter-intuitive consequence that what is true for one person or group may not be true for another. He fluctuated between Peirce's identification of truth with what will be believed under ideal conditions, and Dewey's strategy of avoiding the topic of truth and talking instead about justification. But for my present purpose—which is to evaluate the view of religious belief which James offered in his essay "The Will to Believe"—it is not necessary to decide between these strategies. So I can postpone for later lectures what pragmatists should say about truth. I need consider only the question of whether the religious believer has a right to her faith—whether this faith conflicts with her intellectual responsibilities.

It is a consequence of James's utilitarian view of the nature of obligation that *the obligation to justify one's beliefs arises only when one's habits of action interfere with the fulfillment of others' needs.* Insofar as one is engaged in a private project, that obligation lapses. The underlying strategy of James's utilitarian / pragmatist philosophy of religion is to *privatize* religion. This privatization allows him to construe the supposed tension between Science and Religion as the illusion of opposition between cooperative endeavors and private projects.

On a pragmatist account, scientific inquiry is best viewed as the attempt to find a single, unified, coherent description of the world—the description which makes it easiest to predict the consequences of events and actions, and thus easiest to gratify certain human desires. When pragmatists say that "creationist science"† is *bad* science, their point is that it subordinates these de-

---

*William James, *Pragmatism* (Cambridge, MA: Harvard University Press, 1979), 42.

†The Spanish translation has a footnote not in the manuscript, which reads, and I translate: "The so-called 'creationist science' is the supposed 'science' that is preached by Protestant fundamen-

sires to other, less widespread, desires. But since religion has aims other than gratification of our need to predict and control, it is not clear that there need be a quarrel between religion and orthodox, atoms-and-void, science, any more than between literature and science. Further, if a private relation to God is not accompanied with the claim to knowledge of the Divine Will, there may be no conflict between religion and utilitarian ethics. A suitably privatized form of religious belief might dictate neither one's scientific beliefs nor anybody's moral choices save one's own. That form of belief would be able to gratify a need without threatening to thwart any needs of any others, and would thus meet the utilitarian test.

W. K. Clifford, James's chosen opponent in "The Will to Believe," thinks that we have a duty to seek the truth, distinct from our duty to seek happiness. His way of describing this duty is not as a duty to get reality right, but rather as a duty not to believe without evidence. James quotes him as saying, "If [a] belief has been accepted on insufficient evidence, the pleasure is a stolen one . . . It is sinful because it is stolen in defiance of our duty to mankind . . . It is wrong always, everywhere, and for every one, to believe anything upon insufficient evidence" (*WB*, 18).

Clifford asks us to be responsive to "evidence," as well as to human needs. So the question between James and Clifford comes down to: is evidence something which floats free of human projects, or is the demand for evidence simply a demand from other human beings for cooperation on such projects?

The view that evidential relations have a kind of existence independent of human projects takes various forms, of which the most prominent are realism and foundationalism. Realist philosophers say that the only true source of evidence is the world as it is in itself. The pragmatist objections to realism start from the claim that "it is impossible to strip the human element out from even our most abstract theorizing. All our mental categories without exception have been evolved because of their fruitfulness for life, and owe their being to historic circumstances, just as much as do the nouns and verbs

---

talists as a substitute for Darwin's theory of evolution. Its basic dogma consists in affirming that it can be demonstrated scientifically that the explanation of creation that is offered in Genesis is true" (41). This appears to be a clarifying note from the translator for Spanish readers who may not be familiar with "creationist science."

and adjectives in which our languages clothe them" (ECR, 552).* Compare
Nietzsche, *The Will to Power*, sec. 514.) If pragmatists are right about this,
the only question at issue between them and realists is whether the notion
of "the world as it is in itself" can be made fruitful for life. James's criticism
of correspondence theories of truth boil down to the argument that a belief's purported "fit" with the intrinsic nature of reality adds nothing which
makes any practical difference to the fact that it is universally agreed to lead
to successful action.

Foundationalism is an epistemological view which can be adopted by those
who suspend judgment on the realist's claim that reality has an intrinsic nature. A foundationalist need only claim that every belief occupies a place in
a natural, transcultural, transhistorical order of reasons—an order which
eventually lead the inquirer back, eventually, to one or another "ultimate
source of evidence."[1] Different foundationalists offer different candidates for
such sources: for example, Scripture, tradition, clear and distinct ideas, sense-
experience, and common sense. Pragmatists object to foundationalism for
the same reasons as they object to realism. They think that the question of
whether my inquiries trace a natural order of reasons or merely respond to
the demands for justification prevalent in my culture is, like the question of
whether the physical world is found or made, one to which the answer can
make no practical difference.

Clifford's demand for evidence can, however, be put in a minimalist
form—one which avoids both realism and foundationalism, and which con-
cedes to James that intellectual responsibility is no more and no less than
responsibility to people with whom one is joined in a shared endeavor. In its
minimalist form, this demand presupposes only that the meaning of a statement consists in the inferential relations which it bears to other statements.
To use the language in which the sentence is phrased commits one, on this
view, to believing that a statement S is true if and only if one also believes
that certain other statements which permit an inference to S, and still others
which can be inferred from S, are true. The wrongness of believing without
evidence is, therefore, the wrongness of pretending to participate in a common
project while refusing to play by the rules.

* William James, *Essays, Comments, and Reviews* (Cambridge, MA: Harvard University Press,
1987), 552.

This view of language was encapsulated in the positivist slogan that the meaning of a statement is its method of verification. The positivists argued that the sentences used to express religious belief are typically not hooked up to the rest of the language in the right inferential way, and hence can express only pseudo-beliefs. The positivists, being empiricist foundationalists, equated "the right inferential way" with eventual appeal to sense experience. But a non-foundationalist neo-positivist might still put forward the following dilemma: If there are inferential connections, then there is a duty to argue; if there are not, then we are not dealing with a belief at all.

So even if we drop the foundationalist notion of "evidence," Clifford's point can still be restated in terms of the responsibility to *argue*. A minimal Clifford-like view can be summed up in the claim that, although your emotions are your own business, your beliefs are everybody's business. There is no way in which the religious person can claim a right to believe as part of an overall right to privacy. For believing is inherently a public project: all us language-users are in it together. We all have a responsibility to each other not to believe anything which cannot be justified to the rest of us. To be rational is to submit one's beliefs—all one's beliefs—to the judgment of one's peers.

James resists this view. In "The Will to Believe" he argues that there are live, momentous, and forced options which cannot be decided by evidence—cannot, as James put it, "be decided on intellectual grounds." But people who side with Clifford typically rejoin that, where evidence and argument are unavailable, intellectual responsibility requires that options *cease* to be either live or forced. The responsible inquirer, they say, does not *let* herself be confronted by options of the sort James describes. When evidence and argument are unavailable, so, they think, is belief, or at least *responsible* belief. Desire, hope, and other non-cognitive states can legitimately be had without evidence—can legitimately be turned over to what James calls "our passional nature"—but *belief* cannot. In the realm of belief, which options are live and forced is not a private matter. The same options face us all; the same truth-candidates are proposed to everyone. It is intellectually irresponsible either to disregard these options, or to decide between these truth-candidates except by argument from the sort of evidence which the very meanings of our words tell us is required for their support.

This nice sharp distinction between the cognitive and the non-cognitive, between belief and desire, is, however, just the sort of dualism which James needs to blur. On the traditional account, desire should play no role in the fixation of belief. On a pragmatist account, the only point of having beliefs in the first place is to gratify desires. James's claim that thinking is "only there for behavior's sake" (*WB*, 92) is his version of Hume's claim that "reason is, and ought to be, the slave of the passions."

If one accepts either claim, one will have reason to be as dubious as James was of the purportedly necessary antagonism between science and religion. For, as I said earlier, these two areas of culture seem to fulfill two different sets of desires. Science enables us to predict and control, whereas religion offers us a larger hope, and thereby something to live for. To ask "Which of their two accounts of the universe is true?" may be as pointless as asking "Is the carpenter's or the particle physicist's account of tables the true one?" For neither question needs to be answered if we can figure out a strategy for keeping the two accounts from getting in each other's way.

Consider James's characterization of the "religious hypothesis" as that (1) "the best things are the more eternal things" and (2) "that we are better off even now if we believe [1]" (*WB*, 29–30). For the moment I shall disregard the question of whether this suffices to characterize what most religious people believe. I want merely to remark that if you had asked James to specify the difference between accepting this hypothesis (a "cognitive" state) and simply trusting the larger hope (a "non-cognitive" state)—or the difference between believing that the best things are the eternal things and relishing the thought that they are—he might well have replied that such differences do not make much difference.[2] What does it matter, one can imagine him asking, whether you call it a belief, a desire, or a hope, a mood, or some complex of these, so long as it has the same cash value in directing action? We know what religious faith is, we know what it does for people. People have a right to have such faith, just as they have a right to fall in love, to marry in haste, and to persist in love despite endless sorrow and disappointment. In all such cases, what James called "our passional nature," and what I should call "our right to privacy," asserts its rights.

I suggest that we reinterpret James's intellect-passion distinction so as to make it coincide with a distinction between the public and the private, between what needs justification to other human beings and what does not. A business proposal, for example, needs such justification, but a marriage proposal (in our romantic and democratic culture) does not. Such an ethics will defend religious belief by saying, with Mill, that our right to happiness is limited only by others' rights not to have their own pursuits of happiness interfered with. This right to happiness includes the rights to faith, hope, and love—intentional states which typically should not have to be justified to our peers. Our intellectual responsibilities are responsibilities to cooperate with others on common projects designed to promote the general welfare (projects such as constructing a unified science, or a uniform commercial code), and not to interfere with their private projects. For the latter—projects such as getting married or getting religion—the question of intellectual responsibility does not arise.

James's critics will hear this riposte as an admission that religion is not a cognitive matter, and that his "right to believe" is a misnomer for "the right to yearn" or "the right to hope" or "the right to take comfort in the thought that . . ." But James is not making, and should not make, such an admission. He is, rather, insisting that the impulse to draw a sharp line between the cognitive and the non-cognitive, and between beliefs and desires, even when this explanation is relevant neither to the explanation or the justification of behavior, is a residue of the false (because useless) belief that we should engage in two distinct quests—one for truth and the other for happiness. Only that belief could persuade us to say *amici socii, sed magis amica veritas.** To be thoroughly anti-authoritarian in one's view of knowledge and inquiry is never to be tempted to say anything like that. The most one can say is something like: *amici socii, sed forse magis amici socii futuri.*†

---

* This expression could be translated as: "our consociates [colleagues] are our friends, but truth is our greater friend."
† This expression could be translated as: "our present consociates [colleagues] are our friends, but perhaps our better friends will be our future consociates [colleagues]."

2

Pragmatism as Romantic Polytheism

/

In 1911 a book appeared in Paris titled *Un romantisme utilitaire: Etude sur le mouvement pragmatiste*. This was the first of three volumes on the subject by René Berthelot, a philosopher who had been struck by the resemblances between the views of James, Nietzsche, Bergson, Poincaré, and certain Catholic Modernists. Berthelot, a convinced Cartesian, disliked and distrusted all these thinkers, but he wrote about them with acuity, verve, and insight. He traced the romantic roots of pragmatism back behind Emerson to Schelling and Hölderlin,[1] and the utilitarian roots to the influence of Darwin and Spencer.[2] "In all its different forms," Berthelot said, "pragmatism reveals itself to be a romantic utilitarianism: that is its most obviously original feature and also its most private vice and its hidden weakness."[3]

Berthelot was probably the first to use the term "a German Pragmatist" of Nietzsche, and the first to emphasize the resemblance between Nietzsche's view of truth and those of the American pragmatists. This resemblance— frequently noted since, notably in a seminal chapter of Arthur Danto's book on Nietzsche—is most evident in the *The Gay Science*. There Nietzsche says, "We do not even have any organ at all for *knowing*, for 'truth'; we 'know' . . . just as much as may be *useful* in the interest of the human herd."[4] [Wir haben eben gar kein Organ fuer das *Erkennen*, fuer die 'Wahrheit'; wir 'wissen' . . .

This lecture was first published in Morris Dickstein, ed., *The Revival of Pragmatism: New Essays on Social Thought* (Durham, NC: Duke University Press, 1998), and was reprinted in Richard Rorty, *Philosophical Papers*, vol. 4: *Philosophy as Cultural Politics* 27–41 (Cambridge: Cambridge University Press, 2007), referenced here as *PCP*. My editorial annotation in the footnotes refers to this more recent version. Rorty's footnotes appear here as endnotes.

gerade so viel, als es im Interesse der Menschen-Herde, der Gattung, *nuetzlich* sein mag.]* This Darwinian view lies behind James's claim that "thinking is for the sake of behavior" and his consequent definition of truth as "the good in the way of belief." That definition amounts to accepting Nietzsche's claim that human beings should be viewed, for epistemological purposes, as what Nietzsche called "clever animals." Beliefs are to be judged solely by whether they get believers what they want.†

James and Nietzsche did for the word "true" what John Stuart Mill had done for the word "right." Just as Mill said that there is no ethical motive apart from the desire for the happiness of human beings, so James and Nietzsche say that there is no will to truth distinct from the will to happiness. All three philosophers think that transcendental terms like "true" and "right" gain their meaning from their use, and that their only use is to evaluate human beings' methods of achieving happiness. Nietzsche, to be sure, had no use for Mill, but this was a result of arrogant ignorance, which resulted in a failure to grasp the difference between Mill and Bentham.‡

James, who dedicated his first philosophical treatise to Mill's memory, wanted to develop not only the debunking, Benthamite strain in Mill's thought but the romantic, Coleridgean strain as well. The latter led Mill to choose an epigraph from Wilhelm von Humboldt for *On Liberty*: "The grand, leading principle, towards which every argument unfolded in these pages directly converges, is the absolute and essential importance of human development in its richest diversity." As a romantic utilitarian, Mill wanted to avoid being the reductionist Bentham had seemed to be, and to defend a secular culture against the familiar charge of blindness to higher things.§ This led him, as M. H. Abrams has pointed out, to share Arnold's view that literature could take the place of dogma. Abrams quotes Alexander Bain as saying of

---

* The German text was moved into footnote 3 in *PCP*, 27.
† These last two sentences are modified and begin the next paragraph; see *PCP*, 28. There, the next paragraph begins with, "That Identification amounts to accepting Nietzsche's claim that human beings should be viewed, for epistemological purposes, as what Nietzsche called 'clever animals.'"
‡ This last sentence begins the next paragraph in *PCP*, 28.
§ In *PCP* the paragraph ends here, and the next one begins with "This led him, as M. H. Abrams has pointed out" (28).

Mill that "he seemed to look upon Poetry as a Religion, or rather as Religion and Philosophy in One."[5]

Abrams quotes a letter of Mill's which says that "the new utilitarianism"—his own as opposed to Bentham's—holds "Poetry not only on a par with, but the necessary condition of, any true and comprehensive philosophy."[6]* Abrams argues that Mill and Arnold, despite their differences, drew the same moral from the English Romantics: that poetry could and should take on "the tremendous responsibility of the functions once performed by the exploded dogmas of religion and religious philosophy."[7] The exploded dogmas included the claim that, whereas there can be many great poems, there can be only one true religion, because only one true God. Poetry cannot be a substitute for a monotheistic religion, but it can serve the purposes of a secular version of polytheism.† A kind of polytheism is recommended in the famous passage near the end of *The Varieties of Religious Experience* at which James says,

> If an Emerson were forced to be a Wesley, or a Moody forced to be a Whitman, the total human consciousness of the divine would suffer. The divine can mean no single quality, it must mean a group of qualities, by

---

* In PCP this last sentence reads: "Abrams also quotes a letter of Mill's which says that 'the new utilitarianism'—his own as opposed to Bentham's—holds Poetry not only on a par with, but the necessary condition of, any true and comprehensive Philosophy" (28).

† In PCP, the paragraph ends here, and a new paragraph is inserted:

> The substitution of poetry for religion as a source of ideals, a movement that began with the Romantics, seems to me usefully described as a return to polytheism. For if, with the utilitarians, you reject the idea that a non-human authority can rank human needs, and thus dictate moral choices to human beings, you will favor the idea, characteristic of the evangelical Christians whom Arnold thought of as "Hebraist," that it suffices to love God and keep his commandments. You will substitute what Arnold called the idea of "a human nature perfected on all its sides." Different poets will perfect different sides of human nature, projecting different ideals. A romantic utilitarian will probably drop the idea of diverse immortal persons, such as the Olympian deities, but she will retain the idea that there are diverse, conflicting, but equally valuable forms of human life.

> A polytheism of this sort is recommended in a famous passage near the end of *Varieties of Religious Experience* at which James says:

Rorty cites Matthew Arnold, *Culture and Anarchy*, ed. Samuel Lipman (New Haven, CT: Yale University Press, 1994), 37. See *PCP*, 29.

being champions of which in alternation, different men may all find worthy missions. Each attitude being a syllable in human nature's total message, it takes the whole of us to spell the meaning out completely.[8]

James's loose use of the term "the divine" makes it pretty much equivalent to "the ideal." In this passage he is doing for theology what Mill did for politics when he said that "human development in its richest diversity" is the aim of social institutions.

There is a passage in Nietzsche in praise of polytheism which complements the one I have just quoted from James. In section 143 of *The Gay Science* he argues that morality—in the wide sense of the need for acceptance of binding laws and customs—entails "hostility against the impulse to have an ideal of one's own." But, he says, the pre-Socratic Greeks provided an outlet for individuality by permitting human beings "to behold, in some distant overworld, a *plurality of norms:* one god was not considered a denial of another god, nor blasphemy against him." [Aber ueber sich und ausser sich, in einer fernen Ueberwelt, durfte man eine *Mehrzahl von Normen* sehen; der eine Gott war nicht die Leugnung oder Laesterung des anderen Gottes.] In this way, Nietzsche says, "the luxury of individuals was first permitted; it was here that one first honored the rights of individuals." For in pre-Socratic polytheism "the free-spiriting and many-spiriting of man attained its first preliminary form—the strength to create for ourselves our own new eyes." [Hier erlaubte man sich zuerst Individuen, hier ehrte man zuerst das Recht von Individuen. . . . In Polytheismus lag die Freigeisterei und Vielgeisterei des Menschen vorgebildet; die Kraft, sich neue und eigne Augen zu schaffen.]*

I can sum up what I have been saying by offering a definition of "polytheism" which covers Nietzsche and James.† You are a polytheist if you think that there is no actual or possible object of knowledge which would permit you to commensurate and rank all human needs. Isaiah Berlin's doctrine of incommensurable human values is, in my sense, a polytheistic manifesto. To be a polytheist in this sense you do not have to believe that there are non-human persons with power to intervene in human affairs. All you need do is to abandon what Heidegger calls "the onto-theological tradition."

---

* In *PCP* the German citation has been moved into footnote 7, p. 30.

† In *PCP* this reads: "Here is a definition of 'polytheism' that covers both Nietzsche and James" (30).

This is the tradition that tells you that we should try to find a way of making everything hang together which will tell all human beings what to do with their lives, and tell all of them the same thing.

Polytheism, in the sense in which I have defined it, is pretty much coextensive with romantic utilitarianism. For once one sees no way of ranking human needs other than playing them off against one another, human happiness becomes all that matters, and Mill's *On Liberty* provides all the ethical instruction one needs.* Polytheists agree with Mill and Arnold that poetry should take over the role which religion has played in the formation of individual human lives, and that nothing should take over the function of the churches. Poets are to polytheism what the priests of a universal church are to monotheism. So once you become polytheistic, you are likely to turn away not only from priests, but from such priest-substitutes as metaphysicians and physicists. But such a turn is compatible with two different attitudes toward those who retain a monotheistic faith. One can see them as Nietzsche did, as blind, weak, fools. Or one can see them as James and Dewey did, as people who are so spell-bound by the work of one poet as to be un-

---

* The rest of this paragraph does not appear in *PCP*. A different paragraph has been added:

> Mill's *On Liberty* provides all the ethical instruction you need—all the philosophical advice you are ever going to get about your responsibilities to other human beings. For human perfection becomes a private concern, and our responsibility to others becomes a matter of permitting them as much space to pursue these private concerns—to worship their own gods, so to speak—as is compatible with granting an equal amount of space to all. The tradition of religious toleration is extended to moral toleration.
>
> This privatization of perfection permits James and Nietzsche to agree with Mill and Arnold that poetry should take over the role that religion has played in the formation of individual lives. They also agree that nobody should take over the function of the clergy. For Poets are to a secularized polytheism what the priests of a universal church are to monotheism. Once you become polytheistic, you will turn away not only from priests but from such priest-substitutes as metaphysicians and physicists—from anyone who purports to tell you how things *really* are, anyone who invokes the distinction between the true world and the apparent world that Nietzsche ridiculed in *Twilight of the Idols*. Both monotheism and the kind of metaphysics or science that purports to tell you what they world is *really* like are replaced with democratic politics. A free consensus about how much space for private perfection we can allow each other takes the place of the quest for "objective" values, the quest for a ranking of human needs that does not depend upon such consensus. (*PCP*, 30–31)

able to appreciate the work of other poets. One can be, like Nietzsche, aggressively atheist, or one can, like Dewey, see such aggressive atheism as itself a version of monotheism, as having "something in common with traditional supernaturalism."[9]

These contrasting attitudes toward religious belief will be my principal topic in what follows. But first I want to try to clear away another difficulty which faces any attempt to put Nietzsche and the American pragmatists in the same box: their dramatically opposed attitudes toward democracy.[*]

Nietzsche was a utilitarian only in the sense that he saw no goals for human beings to pursue other than human happiness. He had no interest in the greatest happiness of the greatest number, but only in that of a few exceptional human beings—those with the capacity to be *greatly* happy. Democracy—which he called "Christianity for the people"—seemed to him a way of trivializing human existence. By contrast, James and Dewey took for granted, as Mill had, the Christian ideal of universal human fraternity. Echoing Mill, James wrote "Take any demand, however slight, which any creature, however weak, may make. Ought it not, for its own sole sake, to be desired?" (*WB*, 149)[†]

Romantic utilitarianism, pragmatism, and polytheism are equally compatible with enthusiasm for democracy and with contempt for democracy. The frequent complaint that a philosopher who holds the pragmatic theory of truth cannot give you a reason not to be a facist is perfectly justified. But neither can she give you a reason to be one. Once you become a polytheist in

---

[*] This last paragraph has been deleted from *PCP*. Instead, Rorty has added two new paragraphs, which read: "So far I have been playing along with Berthelot's emphasis on the similarities between Nietzsche and the American pragmatists. Now I want to turn to the two most oblivious differences between them: their attitude toward democracy and their attitude toward religion. Nietzsche thought democracy was "Christianity for the people"—Christianity deprived of the nobility of spirit of which Christ himself, and perhaps a few of the more strenuous saints, had been capable. Dewey thought of democracy as Christianity cleansed of the hieratic, exclusionist elements. Nietzsche thought those who believed in a traditional monotheistic God were foolish weaklings. Dewey thought of them as so spellbound by the work of one poet as to be unable to appreciate the work of other poets. Dewey thought that the sort of "aggressive atheism" on which Nietzsche prided himself is unnecessarily intolerant. It has, he said, "something in common with traditional supernaturalism." Here Rorty is quoting Dewey's work "A Common Faith," in Dewey, *Later Works, 1925-1953*, vol. 9: *1933-1934*, ed. Jo Ann Boydston (Carbondale: Southern Illinois University Press, 1986), 36.

[†] William James, *The Will to Believe* (Cambridge, MA: Harvard University Press, 1979), 149.

the sense I just defined, you have to give up on the idea that philosophy can help you choose among the various deities, and the various forms of life, which are on offer. The choice between enthusiasm and contempt for democracy becomes a choice between, for example, Walt Whitman and Robinson Jeffers, rather than between competing sets of philosophical arguments.

Those who find the pragmatist identification of truth with what is good to believe morally offensive often say that Nietzsche, rather than James and Dewey, drew the proper inference from the abandonment of the idea of an object of knowledge which tells one how to rank human needs. Those who think of pragmatism as a species of irrationalism, and of irrationalism as selling the pass to fascism, say that James and Dewey were blind to the anti-democratic consequences of their own ideas, and naive to think that one can be both a good pragmatist and a good democrat.

Such critics make the same mistake that Nietzsche made. They think that the Christian idea of fraternity is inextricable from Platonism. Platonism, in this sense, is the idea that the will to truth is distinct from the will to happiness—or, to be a bit more precise, the claim that human beings are divided between a quest for a lower, animal form of happiness and a higher, God-like form of happiness. Nietzsche mistakenly thought that once you had, with Darwin's help, given up this idea, and gotten comfortable with the idea that you are just a clever animal, you could have no reason to wish for the happiness of all human beings. He was so impressed by the fact that Christianity would have seemed ludicrous to the Homeric heroes that he was unable, except at occasional fleeting moments, to think of Christianity as the work of strong poets. So he assumed that once poetry had replaced religion as the source of ideals, there would be no place for either Christianity or democracy.

Nietzsche would have done better to ask himself whether the Christian ideal of human fraternity—the idea that for Christians there is neither Jew nor Greek, and the related idea that love is the only law—might have been only accidentally associated with Platonism. This idea might have gotten along nicely without the logocentrism of the Gospel of John, and without Augustine's unfortunate decision that Plato had been a prefiguration of Christian truth. In a different, but possible, world, some early Christian might have anticipated James's remark about Emerson and Wesley by writing, "If Caesar were forced to be Christ, the total human consciousness of the divine would suffer."

A Christianity which was merely ethical—the sort which Jefferson and other Enlightenment thinkers commended, and which was later propounded by theologians of the social gospel—might have sloughed off the exclusionism which had characterized Judaism, and viewed Jesus as one incarnation of the divine among others.* The celebration of an ethics of love would then have taken its place within the tolerant polytheism of the Roman Empire, having disjoined the ideal of human brotherhood from the claim to represent the will of an omnipotent and monopolistic Heavenly Father.†

Had they preached such a merely moral and social gospel, the Christians would never have bothered to develop a natural theology. Thirteenth-century Christians would not have worried about whether the Scriptures could be reconciled with Aristotle. Seventeenth-century ones would not have worried about whether they could be reconciled with Newton, nor nineteenth-century [ones] about whether they could be reconciled with Darwin. These hypothetical Christians would have treated Scripture not as "non-cognitive" but as useful for purposes for which Aristotle, Newton, and Darwin were useless. As things in fact were, however, the Christian churches remained obsessed by the Platonic idea that both Truth and God are One. So it was natural, when physical science began to make some progress, that its practitioners should take over this rhetoric, and thereby stir up a war between science and theology—between Scientific Truth and Religious Faith.

I have imagined such a non-Platonic and non-exclusivist form of Christianity in order to emphasize that no chain of inference links the ideal of human fraternity to the ideal of escaping from a world of appearance inhabited by animals to a real world in which you will become as gods. Nietzsche and contemporary criticisms of what they call "irrationalism" have been tricked by Plato into believing that, unless there is such a real world, Thrasymachus and Callicles are unanswerable.‡ But they are unanswerable only in

---

* This sentence reads differently in *PCP*: "might have sloughed off exclusionism by viewing Jesus as one incarnation of the divine among others" (33).

† In *PCP* Rorty has added at the end of this paragraph the following parenthesis: "(not to mention the idea that there is no salvation outside the Christian Church)" (33).

‡ This sentence and the one that follows appeared differently in *PCP*: "Nietzsche and contemporary critics who see Nietzsche and Dewey as holding similar dangerous 'irrationalist' doctrines have been tricked by Plato into believing that, unless there is such a real world, Thrasymachus, Callicles, and Hitler are unanswerable. But they are unanswerable only in the sense

the sense that there are no premises to which they must assent simply by virtue of being rational, language-using—and, a fortiori, no premises which would lead them to agree that they should treat all other human beings as brothers and sisters. Christianity as a strong poem, one poem among many, can be as socially useful as Christianity backed up by the Platonist claim that God and Truth are interchangeable terms.

So far I have been trying to make Berthelot's idea that Nietzsche and the American pragmatists are parts of a single intellectual movement a bit more plausible by arguing that neither of the Americans need infer their devotion to democracy from their pragmatism. I have argued elsewhere that it is the other way around: that if there is an inferential connection between devotion to democracy and an anti-representationalist view of truth and knowledge, it is that the latter is better suited to the purposes of the former than are representationalist theories. But I shall not pursue this point now.*

Rather, I want to turn to the second big difference between Nietzsche, on the one hand, and James and Dewey, on the other: Nietzsche thinks religious belief morally disreputable, and James and Dewey do not. First, I shall put forward six theses, intended as a sketch of a pragmatist philosophy of religion.† Then I shall try to relate these theses to what James and Dewey actually

---

that, *pace* Habermas, there are no premises to which they must assent simply by virtue of being rational, language-using animals" (33).

* Two further paragraphs follow:

> Although I do not think that there is an inferential path that leads from the anti-representationalist view of truth and knowledge common to Nietzsche, James, and Dewey either to democracy or anti-democracy, I do think there is a plausible inference from democratic convictions to such a view. Your devotion to democracy is unlikely to be wholehearted if you believe, as monotheists typically do, that we can have knowledge of an "objective" ranking of human needs that can overrule the results of democratic consensus. But if your devotion is wholehearted, then you will welcome the utilitarian and pragmatist claim that we have no will to truth distinct from the will to happiness.
>
> So much for the disagreement between Nietzsche and his American colleagues about the value of democracy. I turn now to the other big difference between Nietzsche on the one hand and James and Dewey on the other. Nietzsche thinks religious belief is intellectually disreputable; James and Dewey do not. (*PCP*, 33–34)

† Should read "five" as Rorty actually discusses only five theses.

said about belief in God. Finally, I shall [sketch] my defense of Dewey's version of theism against some objections.

(1)* It is an advantage of the anti-representationalist view of belief which James took over from Bain and Peirce—the view that beliefs are habits of action—that it frees us from the responsibility to unify all our beliefs into a single worldview. If our beliefs are all parts of a single attempt to represent a single world, then they must all hang together fairly tightly. But if they are habits of action, then, since the purposes served by action may blamelessly vary, so may the habits we develop to serve those purposes.

(2)† Nietzsche's attempt to "see science through the optic of art, and art through that of life" is part of the same movement of thought as Arnold's and Mill's substitution of poetry for religion, as the necessary complement to science. Both are attempts to make more room for individuality than can be provided either by orthodox monotheism, or by the Enlightenment's attempt to put science in the place of religion as a source of Truth. So the attempt, by Tillich and others, to treat religious faith as "symbolic," and thereby to treat religion as poetic and poetry as religious, and neither as competing with science, is on the right track. But to make it convincing we need to drop the idea that some parts of culture fulfill our need to know the truth and others fulfill lesser aims. The pragmatists' romantic utilitarianism does drop this idea: if there is no will to truth apart from the will to happiness, there is no way to contrast the cognitive with the non-cognitive, the serious with the non-serious.

(3)‡ Pragmatism does, however, permit us to make another distinction, one which takes over some of the work previously done by the old distinction between the cognitive and the non-cognitive. The new distinction is between projects of social cooperation and projects of individual self-development. Intersubjective agreement is required for the former projects, but not for the latter. Science is the paradigm of a

* "First," *PCP*, 34.
† "Second," *PCP*, 34.
‡ "Third," *PCP*, 34.

project of social cooperation. It is the project of improving man's estate by taking account of every possible observation and experimental result in order to facilitate the making of predictions which will come true. Romantic art is one paradigm of a project of individual self-development.* Religion, if it can be disconnected from both science and morals—from both the attempt to predict the consequences of our actions and the attempt to rank human needs—may be another such paradigm.

(4)† The Idea that we should love Truth is largely responsible for the idea that religious belief is "intellectually irresponsible." But there is no such thing as the love of Truth. What has been called by that name is a mixture of the love of reaching intersubjective agreement, the love of gaining mastery over a recalcitrant set of data, the love of winning arguments, and the love of synthesizing little theories into big theories. It is never an objection to a religious belief that there is no evidence for it. The only possible objection to it can be that it intrudes an individual project into a social and cooperative project, and thereby offends against the teachings of *On Liberty*. Such intrusion is a betrayal of one's responsibilities to cooperate with other human beings, not of one's responsibility to Truth or to Reason.

(5)‡ The attempt to love Truth, and to think of it as one, and as capable of commensurating and ranking human needs, is a secular version of the traditional religious hope that allegiance to something big, powerful, and non-human will persuade that powerful being to take your side in your struggle with other people. Nietzsche despised any such hope as a sign of weakness. Pragmatists who are also democrats have a different objection to such hope for allegiance with power: they see it as a betrayal of the ideal of human fraternity which democracy

---

* These two last sentences read differently in *PCP*: "Natural science is a paradigmatic project of social cooperation: the project of improving man's estate by taking account of every possible observation and experimental result in order to facilitate the making of predictions that will come true. Law is another such paradigm. Romantic art, by contrast, is a paradigmatic project of individual self-development" (35).

† "Fourth," *PCP*, 35.

‡ "Fifth," *PCP*, 35.

inherits from Christianity.* For that ideal finds its best expression in the doctrine, common to Mill and James, that every human need should be satisfied unless doing so causes too many other human needs to go unsatisfied. The pragmatist objection to traditional forms of religion is not that they are *intellectually* irresponsible in disregarding the results of natural science. Rather it is that they are *morally* irresponsible in attempting to circumvent the process of achieving democratic consensus about how to maximize happiness.†

I turn now to the question of how this view of religious belief accords with the views of James and Dewey. It would not, I think, have been congenial to James. But I think it might have suited Dewey. So I shall argue that it is Dewey's rather unambitious and half-hearted *A Common Faith*, rather than James's brave and exuberant "Conclusion" to *Varieties of Religious Experience*, that coheres best with the romantic utilitarianism which both accepted.

James says, in that chapter of *Varieties*, that "the pivot round which the religious life revolves . . . is the interest of the individual in his private personal destiny." Science, however, "repudiating the personal point of view," gives us a picture of nature which "has no one distinguishable ultimate tendency with which it is possible to feel a sympathy." The "driftings of the cosmic atoms" are "a kind of aimless weather, doing and undoing, achieving no proper history, and leaving no result" (*VRE*, 387–388).‡ On the view I have just outlined, he should have followed this up by saying, "But we are free to describe the universe in many different ways. Describing it as the drifting of cosmic atoms is useful for the social project of working together to control our environment and improve man's estate. But that description leaves us entirely free to say, for example, that the Heavens proclaim the glory of God."

Sometimes James seems to take this line, as when, with obvious approval, he quotes James Henry Leuba as saying,

---

* In *PCP* this sentence reads: "They see it as a betrayal of the ideal of human fraternity that democracy inherits from the Judeo-Christian religious tradition" (35).

† In *PCP* this paragraph ends: "They sin not by ignoring Mill's inductive methods, but by ignoring his reflections on liberty" (35).

‡ William James, *Varieties of Religious Experience* (hereafter *VRE* in Rorty's text), 387–388.

"*God is not known, he is not understood, he is used*—sometimes as meat-purveyor, sometimes as moral support, sometimes as friend, sometime as an object of love. If he proves himself useful, the religious conscious-ness can ask no more than that. Does God really exist? How does he exist? What is he? are so many irrelevant questions. Not God, but life, more life, a larger, richer, more satisfying life, is, in the last analysis, the end of religion." (*VRE*, 398)

Unfortunately, however, almost immediately after quoting Leuba he says, "we must next pass beyond the point of view of merely subjective utility, and make inquiry into the intellectual content itself" (*VRE*, 399). He then goes on to argue that the material he has gathered together in *Varieties* provides em-pirical evidence for the hypothesis that "*the conscious person is continuous with a wider self through which saving experiences come.*" He calls this "a pos-itive content of religious experience which, it seems to me, *is literally and objectively true as far as it goes*" (*VRE*, 405).*

On the view I have been suggesting, this claim to literal and objective truth is unpragmatic, hollow, and superfluous. James should have rested content with the argument of "The Will to Believe." As I read that essay, it says that we have a right to believe what we like when we are, so to speak, on our own time.[10] But we abandon this right when we are engaged in, for example, a sci-entific or a political project. For when so engaged it is necessary to reconcile our beliefs, our habits of action, with those of others. On our own time, by contrast, our habits of action are nobody's business but our own. A romantic polytheist will rejoice in what Nietzsche called the "free-spiritedness and many-spiritedness" of individuals, and see the only constraint on this freedom and this diversity as the need not to injure others.

James wobbled on the question of whether what he called "the religious hypothesis" was something to be adopted on "passional" or on "intellectual" grounds. This hypothesis says that "the best things are the more eternal things, the overlapping things, the things in the universe that throw the last stone, so to speak, and say the final word" (*WB*, 29–30). In "The Will to Be-lieve" this is put forward as any hypothesis which cannot be accepted on "in-tellectual" grounds. But in the "Conclusions" to *Varieties* the hypothesis

_____

* These two citations are italicized in *VRE*, but not in Rorty's text.

that "God's existence is the guarantee of an ideal order that shall be permanently preserved" (*VRE*, 407) is one for which he has accumulated evidence. There he also says that the least common denominator of religious beliefs is that "The solution [to the problem presented by a "sense that there is *something wrong about us* as we naturally stand"] is that *we are saved from the wrongness* by making proper connection with the higher powers" (*VRE*, 400). Again, he says that "*the conscious person is continuous with a wider self through which saving experiences come*" (*VRE*, 405).*

James should not have made a distinction between issues to be decided by intellect and issues to be decided by emotion. If he had not, he might have wobbled less. What he should have done instead was to distinguish issues which you must resolve cooperatively with others and issues which you are entitled to resolve on your own—issues such that the problem is to conciliate your habits of action with those of others, and issues which are your own business. In the latter, the problem is to get your own habits of action to cohere with each other sufficiently to have a stable and coherent character. But such a character does not require monotheism, or the belief that Truth is One. It is compatible with the idea that you have many different needs, and that the beliefs that help you fill one set of needs are irrelevant to, and need not be made to cohere with, those which help you to fill another set.

Dewey avoided James's mistakes in this area. One reason he did so is that he was much less prone to a sense of guilt than was James. After he realized that his mother had made him unnecessarily miserable by burdening him with a belief in original sin, he simply stopped thinking that, in James's words, "there is *something wrong about us* as we naturally stand." He no longer believed that we could be "*saved from the wrongness* by making proper connection with the higher powers."† He thought that all that was wrong with us was that the Christian ideal of fraternity had not yet been achieved—society had not yet become pervasively democratic. That was not a problem to be solved by making proper connection with higher powers, but a problem of men to be solved by men.

Dewey's steadfast refusal to have any truck with the notion of original sin, and his suspicion of anything that smacked of such a notion, is bound up with

* In *VRE* there are italics for emphasis. Rorty's text omits them, but they have been restored.
† Italics restored.

his lifelong distaste for the idea of authority—the idea that anything has authority over the members of a democratic community save the decisions of that community. This anti-authoritarian motif is perhaps clearest in his early essay "Christianity and Democracy"—to which Alan Ryan has recently called our attention, saying that it is "a dazzling and dazzlingly brave piece of work."[11] Indeed it is. It must have seemed strange to the University of Michigan's Christian Students Association to be told, in 1892, that "God is essentially and only the self-revealing" and that "the revelation is complete only as men come to realize Him." Dewey spelled out what he meant by going on to say,

> Had Jesus Christ made an absolute, detailed and explicit statement upon all the facts of life, that statement would not have had meaning—it would not have been revelation—until men began to realize in their own action the truth he declared—until they themselves began to *live* it.[12]

This amounts to saying that even if a non-human being tells you something, the only way to figure out whether what you have been told is true is to see whether it gets you the sort of life you want. The only way is to apply the utilitarian test for whether the suggestion made proves to be "good in the way of belief." Granted that hearing what such a being has to say may change your wants, nevertheless you test those new wants and that purported truth in the same way: by living them, trying them out in everyday life, seeing whether they make you and yours happier.

Suppose that a source which you believe to be non-human tells you that all men are brothers, that the attempt to make yourself and those you cherish happier should be expanded into an attempt to make all human beings happy. For Dewey, the source of this suggestion is irrelevant. You might have heard it from a god or a guru, but you might just as well have found it carved out by the waves on a sandy beach. It has no validity unless it is treated as an hypothesis, tried out, and found successful. The good thing about Christianity, Dewey is saying, is that it has been found to work.

More specifically, what has been found to work is the Christian idea of fraternity and equality as a basis for social organization. This worked not just as a Thrasymachian device for avoiding pain—what Rawls calls a "mere *modus vivendi*"—but as a source of the kind of spiritual transfiguration which Platonism and the Christian churches have told us would have to wait upon a future intersection of time with eternity.* "Democracy," Dewey says, "is neither a form of government nor a social expediency, but a metaphysic of the relation of man and his experience in nature."[13] The point of calling it a metaphysic is not, of course, that it is an accurate account of the fundamental relation of reality, but that if one shares Whitman's sense of glorious democratic vistas stretching on indefinitely into the future one has everything which Platonists hoped to get out of such an account. For Whitman offers what Tillich called "a symbol of ultimate concern," of something that can be loved with all one's heart and soul and mind.

Plato's mistake, on Dewey's view, was having identified the ultimate object of *eros* with something unique, atemporal, and non-human rather than with an indefinitely expansible pantheon of transitory temporal accomplishments, both natural and cultural. This mistake lent aid and comfort to monotheism, and Dewey shared Nietzsche's sense that "Monotheism, this rigid consequence of the doctrine of one normal human type—the faith in one normal god beside whom there are only pseudo-gods—was perhaps the greatest danger that has yet confronted humanity."[14] When Christianity is detheologized and treated as a merely social gospel, it acquires the advantage which Nietzsche attributes to polytheism:† it makes the most important human achievement "creating for ourselves our own new eyes," and thereby "honors the rights of individuals." As Dewey put it, "Government, business, art, religion, all social institutions have ... a purpose[:] ... to set free and to develop the capacities of human individuals.... [T]he test of their value is the extent to which they educate every individual into the full stature of his possibility."[15] In a democratic society, everybody gets to worship his or her personal symbol of ultimate concern, unless worship of that symbol interferes with the pursuit of happiness by his or her fellow citizens. Accepting that utilitarian constraint, the one Mill formulated in *On Liberty*, is the only obligation imposed by democratic citizenship, the only exception to democracy's commitment to honor the rights of individuals.

---

* *PCP* adds the following sentence: "It makes possible precisely the sort of nobility of spirit that Nietzsche mistakenly thought could be had only by the exceptional few—those who were capable of being greatly happy." The next paragraph begins: "'Democracy,' Dewey says," (39).

† In *PCP*, this sentence begins: "When Christianity is treated as a merely social gospel, it acquires..." (40).

This means that nobody is under any constraint to seek Truth, nor to care, any more than Sherlock Holmes did, whether the earth revolves around the sun or conversely. Scientific theories become, as do theological and philosophical ones, optional tools for the facilitation of individual or social projects. Science thereby loses the position it inherited from the monotheistic priesthood, as the people who pay proper tribute to the authority of something "not ourselves."*

"Not ourselves" is a term which tolls like a bell throughout the text of Arnold's *Literature and Dogma*, and this may be one of the reasons Dewey had a particular dislike for Arnold.[16] Once he got out from under the influence of his mother's Calvinism, Dewey distrusted nothing more than the suggestion that there was a non-human authority to which human beings owed respect. He praised democracy as the *only* form of "moral and social faith" which does *not* rest "upon the idea that experience must be subjected at some point or other to some form of external control: to some 'authority' alleged to exist outside the process of experience."[17]

This passage in an essay of 1939 echoes one written forty-seven years earlier. In "Christianity and Democracy" Dewey had said that "The one claim that Christianity makes is that God is truth; that as truth He is love and reveals Himself fully to man, keeping back nothing of Himself; that man is so one with the truth thus revealed that it is not so much revealed *to* him as *in* him; he is its incarnation."[18] For Dewey, God is in no way Kierkegaard's Wholly Other. Rather, he is whatever human beings come to see through the eyes that they themselves create.

If atheism is interpreted as anti-monotheism, then Dewey was as aggressive an atheist as has ever lived.† The idea that God might have kept something back, that there might be something not ourselves which it was our duty to discover, was as distasteful to him as was the idea that God could tell us which of our needs took priority over others. He reserved his awe for the universe as a whole, "the community of causes and consequences in which we, together with those not born, are enmeshed." "The continuing life of this comprehensive community of beings," he said, "includes all the significant

---

* In *PCP*, this sentence begins: "Scientists thereby lose the position . . ." (40).
† In *PCP*, this sentence reads: "If atheism were identical with anti-monotheism, then Dewey would have been as aggressive an atheist as has ever lived" (41).

achievement of men in science and art and all the kindly offices of intercourse and communication."

Notice, in the passages I have just quoted, the phrase "together with those not born" and also the adjective "continuing." Dewey's distaste for the eternity and stability on which monotheism prides itself is so great that he can never refer to the universe as a whole without reminding us that the universe is still evolving—still experimenting, still fashioning new eyes with which to see itself. Wordsworth's version of pantheism meant a great deal to Dewey, but Whitman's insistence on futurity meant more. Wordsworth's pantheism saves us from what Arnold called "Hebraism" by making it impossible to treat, as Dewey put it, "the drama of sin and redemption enacted within the isolated and lonely soul of man as the one thing of ultimate importance." But Whitman does something more. He tells us that non-human nature culminates in a community of free men, in their collaboration in building a society in which, as Dewey said, "poetry and religious feeling will be the unforced flowers of life."[19] Dewey's God, his symbol of what he called "the union of the ideal and the actual" was the United States of America treated as a symbol of openness to the possibility of as yet undreamt of, ever more diverse, forms of human happiness. Much of what Dewey wrote consists of endless reiteration of a passage in "Democratic Vistas" at which Whitman says,*

> America . . . counts, as I reckon, for her justification and success, (for who, as yet, dare claim success?) almost entirely on the future. . . . For our New World I consider far less important for what it has done, or what it is, than for results to come.[†]

So much for my contrast between James and Dewey, and for my claim that Dewey is the better exponent of a properly pragmatist philosophy of religion. I shall end with an attempt to reply to Dewey's most recent critic, Alan Ryan. Ryan agrees with Sidney Hook that Dewey was trying to stretch the term "God" too far. Toward the end of his discussion of Dewey's treatment of religion he says,

---

* This sentence reads differently in *PCP*: "Much of what Dewey wrote consists of endless reiteration of Whitman's caution that"; see *PCP*, 41.

† *PCP* ends with this quotation from Walt Whitman, *Democratic Vistas*, in *Complete Poetry and Selected Prose* (New York: Library of America, 1982), 929.

As myself an aggressive atheist, I am not persuaded that the *usefulness* of such ways of talking has much bearing on their *truthfulness;* to put it unkindly, one might complain that Dewey wants the social value of religious belief without being willing to pay the epistemological price for it. To put it less unkindly, we may wonder whether in fact, it is possible to have the *use* of a religious vocabulary without the accretion of supernaturalist beliefs that Dewey wishes to sluff off.[20]

Elsewhere Ryan firms up this latter doubt by saying that Dewey "was simply wrong about the religious attitude" because he failed to realize that "the sense of human finitude" and "the proper self-doubt that the doctrine of original sin picks up (and maybe traduces)" are among the "more serious features of traditional religious belief."[21]

Committed pragmatists like myself would not dream of distinguishing between the usefulness of a way of talking and its truth, nor would we imagine that any belief came with an epistemological price tag attached. We are saddened that, after plowing through those thirty-seven volumes, Ryan can still describe the crux between Dewey and his religious critics as follows:

> Although we learn our understanding of the world in a community and employing the resources of a culture, we cannot help asking whether our interpretation of the world is *right*. . . . The fact that we learn to interpret the world by belonging to a community does not answer the question of whether what we say about the world is *mass* projection of our hopes, fears, and whatever else rather than an account of how the world really is.[22]

We who are more convinced by Dewey than Ryan think that this latter question is one the answer to which can make no difference to practice, and therefore should not be asked. The only form of the question which we will buy is: does any other community, culture, or individual genius have a description of the world which suits our communal or individual purposes better?

But this philosophical quarrel is irrelevant to the answer to Ryan's question about whether "it is possible to have the *use* of a religious vocabulary without the accretion of supernaturalist beliefs that Dewey wishes to sluff off." Here one is tempted to answer: It's not only possible, but actual. Dewey did it.

But of course Ryan does not mean "possible," he means "legitimate." Ryan believes that Dewey was "simply wrong about the religious attitude," and not just because he doesn't have a proper sense of human finitude and proper amount of self-doubt. I suspect that Ryan thinks that, just as you probably can't play chess without the queen, you probably can't have a religious attitude without believing that there is a power not ourselves—a power occupying a place in the same causal order as the comets and the quarks—that makes for righteousness.

The big difference, however, between Ryan's and my own sense of what is important about religion is that for him a sense of sin and of the necessary inferiority of the finite and human to the infinite and non-human is necessary for an outlook to be called religious. I see Christianity as working its way from a form of religion in which the notions of obedience, sin, and immortality are central to one in which these notions have all but vanished. Christianity put forward, though it has never been very faithful to, the suggestion that the only form of obedience which God wants is for us to love one another, that worship of him consists precisely in kindness toward each other, and that the only reward we should expect from showing such kindness is that others will show it to us.

If this is one's view of the Christian message, then it becomes possible to see Mill's utilitarianism as a de-theologized version of Christianity. This may seem paradoxical, since utilitarianism was often said, by its nineteenth-century opponents, to be a godless, atheistic, materialistic creed. Those who take this view of utilitarianism and pragmatism will say that the religious should beware of pragmatists bearing gifts. In particular, they should beware of James's suggestion that anybody has a right to believe anything as long as their doing so does not compromise any cooperative enterprise to which they have committed themselves. They claim that utilitarianism is a view which could only be accepted by somebody who was already an atheist—or at least by somebody who had no religious feeling, somebody whose sense of human possibilities is narrow and blinkered.

This claim, however, presupposes that it is essential to religious faith to submit to the authority of something non-human. Insofar as religion consists in such submission, to what is sometimes called "a sacrifice of the intellect," then it is indeed the case that no one who is religious can be either a utilitarian or a pragmatist. But this is a question-begging definition of religion. If "religious faith" is defined narrowly enough, so that it consists in a refusal to take part in some cooperative enterprise such as scientific research or democratic politics because doing so would offend one's conscience, then of course nobody can have such faith and be a utilitarian.

But there are broader and more plausible definitions of "being religious." For example, it is sometimes said that for followers of Christ, love is the only law. Nothing, on this view of Christianity, takes precedence over the duty to be of assistance to one's neighbor, to treat his or her needs with loving kindness. Credal statements and acts of worship are secondary in comparison to this overriding obligation. Theology is not of the essence of Christian belief, for the Christian life is one of service to others, for only such service counts as service to God. To lead a life devoted to such service counts as Christian, and a fortiori as being religious, in the fullest possible sense of the terms "Christian" and "religious." But a life which neglects such service, no matter how many sacraments are received nor how many professions made, does not.

If one takes this view of Christianity, then it is possible to view utilitarianism as a reformulation of the central Christian doctrine. For utilitarianism says that all human beings, or perhaps even all creatures that can suffer pain, are on a moral par—that they all deserve to have their needs satisfied, insofar as this can be done without harm to others. The egalitarianism which runs through Mill's and James's work is a moral attitude which could only flourish in a culture which had been told, century after century, that God's will was for men to treat each other with loving kindness, that all men are brothers, that love is the first commandment. The idea that everybody—black or white, male or female, Christian or heathen, wise or foolish—has rights which deserve respect and consideration is one which, in Europe and America, has traditionally been backed up by appeal to the agapistic strand in the Christian tradition.

If one does see the claim that love is the only law as central to Christianity, then it is plausible to describe the historical development of Christianity in terms of the gradual substitution of love for power as the essential attribute of God. A god of power is an authority; a god of love is a friend. If one thinks of our relation to God as one of awe, worship, and obedience, then one will insist that utilitarianism and pragmatism have their limits: limits set by God's commands. If God has commanded us to worship him under one name rather than another, or commanded us not to suffer a witch to live, or commanded that women be silent in churches, or that a man shall not lie with a man as with a woman, then no pragmatic or utilitarian consideration should have any force to persuade us of any different opinion. Insofar as Christians see their duty of obedience to God as including more than the duty to serve their fellow human beings, they are worshipping a god of power rather than a god of love.

From this point of view, [William Kingdon] Clifford's claim that we have an obligation to Truth—that the pursuit of truth is something different from the pursuit of human happiness—is a version of the religious idea that we owe obedience to a higher power. Truth, considered as correspondence to the Intrinsic Nature of Reality, is the secularist's equivalent of the God of Power. Science, seen as Clifford does rather than as James does, is the Enlightenment's version of the worship of a god of power. But James, by insisting that reality has no intrinsic nature to be respected, is following up on the agapistic strain in Christianity. In saying that our duty to truth amounts to the duty to respect the needs of those fellow creatures with whom we are involved in cooperative activities, pragmatists are following out the line of thought in Christianity which says that love is the only law.

Suppose that a source which you believe to be non-human tells you that all men are brothers, and that your attempt to make yourself and those you cherish happier should be expanded into an attempt to make all human beings happy. For Dewey, your belief that the source of this suggestion is a non-human power is irrelevant. You might have heard the same suggestion from a false messiah, or you might have found it scratched anonymously on a wall. Whatever its source, it has no validity unless it is treated as a hypothesis, tried out, and found successful. The good thing about the Christian doctrine that love is the only law, Dewey is saying, is not that it has been proclaimed from above, but that it works—works according to utilitarian criteria. Living in this way produces more human happiness than would be produced by living in other ways.

It would be pointless to ask whether Dewey is judging Christianity by utilitarian and pragmatist criteria or instead judging utilitarianism and pragmatism by Christian criteria. He is doing both at once, and sees no need to make one act of judgment prior to the other. For he is treating Christianity, utilitarianism, and pragmatism as so many different ways of getting human beings to stand on their own feet, to rely on each other rather than hoping for help from the non-human. They are, in his eyes, three different forms of the attempt to substitute love for obedience. He sees Christianity not as a matter of exchanging worship for a promise of protection from a power not ourselves, but as a way of freeing us to exchange awe for hope and love. He sees utilitarianism and pragmatism as ways of freeing us from the idea that something non-human—be it the mysterious Will of God or the mysterious True Nature of Reality—deserves respect simply because it is so different from us and so unconcerned with our needs. For Dewey, Kierkegaard's Wholly Other is demonic rather than divine, and the worship of the Wholly Other is idolatry, a betrayal of everything which Christ stood for.

If this humanistic version of Christianity seems strange, that may be because it leaves no room for the doctrine which was closest to Kierkegaard's heart: the doctrine of sin. That we are in sin, Kierkegaard tells us, is something so hard for us sinners to realize that only the operation of Grace can make it possible. For Dewey, on the other hand, there is no such thing as sin, no such thing as radical evil. Every evil, Dewey thought, is a name for a lesser good—a good considered and rejected in the process of deliberation. The anti-authoritarianism which was central to the Enlightenment, and of which anti-clericalism was only one facet, finds its ultimate expression in the substitution of the kind of fraternal cooperation characteristic of an ideal democratic society for the idea of redemption from sin. The Enlightenment rationalists substituted the idea of redemption from ignorance by Science for this theological idea, but Dewey and James wanted to get rid of that notion too. They wanted to substitute the contrast between a less useful set of beliefs and a more useful set for the contrast between ignorance and knowledge. For them, there was no goal called Truth to be aimed at; the only goal was the ever-receding goal of still greater human happiness.

I have given you this sketch of Dewey's attempt to appropriate Christianity for his own pragmatic purposes in order to reply to the suggestion that pragmatism begs the question against religion. As I see it, the only question it begs is whether we are in a state of Sin: whether we need to rely on something non-human for our salvation. Anyone who thinks the consciousness of Sin essential to religious faith will have no use for James's and Dewey's way of reconciling science and religion. But for those who are willing to use the term "religious faith" to cover both a religion of obedient submission to non-human power and a religion of love between human beings, this project of reconciliation may have some attractions.

3 & 4

Universality and Truth[1]

1. Is the Topic of Truth Relevant to Democratic Politics?

The question of whether there are any beliefs or desires common to all human beings is of little interest apart from the vision of a utopian, inclusivist, human community—one which prides itself on the different sorts of people it welcomes, rather than on the firmness with which it keeps strangers out. Most human communities are exclusivist: their sense of identity, and the self-images of their members, depend on pride in not being certain other sorts of people: people who worship the wrong god, eat the wrong foods, or have some other perverse, repellent beliefs or desires. Philosophers would not bother trying to show that certain beliefs and desires are found in every society, or are implicit in some ineliminable human practice, unless they hoped to show that the existence of these beliefs demonstrates the possibility of, or the obligation to construct, a planet-wide inclusivist community. In this paper, I shall use "democratic politics" as a synonym for the attempt to bring such a community into existence.

One of the desires said to be universal by philosophers interested in democratic politics is the desire for truth. In the past, such philosophers have typically conjoined the claim that there is universal human agreement on the supreme desirability of truth with the further premises that truth is correspondence to reality, and that reality has an intrinsic nature (that there is, in Nelson Goodman's terms, a Way the World Is). Given these three premises, they proceed to argue that Truth is One, and that the universal human interest in truth provides a motive for creating an inclusivist community. For

These two lectures appeared as one chapter in Rorty, "Universality and Truth," in *Rorty and His Critics*, ed. Robert Brandom, 1–30 (Malden, MA: Blackwell, 2000) (hereafter *RHC*).

such a community would be best suited to accomplishing our desire of discovering the One Truth. The more of that truth we uncover, the more common ground we shall share, and the more tolerant and inclusivist we shall therefore become. The rise of relatively democratic, relatively tolerant societies in the last few hundred years is said to be due to the increased rationality of modern times, where "rationality" denotes the exercise of a truth-oriented faculty.

The three premises I have listed are sometimes said to be "necessitated by reason." But this claim is usually tautologous, for philosophers who say this typically explain their use of the word "reason" by listing those same three premises as "constitutive of the very idea of rationality." They view colleagues who have doubts about one or another of these three premises as "irrationalists." Degrees of irrationality are attributed according to how many of these premises the distrusted philosopher denies, and also according to how little interest he or she shows in democratic politics.[2]

In this paper I shall consider the prospects for defending democratic politics while denying any of the three premises I have listed. I shall be arguing that what philosophers have described as the universal desire for truth is better described as the universal desire for justification.[3] The grounding premise of my argument is that you cannot aim at something, cannot work to get it, unless you can recognize it once you've got it. One difference between truth and justification is that between the unrecognizable and the recognizable. We shall never know for sure whether a given belief is true, but we can be sure that nobody is able to summon up any residual objections to it, that everybody agrees that it ought to be held.

There are, to be sure, what Lacanians call impossible, indefinable, sublime objects of desire. But a desire for such an object cannot be made relevant to democratic politics.[4] On my view, truth is just such an object. It is too sublime, so to speak, to be either recognized or aimed at. Justification is merely beautiful, but it is recognizable, and therefore capable of being systematically worked for. Sometimes, with luck, justification is even achieved. But that achievement is usually only temporary, since sooner or later, with luck, some new objections to the temporarily justified belief will be developed. As I see it, the yearning for unconditionality—the yearning which leads philosophers to insist that we need to avoid "contextualism" and "relativism"—is, indeed, satisfied by the notion of truth. But this yearning is unhealthy because the price of unconditionality is irrelevance to practice. So I think the topic of truth cannot be made relevant to democratic politics, and that philosophers devoted to such politics should forget about truth and stick to the topic of justification.

2. Habermas on Communicative Reason

In order to place my view within the context of contemporary philosophical controversies, I shall begin with some comments on Habermas. Habermas draws his well-known distinction between subject-centered reason and communicative reason in connection with his attempt to separate out what is useful to democratic politics in the traditional philosophical notion of rationality from what is useless. I think that he makes a tactical error when he tries to preserve the notion of unconditionality. Although I think Habermas is absolutely right that we need to *socialize* and *linguistify* the notion of "reason" by viewing it as communicative,[5] I think that we also need to *naturalize* reason by dropping his claim that "a moment of *unconditionality* is built into *factual processes* of mutual understanding."[6]

Habermas, like Putnam, believes that "reason cannot be naturalized."[7] Both philosophers think it important to insist on this point in order to avoid the "relativism" which seems to them to put democratic politics on a par with totalitarian politics. Both think it important to say that the former sort of politics is more *rational* than the latter. I do not think that we should say this, because I do not think that the notion of "rationality" can be stretched this far. We should admit that we have no neutral ground to stand on when we defend such politics against its opponents. If we do not admit this, I think we can rightly be accused of attempting to smuggle our own social practices into the definition of something universal and ineluctable, because presupposed by the practices of any and every language-user. It would be franker, and therefore better, to say that democratic politics can no more appeal to such presuppositions than can anti-democratic politics, but is none the worse for that.

Habermas agrees with the criticism which post-Nietzschean writers have made of "logocentrism," and specifically with their denial that "the linguistic function of representing states of affairs is the sole human monopoly."[8] So do I, but I would extend this criticism as follows: only over-attention to fact-stating would make one think that there was an aim of inquiry called "truth" in addition to that of justification. More generally, only over-attention to fact-stating would make one think that a claim to universal validity is important for democratic politics. Still more generally, abandoning the logocentric idea that *knowledge* is the distinctively human capacity would leave room for the idea that *democratic citizenship* is better suited for that role. The latter is what we human beings should take most pride in, should make central to our self-image.

As I see it, Habermas's attempt to redefine "reason" after deciding that "the paradigm of the philosophy of consciousness is exhausted"[9]—his attempt to redescribe reason as "communicative" through and through—is insufficiently radical. It is a halfway house between thinking in terms of validity-claims and thinking in terms of justificatory practices. It comes down halfway between the Greek idea that human beings are special because they can *know* (whereas other animals can merely cope) and Dewey's idea that we are special because we can take charge of our own evolution, take ourselves in directions which have neither precedent nor justification in either biology or history.[10]

This latter idea can be made to sound unattractive by dubbing it "Nietzschean" and construing it as one more form of the same will to power which was incarnate in the Nazis. I should like to make it sound attractive by dubbing it "American" and construing it as the idea common to Emerson and Whitman, the idea of a new, self-creating community, united not by knowledge of the same truths but by sharing the same generous, inclusivist, democratic hopes. The idea of communal self-creation, of realizing a dream which has no justification in unconditional claims to universal validity, sounds suspicious to Habermas and Apel because they naturally associate it with Hitler. It sounds better to Americans, because they naturally associate it with Jefferson, Whitman, and Dewey.[11] The moral to be drawn, I think, is that this suggestion is neutral between Hitler and Jefferson.

If one wants neutral principles on the basis of which to decide between Hitler and Jefferson, one will have to find a way of replacing Jefferson's occasional references to natural law, and self-evident political truths, by a more up-to-date version of Enlightenment rationalism. This is the role in which Apel and Habermas cast "discourse ethics." Only if one has given up hope for such neutrality will the alternative I have suggested seem attractive.

Whether one gives up that hope should, I think, be decided—at least in part—on the basis of one's view of the sort of argument from performative self-contradiction which is at the heart of that ethics.

I see that argument as weak and unconvincing, but I have nothing better to put in its place. Because I have nothing better, I am inclined to reject the very idea of neutral principles, and ask myself what philosophers might do for democratic politics apart from trying to ground this politics on principles. My answer is: they can get to work substituting hope for knowledge, substituting the idea that the ability to be citizens of the full-fledged democracy which is yet to come, rather than the ability to grasp truth, is what is important about being human. This is not a matter of *Letzbegründung*, but of redescribing humanity and history in terms which makes democracy seem desirable. If doing that is said to be mere "rhetoric" rather than "argument," I should rejoin that it is no more or less rhetorical and argumentative that my opponents' attempt to describe discourse and communication in terms that make democracy seem linked to the intrinsic nature of humanity.

3. Truth and Justification

There are many uses for the word "true," but the only one which could not be eliminated from our linguistic practice with relative ease is the cautionary use.[12] That is the use we make of the word when we contrast justification and truth, and say that a belief may be justified but not true. Outside of philosophy, this cautionary use is used to contrast less-informed with better-informed audiences, and more generally past audiences with future audiences. In non-philosophical contexts, the point of contrasting truth and justification is simply to remind oneself that there may be objections (arising from newly discovered data, or more ingenious explanatory hypotheses, or a shift in the vocabulary used for describing the objects under discussion) which have not occurred to any of the audiences to whom the belief in question has so far been justified. This sort of gesture toward an unpredictable future is made, for example, when we say that our present moral and scientific beliefs may look as primitive to our remote descendants as those of the Greeks look to us.

My grounding premise, that you can only work for what you could recognize, is a corollary of James's principle that a difference has to make a difference to practice before it is worth discussing. The only difference between truth and justification which makes such a difference is, as far as I can see, the difference between old audiences and new audiences. So I take the appropriate pragmatist attitude toward truth to be: it is no more necessary to have a philosophical theory about the nature of truth, or the meaning of the word "true," than it is to have one about the nature of danger, or the meaning of the word "danger." The principal reason we have a word like "danger" in the language is to caution people: to warn them that they may not have envisaged all the consequences of their proposed action. We pragmatists, who think that beliefs are habits of action rather than attempts to correspond to reality, see the cautionary use of the word "true" as flagging a special sort of danger. We use it to remind ourselves that people in different circumstances—people facing future audiences—may not be able to justify the belief which we have triumphantly justified to all the audiences we have encountered.

Given this pragmatist view of the function of the word "true," what about the claim that all human beings desire truth? This claim is ambiguous between the claim that all of them desire to justify their beliefs to some, though not necessarily all, other human beings, and the claim that they all want their beliefs to be true. The first claim seems to me unobjectionable. The second claim, however, seems to me dubious, unless it is merely an alternative formulation of the first. For the only other interpretation which we pragmatists can give to the second claim is that all human beings are concerned about the danger that someday an audience will come into being before which a presently justified belief cannot be justified.

But, in the first place, mere fallibilism is not what philosophers who hope to make the notion of truth relevant to democratic politics want. In the second place, such fallibilism is not, in fact, a feature of all human beings. It is much more prevalent among inhabitants of wealthy, secure, tolerant, inclusivist societies than elsewhere—for these people are brought up to bethink themselves that they might be mistaken, that there are people out there who might disagree with them, and whose disagreements need to be taken into account. If you favor democratic politics, you will want to encourage fallibilism, but there are other ways to do so besides harping on the difference between the conditional character of justification and the unconditional character of truth. One might, for example, harp on the sad fact that many previous communities have betrayed their own interests by being too sure of themselves, and so failing to attend to objections raised by outsiders.

Furthermore, we should distinguish between fallibilism and philosophical skepticism. Fallibilism has nothing in particular to do with the quest for universality and unconditionality. Skepticism does. One will usually not go into philosophy unless one is impressed by the sort of skepticism found in Descartes's *Meditations,* the sort of skepticism which says that the mere possibility of error defeats knowledge-claims. Not many people find this sort of skepticism interesting, but those who do ask themselves: is there any way in which we can ensure ourselves against having beliefs which may be unjustifiable to some future audience? Is there any way in which we can ensure that we have beliefs which are justifiable to any and every audience?

The tiny minority which finds this question interesting consists almost entirely of philosophy professors, and divides into three groups.

(1) Skeptics like [Barry] Stroud say that Descartes's argument from dreams is unanswerable; for the skeptics, there is always an audience, the future self who has awoken from the dream, who will not be satisfied by any justification offered by our present, possibly dreaming, self.

(2) Foundationalists like [Roderick] Chisholm say that, even if we are now dreaming, we cannot be wrong about *certain* beliefs.

(3) Coherentists like [Wilfrid] Sellars say that "all our beliefs are up for grabs, though not all at once."

We pragmatists, who have been impressed by Peirce's criticisms of Descartes, think that both skeptics and foundationalists are led astray by the picture of beliefs as attempts to represent reality, and by the associated idea that truth is a matter of correspondence to reality. So we become coherentists.[13] But we coherentists remain divided about what, if anything, needs to be said about truth. I think that, once one has explicated the distinction between justification and truth by that between present and future justifiability, there is little more to be said. My fellow coherentists—Apel, Habermas, and Putnam—think, as Peirce also did, that there is a lot more to be said, and that saying it is important for democratic politics.[14]

4. "Universal Validity" and "Context-Transcendence"

Putnam, Apel, and Habermas all take over from Peirce an idea which I reject: the idea of convergence upon the One Truth.[15] Instead of arguing that because reality is One, and truth correspondence to that One Reality, Peirceans argue that the idea of convergence is built into the presuppositions of discourse. They all agree that the principal reason why reason cannot be naturalized is that reason is normative and norms cannot be naturalized. But, they say, we can make room for the normative without going back to the traditional idea of a duty to correspond to the intrinsic nature of One Reality. We do this by attending to the universalistic character of the idealizing presuppositions of discourse. This strategy has the advantage of setting aside metaethical questions about whether there is a moral reality to which our moral judgments might hope to correspond, as our physical science supposedly corresponds to physical reality.[16]

Habermas says that every validity claim has "a transcendent moment of universal validity [which] bursts every provinciality asunder" in addition to its strategic role in some context-bound discussion. As I see it, the only truth in this idea is that many claims to validity are made by people who would be willing to defend their claims before audiences other than the one which they are currently addressing. (Not all assertions, obviously, of this sort; lawyers, for example, are quite aware that they fashion their claims to suit the quaint context of a highly local jurisprudence.) But willingness to take on new and unfamiliar audiences is one thing; bursting provinciality asunder is another.

Habermas's doctrine of a "transcendent moment" seems to me to run together a commendable willingness to try something new with an empty boast. To say "I'll try to defend this against all comers" is often, depending upon the circumstances, a commendable attitude. But to say "I can successfully defend this against all comers" is silly. Maybe you can, but you are no more in a position to claim that you can than the village champion is to claim that he can beat the world champion. The only sort of situation in which you would be in a position to say the latter is one in which the rules of the argumentative game are agreed upon in advance—as in "normal" (as opposed to "revolutionary") mathematics, for example.

But in most cases, including the moral and political claims in which Habermas is most interested, there are no such rules. The notion of context-dependence has a clear sense in the sorts of cases I have just mentioned—in provincial law courts and in language-games, such as normal mathematics, which are regulated by clear and explicit conventions. For most assertions, however, neither it nor that of "universal validity" has such a sense. For most assertions—"Clinton is the better candidate," "Alexander came before Caesar," "Gold is insoluble in hydrochloric acid," and the like—it is hard to see why I should ask myself "is my claim context-dependent or universal?" No difference to practice is made by coming down in favor of one alternative rather than the other.

Habermas puts forward an analogue of this distinction between the context-dependent and the universal which might seem more relevant to practice. This analogue is what he calls "the tension between facticity and validity." He views this tension as a central philosophical problem, and says that this tension is responsible for many of the difficulties encountered in theorizing democratic politics.[17] He thinks it a distinctive and valuable feature of his theory of communicative action that it "already absorbs the tension between facticity and validity into its fundamental concepts."[18] It does so by distinguishing between the "strategic" use of discourse and the "use of language oriented to reaching understanding."[19] This latter distinction might seem the one we are looking for: the one which lets us interpret the distinction between context-dependence and universality in a way which makes a difference to practice.

As I see it, however, the distinction between the strategic and non-strategic use of language is just the distinction between cases in which all we care about is convincing others and cases in which we hope to learn something. In the latter set of cases, we are quite willing to give up our present views if we hear something better. These cases are two ends of a spectrum, at one end of which we shall use any dirty trick we can (lying, *omissio veri, suggestio falsi,* etc.) to convince. At the other end we talk to others as we talk to ourselves when we are most at ease, most reflective, and most curious. Most of the time we are somewhere in the middle between these two extremes.

My problem is that I do not see that the two extremes have anything in particular to do with the distinction between context-dependence and universality. "The pure pursuit of truth" is a traditional name for the sort of conversation which takes place at one end of this spectrum. But I do not see what that sort of conversation has to do with universality or with unconditionality.

It is "non-strategic" in the sense that in such conversations we let the wind blow where it listeth, but it is hard to see that the assertions we make in such conversations presuppose something which is not presupposed in the assertions I make when I am at the other end of the spectrum.

Habermas, however, thinks that unless we recognize that "the validity claims raised *hic et nunc* and aimed at intersubjective recognition or acceptance can at the same time overshoot local standards for taking yes / no positions," we shall not see that "this transcendent moment alone distinguishes the practices of justification oriented to truth claims from other practices that are regulated merely by social convention."[20] This passage is a good example of what seems to me Habermas's undesirable commitment to the logocentric distinction between opinion and knowledge—a distinction between mere obedience to *nomoi,* even the sort of *nomoi* which would be found in a utopian democratic society, and the kind of *phusei* relation to reality which is provided by the grasp of truth. Both the opinion-knowledge and the *nomos-physis* distinction appear to Deweyans as remnants of Plato's obsession with the kind of certainty found in mathematics, and, more generally, with the idea that the universal, being somehow eternal and unconditional, somehow provides an escape from what is particular, temporal, and conditioned.

In this passage Habermas is, I take it, using the term "practices of justification oriented to truth claims" to refer to the nicer end of the spectrum I described above. But from my point of view, truth has nothing to do with it. These practices do not transcend social convention. Rather, they are regulated by certain *particular* social conventions: those of a society even more democratic, tolerant, leisured, wealthy and diverse than our own—one in which inclusivism is built into everybody's sense of moral identity. In this society, everybody always welcomes strange opinions on all sorts of topics. These are also the conventions of certain lucky parts of contemporary society: for example, of university seminars, of summer camps for intellectuals, and so on.[21]

Perhaps the most far-reaching difference between Habermas and me is that pragmatists like myself sympathize with the anti-metaphysical, "postmodern" thinkers he criticizes when they suggest that the idea of a distinction between social practice and what transcends such practice is an undesirable remnant of logocentrism. Foucault and Dewey can agree that, whether or not inquiry is always a matter of "power," it never transcends social practice. Both would say that the only thing that can transcend a social practice is another social practice, just as the only thing that can transcend a present audience is a future audience. Similarly, the only thing that can transcend a discursive strategy is another discursive strategy—one aimed at other, better, goals. But, because I do not know how to aim at it, I do not think that "truth" names such a goal. I know how to aim at greater honesty, greater charity, greater patience, greater inclusiveness, and so on. I see democratic politics as serving such concrete, describable goals. But I do not see that it helps things to add "truth" or "universality" or "unconditionality" to our list of goals, for I do not see what we will do differently depending upon whether or not we make such additions.

It may sound at this point as if the difference between me and Habermas is one that makes no difference to practice: we both have the same utopias in mind, and we both engage in the same sort of democratic politics. So why quibble about whether to call utopian communication practices "oriented to truth" or not? Why quibble about the relevance of truth to democratic politics? The answer is that Habermas thinks that it does make a difference to practice, because he gets to make an argumentative move which is not open to me: he gets to accuse his opponents of performative self-contradiction. Habermas thinks that "the universal discourse of an unbounded community of interpretation" is "unavoidably assumed" by anybody, even me, who gets into an argument. He says that "Even if these presuppositions have an *ideal* content that can only be approximately satisfied, all participants must *de facto* accept them [the presuppositions of communication] whenever they assert or deny the truth of a statement in any way and would like to enter into argumentation aimed at justifying this validity claim."[22]

But what about somebody who is outraged (as are many trustees of American universities) by the social conventions of the better parts of the better universities—places where even the most paradoxical and unpromising claims are seriously discussed, and in which feminists, atheists, homosexuals, blacks, etc. are taken seriously as moral equals and conversational partners? I take it that on Habermas's view such a person will be *contradicting* themselves if they offer *arguments* to the effect that these conventions should be replaced with other, more exclusivist, conventions. By contrast, I cannot tell the narrow-minded trustee that he is contradicting himself. I can only try to wheedle him into greater tolerance by the usual indirect means: giving examples of present platitudes which were once paradoxes, of the contributions to culture made by black and female homosexual atheists, and so on.[23]

The big question is whether anybody has ever been convinced by the charge of performative self-contradiction. I do not think that there are many clear examples of such a charge being taken to heart. If you tell a bigot of the sort I've sketched that he is committed to making context-surpassing validity claims, to aiming at truth, he will probably agree that that is exactly what he is doing. If you tell him that he cannot make such claims and still balk at the paradoxes or the people at whom he balks, he will probably not get the point. He will say that people who advance such paradoxes are too crazy to argue with or about, that women have a distorted view of reality, and the like. He will think it irrational or immoral, or both, to take such paradoxes and people seriously.[24]

I cannot see much difference between the bigot's reaction to me and Habermas and Habermas's and my reactions to him. I cannot see that anything like "communicative reason" favors our reactions rather than his. This is because I do not see why the term "reason" is not as much up for grabs as the term "academic freedom" or "morality" or "pervert," nor how the anti-foundationalist coherentism which Habermas and I share can make room for a non-recontextualizable, non-relativizable, conversation-stopper called "performative self-contradiction." What the bigot and I do, and I think should do, when told that we have violated a presupposition of communication is to haggle about the meanings of the terms used in stating the purported presupposition—terms like "true," "argument," "reason," "communication," "domination," etc.[25]

This haggling will, with luck, eventually turn into a mutually profitable conversation about our respective utopias—our respective ideas about what an ideal society, empowering an ideally competent audience, would look like. But this conversation is not going to end with the bigot's reluctant admission that he has entangled himself in a contradiction. Even if I should, *mirabile dictu,* succeed in convincing him of the worth of my utopia, his reaction will be to regret his own previous lack of curiosity and imagination, rather than to regret his failure to spot his own presuppositions.

5. Context-Independence without Convergence: Albrecht Wellmer's View

I agree with Apel and Habermas that Peirce was right in telling us to talk about discourse rather than about consciousness, but I think that the *only* ideal presupposed by discourse is that of being able to justify your beliefs to a *competent* audience. As a coherentist, I think that if you can agree with other members of such an audience about what is to be done, then you do not have to worry about your relation to reality. But everything depends upon what constitutes a competent audience. Unlike Apel and Habermas, the moral I draw from Peirce is that we philosophers who are concerned with democratic politics should leave truth alone, as a sublimely undiscussable topic, and instead turn to the question of how to persuade people to broaden the size of the audience they take to be competent, to increase the size of the relevant community of justification. The latter project is not only relevant to democratic politics, it pretty much *is* democratic politics.

Apel and Habermas think that the demand to maximize the size of this community is already, so to speak, built into communicative action. This is the cash value of their claim that every assertion claims universal validity.[26] Albrecht Wellmer, who, like me, rejects the convergentism which Habermas and Apel share with Putnam, nevertheless accepts their claim that our truth claims "transcend the context—the local or cultural context—in which they are raised."[27] He opposes this claim to my own ethnocentrism, and interprets the latter as denying some things he thinks it important to affirm: in particular, that "the arguments for supporting and critically developing democratic-liberal principles and institutions" are "good arguments,"[28] even though they do not convince everybody.*

My problem with Wellmer, Apel, and Habermas is that I do not see what the pragmatic force of saying that an argument which, like all other arguments, convinces certain people and not others is a "good argument." This seems like saying that a tool which, like all tools, is useful for certain purposes but not others is a good tool. Imagine the surgeon who says, after unsuccessfully attempting to dig a tunnel out of his prison cell with his scalpel, "Still, it's a good tool." Then picture him saying, after unsuccessfully trying to convince his guards to let him escape so that he may resume his position as leader of the resistance, "Still, they are good arguments."

My problem is intensified when I ask myself whether my truth claims "transcend my local cultural context." I have no clear idea whether they do

---

* This last sentence, which begins right after the citation from Wellmer, does not appear in the Spanish translation, although it does appear in the manuscript.

or not, because I cannot see what "transcendence" means here. I cannot even see what the point of taking my assertion as "making a truth claim" is. When I believe that *p,* and express this belief by asserting it in the course of a conversation, am I making a *claim?* What is the force of saying that I am? What does saying so add to saying that I am (to speak with Peirce) informing my interlocutor about my habits of action, giving her hints about how to predict and control my future conversational and non-conversational behavior? Depending on the situation at hand, I may also be inviting her to disagree with me by telling me about her different habits of action, suggesting that I am prepared to give reasons for my belief, trying to make a good impression on her, and a thousand other things. As Austin reminded us, there are lots of things I do when I make an assertion which can be interpreted as part of the give and take between me and my interlocutor. This give and take is a matter of, roughly, the reciprocal adjustment of our behavior, the strategic coordination of that behavior in ways which may prove to be mutually profitable.

Of course, if somebody asks me, after I have asserted *p,* whether I believe *p* to be true, I shall say "yes." But I shall wonder, with Wittgenstein, what the point of his question is. Is he questioning my sincerity? Is he expressing incredulity about my ability to offer reasons for my belief? I can try to straighten things out by asking him to spell out why he asks. But if he replies: "I just wanted to be sure you were making a context-transcendent truth claim," I shall be baffled. What does he want to be reassured about, exactly? What would it be like for me to make a context-*dependent* assertion? Of course, in the trivial sense that an assertion may not always be a propos, all assertions are context-dependent. But what would it mean for the proposition asserted to be context-dependent, as opposed to the speech-act being context-dependent?

I am not sure how people like Habermas and Wellmer, who have given up on correspondence theories of truth and consequently cannot distinguish between a claim to report a habit of action and a claim to represent reality, can draw this distinction between context-dependence and context-independence. My best guess is that they believe that, in Wellmer's words, "Whenever we raise a truth claim on the basis of what we take to be good arguments or compelling evidence we *take* the epistemic conditions prevailing here and now to be ideal in the following sense: we presuppose that no arguments or evidences will come up in the future which would put our own truth claim into question." Or, as Wellmer also puts it, "relying upon reasons or evidences as compelling means to exclude the possibility of being proved wrong as time goes on."[29]

If that is what it takes to make a context-transcendent truth claim, then I have never made one. I would not know how to exclude the possibility Wellmer describes. Nor would I know how to presuppose that no arguments or evidence will turn up in the future which will cast doubt on my belief. Relying once again on the fundamental pragmatist principle that any difference has to make a difference to practice, I want to know whether this "excluding" and "presupposing" are things I can decide to do or not to do. If they are, I want to know more about how to go about doing them. If they are not, they seem to me empty.

I can make my point in another way by asking: What is the difference between a metaphysician, committed to a correspondence theory of truth, telling me that, whether I know it or will admit it or not, my assertions automatically, willy-nilly, amount to a claim to represent reality accurately, and my fellow Peirceans telling me that they automatically, willy-nilly, amount to an exclusion of possibilities, or a presupposition about what the future holds? In both cases I am being told that I presuppose something which, even after considerable reflection, I do not think I believe. But the notion of "presupposition," when it is extended to beliefs which the purported presupposer stoutly denies, becomes hard to distinguish from the notion of "redescription of person A in person B's." If A can explain what I am doing and why I am doing it in her own terms, what right has B got to keep on saying "No, what A is *really* doing is . . ."? In the case at hand, we Deweyans think we have a perfectly good way of describing our own behavior—behavior of which Habermas approves—in ways which eschew terms like "universal" and "unconditional" and "transcendence."

It seems to me in the spirit of Peirce's criticism of Descartes's "make-believe doubt" to raise the question of whether we are not dealing here with "make-believe transcendence"—a sort of make-believe response to a make-believe doubt. Real doubt, Peirce said, comes when some concrete difficulty is envisaged if one acts according to the habit which is the belief. (Such a difficulty might be, for example, having to cease asserting, and believing, some relevant but conflicting proposition.) Real transcendence, I should say, occurs when I say "I am prepared to justify this belief not just to people who share the following premises with me, but to lots of other people who do not share those premises but with whom I share certain others."[30] The question of whether I am so prepared is a concrete practical question, whose answer I determine by, for example, imaginatively previewing various other audiences' responses to my assertion that p, and my subsequent behavior.

But such experiments in imagination obviously have limits. I cannot imagine myself defending my assertion to *any possible* audience. In the first place, I can usually dream up audiences to whom it would be pointless to try to justify my belief. (Try defending beliefs about justice to Neanderthals or to Nazi prison guards, or about quarks to Aristotle, or about trigonometry to three-year-olds.) In the second place, no good pragmatist should ever use the term "all possible." He does not know how to imagine or to discover the bounds of possibility. Indeed, he cannot figure out what the point of attempting such feats could be. Under what concrete circumstances would it be important to consider the difference between "all the X's I can think of" and "all possible X's"?[31] How could this difference make a difference to practice?

I conclude that Wellmer's way of distinguishing between context-dependent and context-independent claims cannot be made plausible, at least to pragmatists. Since I can think of no better way, I think that we should ask why Wellmer, Apel, and Habermas think this distinction worth drawing. The obvious answer is that they want to avoid the "relativism" which contextualism purportedly entails. So I turn now to what Wellmer calls "the antinomy of truth"[32]—the clash between relativist and absolutist intuitions.

6. Must Pragmatists Be Relativists?

Toward the beginning of his "Truth, Contingency and Modernity" Wellmer writes as follows:

> If there is irresolvable disagreement about the possibility of justifying truth claims, about standards of argumentation or evidential support, e.g., between members of different linguistic, scientific or cultural communities, may I still suppose that there *are*—somewhere—the *correct* standards, the *right* criteria, in short that there is an *objective* truth of the matter? Or should I rather think that truth is "relative" to cultures, languages, communities or even persons? While relativism (the second

alternative) appears to be inconsistent, absolutism (the first alternative) seems to imply metaphysical assumptions. Let's call this the antinomy of truth. Much important philosophical work has been done in the last decades to resolve this antinomy of truth; either by trying to show that absolutism need not be metaphysical or by trying to show that the critique of absolutism need not lead to relativism.[33]

My problem with Wellmer's antinomy is that I do not think that denying that there are "the *correct* standards" should lead anybody to say that *truth* (as opposed to justification) is "relative" to something. As far as I can see, nobody would think that the critique of absolutism leads to relativism unless she thought that the only reason for justifying our beliefs to each other is that such justification makes it more likely that our beliefs are true.

I do not think that there is any reason to think that such justification makes it more likely that our beliefs are true.[34]* But I do not think it is a cause for concern, since I do not think our practice of justifying our beliefs needs justification. If I am right that the only indispensable function of the word "true" (or any other indefinable normative term, such as "good" or "right") is to caution, to warn against danger by making gestures toward unpredictable situations (future audiences, future moral dilemmas, etc.), then it does not make much sense to ask whether or not justification leads to truth. Justification to more and more audiences leads to less and less danger of rebuttal, and thus to less and less need for caution. ("If I convinced *them,*" we often say to ourselves, "I should be able to convince *anybody.*") But one would only say that it leads to *truth* if one could somehow project from the conditioned to the unconditioned—from all imaginable to all possible audiences.

Such a projection makes some sense if one believes in convergence. For such a belief sees the space of reasons as finite and structured, so that as more and more audiences are satisfied, more and more members of a finite set of possible objections are eliminated. One will be encouraged to see the space of

---

*In *RHC*, this paragraph begins, "I have argued elsewhere that there is no reason to think that such justification makes this more likely." Then there is a new endnote, 34, that reads: "See 'Is truth a goal of inquiry? Donald Davidson vs. Crispin Wright' reprinted in my *Truth and Progress*." See Richard Rorty, "Is Truth a Goal of Inquiry? Donald Davidson vs. Crispin Wright," in *Philosophical Papers*, vol. 3: *Truth and Progress*, 19–42 (Cambridge: Cambridge University Press, 1998).

reasons in this way if one is a representationalist, because one will see reality (or at least the spatio-temporal hunk of it relevant to most human concerns) as finite and as constantly shoving us out of error and toward truth, discouraging inaccurate representations of itself and thereby producing increasingly accurate ones.[35] But if one does not take knowledge to be accurate representation of reality, nor truth as correspondence to reality, then it is harder to be a convergentist, and harder to think of the space of reasons as finite and structured.

Wellmer, it seems to me, wants to project from the conditioned (our various experiences of success in justifying our beliefs) to the unconditioned (truth). The big difference between me and Wellmer is that I think that the answer to the question "Do our democratic and liberal principles define just *one* possible political language game among others?" is an unqualified "yes." Wellmer, however, says that "a qualified 'no' can be justified, and by justification I now mean not justification *for us,* but justification, *period.*"[36]

As I see it, the very idea of "justification *period*" commits Wellmer to the thesis that the logical space of reason-giving is finite and structured. So I should urge him to abandon the latter thesis for the same reasons that he abandoned Apel's and Habermas's convergentism. But, oddly enough, these reasons are pretty much the reasons he gives for giving his "qualified 'no.'" His central point in defense of this answer is one which I whole-heartedly accept: viz., that the very idea of incompatible, and perhaps reciprocally unintelligible, language-games is a pointless fiction, and that in real cases representatives of different traditions and cultures can always find a way to talk over their differences.[37] I entirely agree with Wellmer that "rationality—in any relevant sense of the word—cannot end at the borderline of closed language games (since there is no such thing)."[38]

Our disagreement starts when, after a semi-colon, Wellmer finishes his sentence with "but then the ethnocentric contextuality of all argumentation is quite well compatible with the raising of truth claims which transcend the context—the local or cultural context—*in* which they are raised and in which they can be justified." I should have finished that same sentence by saying "but then the ethnocentric contextuality of all argumentation is quite well compatible with the claim that a liberal and democratic society can bring together, include, all sorts of diverse *ethnoi.*" I see no way to get from the premise that there are no such things as mutually unintelligible standards of argument to the conclusion that the claims of democratic societies are "context-transcendent."*

Here is a way of summing up the difference between me and Wellmer. We agree that one reason to prefer democracies is that they enable us to construct ever bigger and better contexts of discussion. But I stop there, and Wellmer goes on. He adds that this reason is not just a justification of democracy *for us,* but "a justification, *period.*" He thinks that "the democratic and liberal principles of modernity" should "*pace* Rorty" be "understood in a universalistic sense."[39]

My problem, of course, is that I do not have the option of understanding them that way. Pragmatists like me can't figure out how to tell whether we are understanding a justification as just a "justification for us" or as a "justification, *period.*" This strikes me as trying to tell whether I think of my scalpel or my computer as "a good tool for this task" or as "a good tool, *period.*"

At this point, however, one could imagine Wellmer rejoining with, "Then so much the worse for pragmatism. Any view which makes you unable to understand a distinction everybody else understands must have something wrong with it." My rebuttal would be: you are only entitled to that distinction as long as you can back it up with a distinction between what seem good reasons to us and what seem good reasons to something like an ahistorical Kantian tribunal of reason. But you deprived yourself of *that* possibility when you gave up on convergentism, and thus gave up the non-metaphysical substitute for such a tribunal—viz., the idealization called the "undistorted communication situation."

I agree with Wellmer that "democratic and liberal institutions are the only ones which could possibly coexist with a recognition of contingency and still reproduce their own legitimacy," at least if one takes "reproduce their own legitimacy"[40] to mean something like "make its view of the situation of human beings in the universe hang together with its political practice." But I don't think that the recognition of contingency serves as a "justification, *period*" for democratic politics because I don't think that it does what Wellmer says:

---

* This last sentence is missing from the Spanish translation, but it appears both in the manuscript and *RHC*, 12.

namely, "destroys the intellectual bases of dogmatism, foundationalism, authoritarianism and of moral and legal inequality."[41]

This is because I don't think that dogmatism or moral inequality *have* "intellectual bases." If I am a bigoted proponent of the inequality of blacks, women, and homosexuals to straight white males, I need not necessarily appeal to the denial of contingency by invoking a metaphysical theory about the true nature of human beings. I could, but I might also, when it came to philosophy, be a pragmatist. A bigot and I can say the same Foucauldian / Nietzschean thing: that the only real question is one of power, the question of which community is going to inherit the earth, mine or my opponent's. One's choice of a community for that role is intertwined with one's sense of what counts as a competent audience.[42]

The fact that there are no mutually unintelligible language games does not, in itself, do much to show that disputes between racists and anti-racists, democrats and fascists, can be decided without resort to force. Both sides may agree that, although they understand what each other says perfectly well, and share common views on most topics (including, perhaps, the recognition of contingency), there seems no prospect of reaching agreement on the particular issue at hand. So, both sides say as they reach for their guns, it looks as if we'll have to fight it out.

My answer to Wellmer's question about whether our "democratic and liberal principles define just *one* possible political language game among others" is "yes, if the force of the question is to ask whether there is something in the nature of discourse which singles this game out." I cannot see what other force the question could have, and I think we have to rest content with saying that no philosophical thesis, either about contingency or about truth, does anything *decisive* for democratic politics.

By "decisive" I mean doing what Apel and Habermas want to do: convicting the anti-democrat of a performative self-contradiction. The most that an insistence on contingency can do for democracy is to supply one more debating point on the democratic side of the argument, just as the insistence that (for example) only the Aryan race is in tune with the intrinsic, necessary nature of things can supply one more debating point on the other side. I cannot take the latter point seriously, but I do not think that there is anything self-contradictory in the Nazi's refusal to take me seriously. We may both have to reach for our guns.

7. Is Reason Unified by Universalistic Presuppositions?

Unlike Habermas, I do not think that disciplines like philosophy, linguistics, and developmental psychology can do much for democratic politics. I see the development of the social conventions in which Habermas and I both rejoice as a lucky accident. Still, I should be happy to think that I was wrong about this. Maybe the gradual development of those conventions *does*, as Habermas thinks, illustrate a universal pattern of phylo- or onto-genetic development, a pattern captured by the rational reconstruction of competences offered by various human sciences and illustrated by the transition from "traditional" to modern, "rationalized" societies.[43]

But, unlike Habermas, I should be unperturbed if the offers currently made by the human sciences were withdrawn: if Chomsky's universalistic ideas about communicative competence were repudiated by a connectionist revolution in artificial intelligence,[44] if Piaget's and Kohlberg's empirical results proved to be unduplicatable, and so on. I do not see that it matters much whether there is a universal pattern here. I do not much care whether democratic politics are an expression of something deep, or whether they express nothing better than some hopes which popped from nowhere into the brains of a few remarkable people (Socrates, Christ, Jefferson, etc.)* and which, for unknown reasons, became popular.

Habermas and Apel think that the way to create a cosmopolitan community is to study the nature of something called "rationality" which all human beings share, something already present within them but insufficiently acknowledged. That is why they would be depressed if the offers made by Chomsky, Kohlberg, etc., were, in the course of time, withdrawn. But suppose we say that all that rationality amounts to—all that marks human beings off from other species of animals—is the ability to use language and thus to have sentential attitudes—beliefs and desires. It seems plausible to add that there is no more reason to expect all the organisms which share this ability to form a single community of justification than to expect such a community to unite all the organisms able to walk long distances, or to remain monogamous, or to digest vegetables. One will not expect such a single community of

---

*This parenthesis with the names of Socrates, Christ, Jefferson, etc. does not appear in the Spanish translation, although it does appear in the manuscript and in *RHC*.

justification to be created by the ability to communicate if one takes the ability to use language to be, like the prehensile thumb, just one more gimmick which organisms have developed to increase their chances of survival.

If we combine this Darwinian point of view with the holistic attitude toward intentionality and language-use found in Wittgenstein and Davidson, we shall say that there is no language-use without justification, no ability to believe without an ability to argue about what beliefs to have. But this is not to say that the ability to use language, to have beliefs and desires, entails a desire to justify one's belief to *every* language-using organism one encounters. It is not to say that any language-user who comes down the road will be treated as a member of a competent audience.

On the contrary, human beings usually divide up into mutually suspicious (*not* mutually unintelligible) communities of justification—mutually exclusive groups—depending upon the presence or absence of sufficient overlap in belief and desire. The principal source of conflict between human communities is the belief that I have no reason to justify my beliefs to you, and none in finding out what alternative beliefs you may have, because you are an infidel, a foreigner, a woman, a child, a slave, a pervert, or an untouchable. In short, you are not "one of us," not one of the *real* human beings, the *paradigm* human beings, the ones whose persons and opinions are to be treated with respect.

The philosophical tradition has tried to stitch exclusivist communities together by saying: there is more overlap between infidels and true believers, masters and slaves, men and women, than you might think. For, as Aristotle said, all human beings by nature desire to know. This desire brings them together in a universal community of justification. To a pragmatist, however, this Aristotelian dictum seems thoroughly misleading. It runs together three different things: the need to make one's beliefs coherent, the need for the respect of one's peers, and curiosity.

We pragmatists think that the reason people try to make their beliefs coherent is not that they love truth but that* they cannot help doing so. Our minds can no more stand incoherence than our brains can stand whatever the neuro-chemical substrate of such coherence may be. Just as our neural

---

* In the manuscript Rorty has crossed out "because" and overwritten "that." "Because" remained in *RHC*; see 15.

networks are, presumably, both constrained and in part constructed by something like the algorithms used in parallel distributed processing of information by computer programmers, so our minds are constrained by the need to tie our beliefs and desires together into a reasonably perspicuous whole.[45] That is why we cannot "will to believe"—believe what we like, regardless of what else we believe. It is why, for example, we have such a hard time keeping our religious beliefs in a separate compartment from our scientific ones, and in isolating our respect for democratic institutions from our contempt for many (even most) of our fellow voters.

The need to make one's beliefs coherent is, for reasons familiar from Hegel, Mead, and Davidson, not separable from the need for the respect of our peers. We have as hard a time tolerating the thought that everybody but ourselves is out of step as we do the thought that we believe both *p* and not-*p*. We need the respect of our peers because we cannot trust our own beliefs, nor maintain our self-respect, unless we are fairly sure that our conversational interlocutors agree among themselves on such propositions as "He's not crazy," "He's one of us," "He may have strange beliefs on some subjects, but he's basically sound," and so on.

This interpenetration of the need to make one's beliefs coherent among themselves and the need to make them coherent with most of those of one's peers results from the fact that, as Wittgenstein said, to imagine a form of human life we have to imagine agreement in judgments as well as in meanings. Davidson brings out the considerations which support Wittgenstein's insight when he says: "The ultimate source of both objectivity and communication is the triangle that, by relating speaker, interpreter and the world, determines the contents of thought and speech."[46] You would not know what you believed, nor have any beliefs, unless your belief had a place in a network of beliefs and desires. But that network would also not exist were you and others unable to pair off features of your non-human environment with assent to your utterances by other language-users, utterances caused (as are yours) by those very features.

The difference between the use which Davidson (and I) would like to make of Hegel's and Mead's realization that our selves are dialogical all the way down—that there is no private core on which to build—and the use which Apel and Habermas make of this point can be exhibited by looking at the sentence immediately following the one I just quoted from Davidson: "Given this source," Davidson says, "there is no room for a relativized concept of truth."

Davidson's point is that the only sort of philosopher who would take seriously the idea that truth is relative to a context, and particularly to a choice between human communities, is one who thinks that he or she can contrast "being in touch with a human community" with "being in touch with reality." But Davidson's point about there being no language without triangulation means that this contrast cannot be drawn. You cannot have any language, or any beliefs, without being in touch with both a human community *and* non-human reality. There is no possibility of agreement without truth, nor of truth without agreement.

Most of our beliefs must be true, Davidson says, because an ascription to a person of mostly false beliefs would mean either that we had mistranslated the person's marks and noises or that she did not in fact have any beliefs, was not in fact speaking a language. Most of our beliefs must be justified in the eyes of our peers for a similar reason: if they were not justified—if our peers could not attribute to us a largely *coherent* web of beliefs and desires—they would have to conclude either that they had misunderstood us or that we did not speak their language. Coherence, truth, and community go together, not because truth is to be defined in terms of coherence rather than correspondence, in terms of social practice rather than in terms of coping with non-human forces, but simply because to ascribe a belief is automatically to ascribe a place in a largely coherent set of mostly true beliefs.

But to say that there is no contact, via belief and desire, with reality—no truth—without community is as yet to say nothing about what sort of community is in question. A radically exclusivist community—made up only of the priests, or the nobles, or the males, or the whites—is quite as good as any other sort of community for Davidsonian purposes. This is the difference between what Davidson thinks you can get out of reflection on the nature of discourse and what Apel and Habermas think you can get out of it. The latter philosophers think that you can get something more out of such reflection than the fact that there are neither beliefs nor persons nor truth without justification in the eyes of a community. They think you can get an argument in favor of the inclusivist project—an argument which says that people who resist this project involve themselves in performative self-contradictions.

By contrast, Davidson thinks that any community of justification will do to make you a language-user and a believer, no matter how "distorted" Apel and Habermas take communication within that community to be. From Davidson's point of view, philosophy of language runs out before we reach the moral imperatives which make up Apel's and Habermas's "discourse ethics."

Apel and Habermas run together the need for coherence and for justification which is required if one is to use language at all, and a commitment to what they call "universal validity," a commitment which can only be consistently acted upon by aiming at the sort of domination-free communication which is impossible as long as there are human communities which remain exclusivist. Davidson and I have no use for the claim that any communicative action contains a claim to universal validity, because this so-called "presupposition" seems to us to have no role to play in the explanation of linguistic behavior.

It does, to be sure, play a part in the explanation of the behavior, linguistic and other, of a small minority of human beings—those who belong to the liberal, universalistic, inclusivist, tradition of the European Enlightenment. But this tradition, to which Davidson and I are as much attached as Apel and Habermas, derives no support from reflection on discourse as such. We language-users who belong to this minority tradition are morally superior to those who do not, but those who do not are no less coherent in their use of language.

Apel and Habermas invoke the presupposition of universal validity to get from a commitment to justification to a willingness to submit one's beliefs to the inspection of any and every language-user—even a slave, even a black, even a woman. They see the desire for truth, construed as the desire to claim universal validity, as the desire for universal justification. But as I see it, they are inferring invalidly from "You cannot use language without invoking a consensus within a community of other language-users" to "You cannot use language consistently without enlarging that community to include all users of language."

Because I see this inference as invalid, I think that the only thing which can play the role in which Aristotle, Peirce, Apel, and Habermas have cast the desire for knowledge (and thus for truth) is *curiosity*. I use this term to mean the urge to expand one's horizons of inquiry—in all areas, ethical as well as logical and physical—so as to encompass new data, new hypotheses, new terminologies, and the like. This urge brings cosmopolitanism, and democratic politics, in its train. The more curiosity you have, the more interest you will have in talking to foreigners, infidels, and anybody else who claims to know something you do not know, to have some ideas you have not yet had.

8. Communicating or Educating?

If one sees the desire and possession of both truth and justification as inseparable from using language, while still resisting the thought that this desire can be used to convict members of exclusivist human communities of performative self-contradiction, then one will see inclusivist communities as based on contingent human developments such as the twitchy curiosity of the sort of eccentrics we call "intellectuals," the desire for intermarriage beyond tribal or caste boundaries produced by erotic obsession, the need to trade across such boundaries produced by lack of (for example) salt or gold within one's own territory, the possession of enough wealth, security, education, and independence so that one's self-respect no longer depends upon membership in an exclusivist community (on, e.g., *not* being an infidel or a slave or a woman), and the like. The increased communication between previously exclusivist communities produced by such contingent human developments may gradually *create* universality, but I cannot see any sense in which it recognizes a previously existent universality.

Philosophers like Habermas, who worry about the anti-Enlightenment overtones of the views they call "contextualist," think that since justification is an obviously context-relative notion—one justifies to a given audience, and the same justification will not work for all audiences—it endangers the ideal of human fraternity. Habermas regards contextualism as "only the flipside of logocentrism."[47] He sees contextualists as negative metaphysicians infatuated by diversity, and says that "The metaphysical priority of unity above plurality and the contextualistic priority of plurality above unity are secret accomplices."[48]

I agree with Habermas that it is as pointless to prize diversity as to prize unity, but I disagree with him that we can use the pragmatics of communication to do the job which metaphysicians hoped to achieve by appealing to the Plotinian One or to the transcendental structure of self-consciousness. My reasons for disagreement are those offered by Michael Walzer, Thomas

McCarthy, Seyla Benhabib, Wellmer, and others—reasons nicely summed up in an article by Michael Kelly.[49] Habermas argues for the thesis that

> the unity of reason only remains perceptible in the plurality of its voices—as the possibility in principle of passing from one language to another—a passage that, no matter how occasional, is still comprehensible. This possibility of mutual understanding, which is now guaranteed only procedurally and is realized only transitorily, forms the background for the existing diversity of those who encounter one another—even when they fail to understand one another.[50]

I agree with Habermas—against Lyotard, Foucault, and others—that there are no incommensurable languages, that any language can be learned by one who is able to use any other languages, that Davidson is right in denouncing the very idea of a conceptual scheme. But I disagree with him about the relevance of this point to the utility of the ideas of "universal validity" and "objective truth."

Habermas says that "what the speaker, here and now in a given context, asserts as valid transcends, *according to the sense of his claim,* all context-dependent, merely local standards of validity."[51] As I said above, I cannot see what "transcends" means here. If it means that he is claiming to say something true, then the question is whether it makes any difference whether you say that a sentence *S* is true or whether you simply offer a justification for it by saying "here are my reasons for believing *S.*" Habermas thinks there is a difference because he thinks that when you assert *S,* you claim truth, you claim to represent the real, and that reality transcends context. "With the concept of reality, to which every representation necessarily refers, we presuppose something transcendent."[52]

Habermas tends to take for granted that truth-claims are claims to represent accurately, and to be suspicious of those who, like Davidson and myself, give up on the notion of linguistic representation. He follows Sellars in being a coherentist rather than a skeptic or a foundationalist, but he is dubious about the move I want to make from coherentism to anti-representationalism. He commends Peirce over Saussure because Peirce examines "expressions from the point of view of their possible truth *and,* at the same time, from that of their communicability." He goes on to say that from the perspective of its capacity for being true, an assertoric sentence stands in an epistemic relation to something in the world—it represents a state of affairs. At the same time, for the perspective of its employment in a communicative act, it stands in a relation to a possible interpretation by a language-user—it is suitable for the transmission of information.[53]

My own view, which I take from Davidson, is that you can give up the notion of an "epistemic relation to something in the world," and just rely on the ordinary causal relations which bind utterances together with the utterers' environments. The idea of representation, on this view, adds nothing to the notion of the transmission of information. Or, more exactly, it adds nothing to the notion of "taking part in the discursive practice of justifying one's assertions."

Habermas sees Putnam as, like himself, defending a third position against the metaphysics of unity on the one hand and the enthusiasts for incommensurability on the other. He defines this third position as "the humanism of those who continue the Kantian tradition by seeking to use the philosophy of language to save a concept of reason that is skeptical and postmetaphysical."[54] Putnam and Habermas have offered similar criticisms of my attempt to get rid of a specifically epistemic concept of reason—the concept according to which one is rational only if one tries to represent reality accurately—and to replace it by the purely moral ideal of solidarity. My central disagreement with both Habermas and Putnam is over the question of whether the regulative ideas of "undistorted communication," or "accurate representation of reality" can do any more for the ideals of the French Revolution than the bare, context-dependent notion of "justification."

Some people care about defending their assertions only to a few people, and some care, or say they care, about defending their assertions to everyone. I am not thinking here of the distinction between specialized, technical discourse and non-technical discourse. Rather, the distinction I want is the one between people who want to defend their views to all people who share certain attributes—for example, devotion to the ideals of the French Revolution, or membership in the Aryan race—and those who say they want to justify their view to every actual and possible language-user.

There are certainly people who say that the latter is what they want. But I am not sure that they really mean it. Do they want to justify their views to language-users who are four years old? Well, perhaps they do in the sense that they would like to educate four-year-olds to the point at which they could appreciate the arguments for and against views in question. Do they want to justify them to intelligent but convinced Nazis, people who believe that the first thing to find out is whether the view under discussion is tainted by the Jewish ancestor of its inventors or propounders? Well, perhaps they do in the sense that they would like to convert these Nazis into people who have doubts about the advisability of a Jew-free Europe and infallibility of Hitler, and therefore are more or less willing to listen to arguments for positions associated with Jewish thinkers. But in both of these cases what they want seems to me best described not as wanting to justify their view to everybody, but as wanting to create an audience to whom they would have a sporting chance of justifying their view.

Let me use the distinction between arguing with people and educating people to abbreviate the distinction I have just drawn: the distinction between proceeding on the assumption that people will follow your arguments and knowing that they cannot but hoping to alter them so that they can. If all education were a matter of argument, this distinction would collapse. But, unless one broadens the term "argument" beyond recognition, a lot of education is not. In particular, a lot of it is simple appeal to sentiment. The distinction between such appeal and argument is fuzzy, but I take it nobody would say that making an unregenerate Nazi watch films of the opening of the concentration camps, or making her read *The Diary of Anne Frank*, counts as *arguing* with her.

People interested in democratic politics both cherish the ideal of human fraternity and cherish the idea of the universal availability of education. When asked about the education we have in mind, we often say that it is an education in critical thinking, in the ability to talk over the pros and cons of any view. We oppose critical thinking to ideology, and say that we oppose ideological education of the sort which the Nazis inflicted on German youth. But we thereby leave ourselves wide open to Nietzsche's scornful suggestion that we are simply inculcating our own ideology: the ideology of what he called "Socratism." The issue between Habermas and me boils down to a disagreement about what to say to Nietzsche at this point.

I should reply to Nietzsche by conceding that there is no non-local, non-contextual way to draw the distinction between ideological education and non-ideological education, because there is nothing to my use of the term "reason" that could not be replaced by "the way we vet Western liberals, the heirs of Socrates and the French Revolution, conduct ourselves." I agree with Alasdair MacIntyre and Michael Kelly that all reasoning, both in physics and ethics, is tradition-bound.

Habermas thinks that this is an unnecessary concession, and more generally that my cheerful ethnocentrism can be avoided by thinking through what he calls "the symmetrical structure of perspectives built into every speech situation."[55] The issue between Habermas and myself thus comes to a head when he takes up my suggestion that we drop the notions of rationality and objectivity, and instead just discuss the kind of community we want to create. He paraphrases this suggestion by saying that I want to treat "the aspiration for objectivity" as "simply the desire for as much intersubjective agreement as possible, namely, the desire to expand the referent of 'for us' to the greatest possible extent." He then paraphrases one of Putnam's objections to me by asking: "can we explain the possibility of the critique and self-critique of established practices of justification if we do not take the idea of the expansion of our interpreted horizon seriously *as an idea,* and if we do not connect this idea with the intersubjectivity of an agreement that allows precisely for the distinction between what is current 'for us' and what is current 'for them'?"[56]

Habermas enlarges on this point by saying

The merging of interpretive horizons . . . does not signify an assimilation to "us"; rather, it must mean a convergence, steered through learning, of "our" perspective and "their" perspective—no matter whether "they" or "we" or both sides have to reformulate established practices of justification to a greater or lesser extent. For learning itself belongs neither to us nor to them; both sides are caught up in it in the same way. Even in the most difficult processes of reaching understanding, all parties appeal to the common reference point of a possible consensus, even if this reference point is projected in each case from within their own contexts. For, although they may be interpreted in various ways and applied according to different criteria, concepts like truth, rationality or justification play the *same* grammatical role in *every* linguistic community.[57]

The nub of the argument is, I think, a disagreement about how much help for democratic politics can be gotten out of what Habermas here calls "grammar." As I said earlier, I think that all that we can get out of the grammar of "true" and "rational" is what we can get out of a rather thin idea of "justification." This thin idea is the one we get when we answer the question "where does the line come between causing people to adjust their behavior by persuasion—by working on their beliefs and desires—and doing so by other means?" Unlike Foucault and some others, I think that it is both possible and important to draw a line here. I do not think it helpful to extend the term "violence" as widely as Foucault extended it. Whatever we are doing when we make Nazis look at pictures of concentration camp survivors, it is not violence, any more than it was violence to educate the Hitler Youth to believe that Jews were worthless vermin.

The inevitable fuzziness of the line between persuasion and violence causes problems, however, when we come to the question of education. We are reluctant to say that the Nazis used *persuasion* on the Hitler Youth, since we have two criteria of persuasion. One is simply using words rather than blows or other forms of physical pressure. One can imagine, with a bit of distortion of history, that, in this sense, only persuasion was employed on the Hitler Youth. The second criterion of persuasion includes abstention from words like "Stop asking these stupid questions about whether there aren't some good Jews, questions which make me doubt your Aryan consciousness and ancestry, or the Reich will find another use for you!" and not assigning *Der Stuermer* to one's students.

Un-Socratic methods of this latter sort are the kind which Habermas would say do not respect the symmetrical relationships of participants in discourse. Habermas clearly thinks that there is something in the grammar of "concepts like truth, rationality and justification" which tell us not to use methods of the latter sort. He would presumably grant that use of such words is language-use, but he needs a category of "distorted language-use" or "distorted communication" to explain that it is, so to speak, ungrammatical language-use. Immediately after the passage I quoted about grammar, Habermas says

All languages offer the possibility of distinguishing between what is true and what we hold to be true. The *supposition* of a common objective world is built into the pragmatics of every single linguistic usage. And the dialogue roles of every speech situation enforce a symmetry in participant perspectives.

A bit later he says, "From the possibility of reaching understanding linguistically, we can read off a concept of situated reason that is given voice in validity claims that are both context-dependent and transcendent." He then approvingly quotes Putnam as saying, "Reason is, in this sense, both immanent (not to be found outside of concrete language games and institutions) and transcendent (a regulative idea that we use to criticize the conduct of all activities and institutions."[58]

It seems to me that the regulative idea that we—we vet liberals, we heirs of the Enlightenment, we Socratists—most frequently use to criticize the conduct of various conversational partners is that of "needing education in order to outgrow their primitive fears, hatreds, and superstitions." This is the concept the victorious Allied armies used when they set about re-educating the citizens of occupied Germany and Japan. It is also the one which was used by American schoolteachers who had read Dewey and were concerned to get students to think "scientifically" and "rationally" about such matters as the origin of the species and sexual behavior (that is, to get them to read Darwin and Freud without disgust and incredulity). It is a concept which I, like most Americans who teach humanities or social science in colleges and universities, use when we hope that the students who enter as bigoted religious fundamentalists will leave college with views more like our own.

What is the relation of this idea to the regulative idea of "reason" which Putnam believes to be transcendent and which Habermas believes to be discoverable within the grammar of concepts ineliminable from our description of the making of assertions? The answer to that question depends upon how much the re-education of Nazis and fundamentalists has to do with merging interpretive horizons and how much with replacing such horizons. The fundamentalist parents of our fundamentalist students think that the entire "liberal Establishment" is engaged in a conspiracy. Had they read Habermas, these people would say that the typical communication situation in American college classrooms is no more *Herrschaftsfrei* than that in the Hitler Youth camps.

These parents have a point. Their point is that we liberal teachers no more feel in a symmetrical communication situation when we talk with our fundamentalist students than do kindergarten teachers with their students. In both college classrooms and kindergartens, it is equally difficult for the teachers to feel that what is going on is what Habmermas calls a "convergence, steered through learning, of 'our' perspective *and* 'their' perspective—no matter whether 'they' or 'we' or both sides have to reformulate established practices of justification to a greater or lesser extent."[59] When we American college teachers encounter religious fundamentalists, we do not consider the possibility of reformulating our own practices of justification so as to give more weight to the authority of the Christian Scriptures. Instead, we do our best to convince these students of the benefits of secularization. We assign first-person accounts of growing up homosexual to our homophobic students for the same reasons that German schoolteachers in the postwar period assigned *The Diary of Anne Frank*.

Putnam and Habermas can rejoin that we teachers do our best to be Socratic, to get our job of re-education, secularization, and liberalization done by conversational exchange. That is true up to a point, but what about assigning books like *Black Boy, The Diary of Anne Frank,* and *A Boy's Life?** The racist or fundamentalist parents of our students say that in a truly democratic society the students should not be forced to read books by such people—black people, Jewish people, homosexual people. They will protest that these books are being jammed down their children's throats. I cannot see how to reply to this charge without saying something like "There are credentials for admission to our democratic society, credentials which we liberals have been making steadily more stringent by doing our best to excommunicate racists, male chauvinists, homophobes, and the like. You have to be *educated* in order to be a citizen of our society, a participant in our conversation, someone with whom we can envisage merging our horizons. So we are going to go right on trying to discredit you in the eyes of your children, trying to strip your fundamentalist religious community of dignity, trying to make your views seem silly rather than discussable. We are not so inclusivist as to tolerate intolerance such as yours."

I have no trouble offering this reply, since I do not claim to make the distinction between education and conversation on the basis of anything

---

* In the published translation, *A Boy's Life* has been replaced by *Becoming a Man;* see Robert Brandom, ed., *Rorty and His Critics,* 22.

except my loyalty to a particular community, a community whose interests required re-educating the Hitler Youth in 1945 and require re-educating the children of southwestern Virginia in 1993. I don't see anything *Herrschafts-frei* about my handling of my fundamentalist students. I think those students are lucky to find themselves under the *Herrschaft* of people like me, and to have escaped from that of their rather frightening and dangerous parents. But I think that the handling of such students is a problem for Putnam and Habermas. It seems to me that I am just as provincial and contextualist as the Nazi teachers who made their students read *Der Stürmer;* the only difference is that I serve a better cause. I come from a better province.

I recognize, of course, that domination-free communication is only a regulative ideal, never to be attained in practice. But unless a regulative ideal makes a difference to practice, it is not good for much. So I ask: is there an ethics of discourse which lets me assign the books I want to assign but makes no reference to the local and ethnocentric considerations which I should cite to justify my pedagogic practices? Can you get such an ethics out of the notions of "reason, truth, and justification," or do you have to load the dice? Can I invoke universalistic notions in defense of my action, as well as local ones?

Like MacIntyre, Benhabib, Kelly, and others, I think that you have to smuggle some provinciality into your universals before they do you any good. We think this for the same sorts of reasons as Hegel thought that you had to smuggle in some provinciality—some ethical substance—before you could get any use out of Kant's notion of "unconditional moral obligation." In particular, you have to smuggle in some rule like "No putative contribution to a conversation can be rejected simply because it comes from somebody who has some attribute which can vary independently of his or her opinions—an attribute like being Jewish, or black, or homosexual."

I call this rule "provincial" because it violates the intuitions of a lot of people outside the province in which we heirs of the Enlightenment run the educational institutions.[60] It violates what they would describe as their *moral* intuitions. I am reluctant to admit that these are moral intuitions, and should prefer to call them revolting prejudices. But I do not think that anything in the grammar of the terms "moral intuition" and "prejudice" helps us reach agreement on this point. Nor will a theory of rationality do so.

9. Do We Need a Theory of Rationality?

As I remarked earlier, Habermas thinks that "the paradigm of the philosophy of consciousness is exhausted" and also that "the symptoms of exhaustion should dissolve with the transition to the paradigm of mutual understanding."[61] My own view is that that the fruitfulness of the topics Weber suggested—modernity and rationality—have also been exhausted. I think that the symptoms of this exhaustion might dissolve if we stopped talking about the transition from tradition to rationality, stopped worrying about falling back from rationality by becoming relativistic or ethnocentric, and stopped contrasting the context-dependent with the universal.

This would mean explicitly abandoning the hope that philosophy can stand above politics, abandoning the hopeless question "How can philosophy find politically neutral premises, premises which can be justified to anybody, from which to infer an obligation to pursue democratic politics?" Dropping that question would let us admit that, in Wellmer's formula, "democratic and liberal principles define just *one* possible language game among others." Such an admission would be in line with the Darwinian idea that the inclusivist project is no more rooted in something larger than itself than, say, the project of replacing ideographic by alphabetic writing, or of representing three spatial dimensions on a two-dimensional surface. All three of these were good, immensely fruitful ideas, but none of them need universalistic backup. They can stand on their own feet.[62]

If we abandoned the idea of philosophy which manages to be both politically neutral and politically relevant, we could start asking the question: "Given that we want to be ever more inclusivist, what should the public rhetoric of our society be like? How different should it be from the public rhetoric of previous societies?" Habermas's implicit answer to this question is that we should hang on to a good many Kantian ideas about the connection between universality and moral obligation. Dewey, however, was willing to move much further away from Kant. Though he would have heartily agreed with Habermas that Aristotle's political vocabulary was unable to capture the spirit of democratic politics, he did not like the distinction between morality and prudence which Habermas thinks essential, and on this point he would have thought Aristotle preferable.[63] Dewey thought that the Kantian notion of "unconditional obligation," like the notion of unconditionality itself (and of universality, insofar as that idea is implicitly accompanied by that of un-conditional necessity),[64] could not survive Darwin.

Whereas Habermas thinks that we need "the reconstructive sciences de-signed to grasp universal competences" in order to break out of "the herme-neutic circle in which the *Geisteswissenschaften,* as well as the interpretive social sciences, are trapped,"[65] Dewey did not feel trapped. This was because he saw no need to resolve a tension between facticity and validity. He saw that tension as a philosopher's fiction, a result of separating out two parts of a sit-uation for no good (i.e., no practical) reason, and then complaining that you cannot put them back together again. For him, all obligations were situational and conditional.

This refusal to be unconditional led Dewey to be charged with "relativism." If "relativism" just means failure to find a use for the notion of "context-independent validity," then this charge was entirely justified. But no roads lead from this failure to an inability to engage in democratic politics, unless one thinks that such politics require us to deny that, in Wellmer's formula, "democratic and liberal principles define just *one* possible language game among others." The question about universality is, for Dewey, just the ques-tion of whether democratic politics can start from an affirmation, rather than a denial, of that claim.

I do not think that we can get much further in debating this question by talking about either modernity or reason. The question of whether Hegel should have stuck to the topic of reason by developing a theory of communi-cative reason, or should instead have dropped the topic and simply politicized philosophy, is not going to be settled by looking more closely at the grammar of words like "true" and "rational" and "argument." Neither is the question of whether philosophers like Annette Baier are right in suggesting that we set Kant aside and go back to Hume's attempt to describe reason in terms of con-ditioned sentiment rather than unconditional obligation.[66]

But although we do not, if I am right, need a theory of rationality, we do need a narrative of maturation. As I see it, the deepest disagreement between Habermas and myself is about whether the distinction between the uncon-ditional and the conditional in general, and the distinction between morality and prudence in particular, is a mark of maturity or a transitional stage on the way to maturity. One of the many points on which Dewey agreed with Nietzsche was that it was the latter. Dewey thought that the desire for universality, unconditionality, and necessity was undesirable, because it led one away from the practical problems of democratic politics into a never-never land of theory. Kant and Habermas think that it is a desirable desire, one which one shares only when one reaches the highest level of moral development.[67]

In this paper, I have tried to show how things look when one puts democratic politics in the context of Dewey's narrative of maturation. I cannot offer anything remotely approaching a knock-down argument, based on commonly accepted premises, for this narrative. The best I could do by way of further defense of my view would be to tell a fuller story, encompassing more topics, in order to show how post-Nietzschean European philosophy looks from a Deweyan angle, rather than a universalistic one. (This is something I have tried to do, in bits and pieces, elsewhere.) I think that narratives are a perfectly fair means of persuasion, and that Habermas's *Philosophical Discourse of Modernity* and Dewey's *The Quest for Certainty* are both admirable illustrations of the power of narratives of maturation.

My reasons for preferring Dewey's are not that I think that Dewey got truth and rationality right, and that Habermas gets them wrong. I think that there is nothing to be gotten right or wrong here. At this level of abstraction, concepts like truth, rationality, and maturity are up for grabs. The only thing that matters is which way of reshaping them will, in the long run, make them more useful for democratic politics. Concepts are, as Wittgenstein taught us, uses of words. Philosophers have long wanted to understand concepts, but the point is to change them so as to make them serve our purposes better. Habermas's, Apel's, Putnam's, and Wellmer's linguistification of Kantian concepts is one suggestion about how to make these concepts more useful. Dewey's and Davidson's thoroughgoing anti-Kantian naturalism is another.

5

Pan-Relationalism

One of the salient facts about contemporary Western philosophy is that non-Anglophones do not read much Anglophone philosophy, and conversely. The gap between so-called "analytic" and so-called "Continental" philosophy shows no signs of being bridged. This seems to me a pity, because I think that the most interesting work being done in these two traditions overlaps to an important extent. Closing this gap might produce an epochal change, in that analytic philosophers might cease to work under the shadow of Kant, and non-analytic philosophers might cease to think that if you abandon Kant's terminology you abandon the Enlightenment's political project. At present, conversation between the two philosophical traditions are typified by dialogues between Kantians (like the one between Rawls and Habermas recently published in *The Journal of Philosophy*).* Dialogues between analytic anti-Kantians like Baier and Davidson and "Continental" anti-Kantians like Lyotard and Derrida are not taking place.

Ceasing to ask modal Kantian questions like "necessary or contingent?," "transcendentally or only empirically real?," "unconditional or merely conditional?" would liberate analytical philosophy from its temptation to take the realist-antirealist debate seriously. It might thus put an end to the constant attempts to remain an empirical realist by dreaming up a still fancier linguistified version of transcendental idealism. Ceasing to think that asking

There does not appear to be a previous English publication of this lecture.
* See Jürgen Habermas, "Reconciliation through the Public Use of Reason: Remarks on John Rawls's Political Liberalism"; and John Rawls, "Political Liberalism: Reply to Habermas"; both in *Journal of Philosophy* 92, no. 3 (1995).

such modal questions is our only safeguard against anti-Enlightenment irrationalism might liberate Habermas from his conviction that Kant remains the official philosopher of bourgeois liberalism. Doing so would enable him to realize that now that we bourgeois liberals have Dewey, we no longer need Kant.

In this lecture I shall try to sketch a way of looking at things which is common to the philosophers I most admire on both sides of the gap. One way to describe this commonality is to say that philosophers as diverse as Davidson and Derrida, Putnam and Latour, Brandom and Foucault, are in the main, and despite occasional backsliding, pan-relationalists. Thinking of things as being what they are by virtue of their relations to other things—in the tradition of Leibniz's monads mirroring the universe and Whitehead's actual entities as a nexus of prehensions—is their way of shaking off the influence of the metaphysical dualisms which we have inherited from the Greeks: the distinctions between essence and accident, substance and property, and appearance and reality. They are trying to replace the various worldpictures constructed with the aid of these Greek oppositions by the picture of a flux of continually changing relations, relations whose terms are themselves dissoluble into a nexus of further relations.[1]

One obvious consequence of their pan-relationalism is to say that they do not make a distinction between intrinsic, non-relational and extrinsic, relational properties. Another is that they have no use for modal distinctions, and in particular for the sort of distinction between necessary and contingent properties which essentialists like Aristotle and Kripke use to draw the line between essence and accident, and which Kantians use to draw the line between conditions of possibility and conditions of actuality. By dropping Leibniz's distinction between the physical and the metaphysical, and Whitehead's distinction between conceptual and physical prehensions, they produce a pan-relationalism in which no relations are more essential to anything than any other, except under some particular description of that thing.

One obvious advantage of pan-relationalism is that it lets one put aside the distinction between subject and object, between the elements in human knowledge contributed by the mind and those contributed by the world. It does so by saying that nothing is what it is under any and every description of it. We can make use of what it is as undescribed, apart from its relations to the human needs and interests which have generated one or another description. This is the move which leads to charges of "idealism" or "linguisticism" or "losing touch with the world" to be brought against the pan-relationalists. They reply to this charge, as I shall be saying later in more detail, by urging that once we cease to describe knowing about something as representing its intrinsic nature accurately, and thereby break representational links to the world, we still have causal links. Anybody who grants that the world has the causal power to change our descriptions of it, they claim, should be immune from accusations of subjectivism and relativism.

Most of the philosophers I have identified as pan-relationalists could, I hope, be persuaded to accept the following argument. A property is simply a hypostatized predicate, so there are no properties which are incapable of being captured in language. Predication is a way of relating things to other things, a way of hooking up bits of the universe with other bits of the universe, or, if you like, as a way of spotlighting certain webs of relationships rather than other webs. All properties, therefore, are hypostatizations of webs of relationships. Whether you think of those relationships realistically, as somehow there before the inventions of the predicates, or whether you think of them anti-realistically, as coming into existence along with such inventions, is a matter of complete indifference. That is a paradigm of the kind of question which pragmatists dismiss as making no difference to practice, and therefore making no difference *tout court*.

My hunch is that the question which arises between realists and anti-realists is one which originates in philosophy's impossible attempt to combine an Aristotelian substance-accident metaphysics with a corpuscularian law-event physics. Once the latter sort of physics takes hold, it makes it possible to see such properties as goodness and redness as relational, and it tempts one to see every description of anything as owing as much to the purposes of the describer as redness owes to the eye of the beholder. But the pull of Aristotelian essentialism tempts one in the opposite direction. It tempts one to follow Descartes in dividing the universe into *res cogitans* and *res extensa*, and thus to conceive of two substances, the subject and the object, struggling for dominance over a third. The third is variously identified as experience, thought, language, or culture. When it is identified as culture, we find philosophers dividing culture down the middle into the parts (for example, art, literature, and politics) where the subject gets the upper hand and the parts (sense-perception of primary qualities—as when John Searle bangs his hand down on his desk—medicine, the natural sciences) where the object wins out. After such a division is made, start taking sides, with, for example, Heidegger and Gadamer giving the palm to the literary culture and Carnap and Searle giving it to the scientific culture. At a final stage, we find cultural politics being mixed up with real politics, as when we are told that respect for natural science will prevent fascist take-overs, or, alternatively, that it will encourage the aggressive use of bio-power by technocrats. Starting out by being adjudicators of culture wars, philosophers quickly take sides and become participants.

I see pan-relationalism as a way of putting a stop to the attempt to divide culture up in this way, by abandoning the picture of subject and object striving for control. To be a pan-relationalist means never using the terms "objective" or "subjective" except in the context of some well-defined expert culture in which we can distinguish between adherence to the procedures which lead the experts to agree and refusal so to adhere. It also means never asking whether a description is better suited to an object than another description without being able to answer the question "what purpose is this description supposed to serve?" That question is never to be answered "to get the object right" or "to represent the object accurately." Pan-relationalists are pragmatists because they do not take such purposes seriously. They cannot do so, because explicating what is meant by getting right or representing accurately requires making some of the objects properties essential and some accidental. If you are a pan-relationalist you are automatically a pragmatist.

So much for a large, vague sketch of what I mean by pan-relationalism. Now I want to offer a suggestion about how to see things from the pan-relationalist point of view. This is that you think of everything as if it were a *number.* The nice thing about numbers, for my present purpose, is just that it is very difficult to think of them as having intrinsic natures. It is hard to think of a number as having an essential core surrounded by a penumbra of accidental relationships. Numbers are an admirable example of something difficult to describe in essentialist, substantialist, language.

To see my point, ask yourself what the essence of the number 17 is—what it is *in itself,* apart from its relationships to other numbers. What is wanted is a description of 17 which is different *in kind* from the following descriptions: less than 22, more than 8, the sum of 6 and 11, the square root of 289, the square of 4.123105, the difference between 1,678,922 and 1,678,905. The tiresome thing about all *these* descriptions is that none of them seem to get closer to the number 17 than do any of the others. Equally tiresomely, there are obviously an infinite number of other descriptions which you could offer of 17, all of which would be equally "accidental" and "extrinsic." None of these descriptions seems to give you a clue to the intrinsic seventeenness of seventeen—the unique feature which makes it the very number that it is. For which of these descriptions you apply is obviously a matter of what purpose you have in mind—the particular situation which caused you to think of the number 17 in the first place.

If we want to be essentialist about the number 17, we have to say, in philosophical jargon, that *all* its infinitely many different relations to infinitely many other numbers are *internal* relations—that is, that none of these relations could be different without the number 17 being different. So there seems to be no way to define the essence of seventeenhood short of finding some mechanism for generating *all* the true descriptions of seventeen, specifying all its relations to *all* the other numbers. Mathematicians can in fact produce such a mechanism by axiomatizing arithmetic, or by reducing numbers to sets and axiomatizing set theory. But if the mathematician then points to his neat little batch of axioms and says, "Behold the essence of seventeen!" we feel cheated. There is nothing very seventeenish about those axioms, for they are equally the essence of 1, of 2, of 289, and of 1,678,922.

At this point, I hope, you will conclude that, whatever sorts of things may have intrinsic natures, numbers do not—that it simply does not pay to be an essentialist about numbers. Pan-relationalism holds that it also does not pay to be essentialist about tables, stars, electrons, human beings, academic disciplines, social institutions, or anything else. We suggest that you think of all such objects as resembling numbers in the following respect: there is nothing to be known about them except an infinitely large, and forever expansible, web of relations to other objects.

There is no point in asking for terms of relations which are not themselves relations, for everything that can serve as the term of a relation can be dissolved into another set of relations, and so on forever. There are, so to speak, relations all the way down and all the way out in every direction; you never reach something which is not just one more nexus of relations. The system of natural numbers is a good model of the universe because in that system it is obvious, and obviously harmless, that there are no terms of relations which are not simply clusters of further relations.

To say that relations go all the way down is a corollary of what Sellars called "psychological nominalism," that is, of the doctrine that there is nothing to be known about anything save what is stated in sentences describing it. For every sentence about an object is an explicit or implicit description of its relation to one or more other objects. So if there is no knowledge by acquaintance, no knowledge which does not take the form of a sentential attitude, then there is nothing to be known about anything save its relations to other things. To insist that there is a difference between a non-relational *ordo essendi* and a relational *ordo cognoscendi* is, inevitably, to recreate the Kantian thing-in-itself. To make that move is to substitute a nostalgia for immediacy, to substitute the hope of salvation by a non-human power for the utopian hopes for a self-made human future. It is to reinvent what Heidegger called "the onto-theological tradition," a tradition which binds Aristotle to Kant, and which cannot survive without modal distinctions.

For psychological nominalists, no description of an object is more a description of the "real" as opposed to the "apparent" object than any other, nor are any of them descriptions of, so to speak, the object's relation to itself—of its identity with its own essence. Some of them, to be sure, are better descriptions than others. But this betterness is a matter of being more useful tools—tools which accomplish some human purpose better than do competing descriptions. All these purposes are, from a philosophical as opposed to a practical point of view, on a par. There is no over-riding purpose called "discovering the truth" which takes precedence. As I was saying yesterday, pragmatists do not think that truth is the aim of inquiry. The aim of inquiry is utility, and there are as many different, useful tools as there are purposes to be served.

In order to show in more detail how things look from a pan-relationalist perspective, I return to my claim that numbers are a good model for objects in general. Common sense—or at least Western common sense—has trouble with this claim because it seems counter-intuitive to say that physical, spatio-temporal, objects dissolve into webs of relations in the way that numbers do. If philosophy dissolves numbers away into relations to other numbers, nobody is going to mourn the loss of their substantial, independent, autonomous reality. But things are different with tables and stars and electrons. Here common sense is inclined to stick in its toes and say that you cannot have relations without something to be related. If there were not a hard, substantial, autonomous table to stand in relation to, e.g., you and me and the chair, or to be constituted out of hard, substantial, elementary particles, there would be nothing to get related and so no relations. There is, common sense insists, a difference between relations and the things that get related, and philosophy cannot break that distinction down.

The pan-relationalist reply to this bit of common sense is pretty much the reply which Berkeley made to Locke's attempt to distinguish primary from secondary qualities—the reply which Peirce cited as the first invocation of the pragmatic principle that every difference must make a difference to practice.[2] The contemporary, linguistified, form of Berkeley's reply is: all that we know about this hard, substantial, table—about the thing that gets related as opposed to its relations—is that certain sentences are true of it. For example, the following sentences: it is rectangular, it is brown, it is ugly, made out of a tree, smaller than a house, larger than a mouse, less luminous than a star, and so on and on. There is nothing to be known about an object except what sentences are true of it. The pan-relationalists' argument thus comes down to saying that since all sentences can do is to relate objects to one another, every sentence which describes an object will, implicitly or explicitly, attribute a relational property to it.[3] So we should substitute a picture of language as a way of hooking objects up to one another for the picture of language as a veil interposed between us and objects.

Essentialists typically rejoin, at this point, that psychological nominalism is a mistake, that we should retrieve what was true in empiricism, and not admit that language provides our only cognitive access to objects. They suggest that we must have some pre-linguistic knowledge of objects, knowledge that cannot be caught in language. This knowledge, they say, is what prevents the table or the number or the human being from being what they call a "mere linguistic construct." To illustrate what he means by non-linguistic knowledge, the essentialist, at this point in the argument, usually bangs his hand on the table, and flinches. He thereby hopes to demonstrate that he has acquired a bit of knowledge, and a kind of intimacy with the table, which escapes the reach of language. He claims that that knowledge of the table's *intrinsic causal powers*, its sheer brute *thereness*, keeps him in touch with reality in a way in which the anti-essentialist is not.

Unfazed by this suggestion that he is out of touch, the anti-essentialist reiterates that if you want to know what the table really, intrinsically, is, the best answer you are going to get is "that of which the following statements are true: it is brown, ugly, painful to banging hands, capable of being stumbled over, made of atoms, and so on and on." The painfulness, the solidity, and the causal powers of the table are on all fours with its brownness and its ugliness. Just as you do not get on more intimate terms with the number 17 by discovering its square root, you do not get on more intimate terms with the table, closer to its intrinsic nature, by hitting it than by looking at it or talking about it. All that hitting it, or decomposing it into atoms, does is to enable you to relate it to a few more things. It does not take you out of language into fact, or out of appearance into reality, or out of a remote and disinterested relationship into a more immediate and intense relationship.

The point of this little exchange is, once again, that the pan-relationalist denies that there is a way to pick out an object from the rest of the universe *except* as the object of which a certain set of sentences is true. With Wittgenstein, he says that ostention only works against the backdrop of a linguistic practice, and that the self-identity of the thing picked out is itself description-relative.[4] Pan-relationalists think that the distinction between things related and relations is just an alternative way of making the distinction between what we are talking about and what we say about it. The latter distinction is, as Whitehead said, just an hypostatization of the relation between linguistic subject and linguistic predicate.

Just as the utterance of a noun conveys no information to people who are unfamiliar with adjectives and verbs, so there is no way to convey information except by relating something to something else. Only in the context of a sentence, we are told on good authority, does a word have meaning. But that means that there is no way of getting behind language to some more immediate non-linguistic form of acquaintance with what we are talking about. Only when linked up with some other parts of speech does a noun have a use, and only as the term of a relation can an object be an object of knowledge. There is no knowledge of the subject without knowledge of what sentences referring to it are true, just as there is no knowledge of a number without knowledge of its relations to other numbers.

Our sense that we can know a thing without knowing its relations to other things is explained away, by pan-relationalist philosophers, as a reflection of the difference between being certain about some familiar, taken-for-granted, obvious relations in which the thing stands and being uncertain about its other relations. Seventeen, for example, starts out by being the sum of seventeen ones, the number between sixteen and eighteen, and so on. Enough such familiar statements, and we begin to think of seventeen as a thing waiting to get related to other things. When we are told that seventeen is also the difference between 1,678,922 and 1,678,905, we feel that we have learned about a rather remote, inessential connection between it and something else, rather than more about *seventeen itself*. But when pressed we have to admit that the relation between 17 and 1,678,922 is no more or less intrinsic than that between 16 and 17. For in the case of numbers, there is no clear sense to be given to the term "intrinsic." We do not really want to say that 17, in the secret depths of its heart, *feels* closer to 16 than to numbers further down the line.

Pan-relationalists suggest that we also brush aside the question of whether the hardness of the table is more intrinsic to the table than its color, or whether the atomic constitution of the star Polaris is more intrinsic to it than its location in a constellation. The question of whether there really are such things as constellations, or whether they are merely illusions produced by the fact that we cannot visually distinguish the distance of stars, strikes anti-essentialists as as bad as the question of whether there really are such things as moral values, or whether they are merely projections of human wishes. They suggest we brush aside all questions about where the thing stops and its relations begin, all questions about where its intrinsic nature starts and its external relations begin, all questions about where its essential core ends and its accidental periphery begins. Pan-relationalists like to ask, with Wittgenstein, whether a chess-board is *really* one thing or sixty-four things, or, with James, whether the Star of David is really one triangle superimposed on another triangle or a hexagon surrounded by six triangles. To ask that question, they think, is to expose its foolishness—its lack of any interesting point. Questions which have a point are those which meet William James's requirement that any difference must *make* a difference. Other questions—such as those about the ontological status of constellations or moral values—are "merely verbal" or, worse yet, "merely philosophical."

The residual essentialism of common sense may rejoin to all this that pan-relationalism is a sort of linguistic idealism: a way of suggesting that there was really nothing there to be talked about before people began talking—that objects are artifacts of language. But this rejoinder is a confusion between the question "How do we pick out objects?" and "Do objects antedate being picked out by us?" The anti-essentialist has no doubt that there were trees and stars long before there were statements about trees and stars. But the fact of antecedent existence is of no use in giving sense to the question "What are trees and stars apart from their relations to other things—apart from our statements about them?" Nor is it of any help in giving sense to the skeptic's claim that trees and stars have non-relational, intrinsic essences which may, alas, be beyond our ken. If that claim is to have a clear meaning, we have to be able to say something more about *what* is beyond our ken, what we are deprived of. Otherwise, we are stuck with Kant's unknowable thing-in-itself. From the pan-relationalist's point of view the Kantian lament that we are forever trapped behind the veil of subjectivity is merely the pointless, because tautologous, claim that something we defined as being beyond our knowledge is, alas, beyond our knowledge.

The essentialist's picture of the relation between language and world drives him back on the claim that the world is identifiable independently of language. That is why he has to insist that the world is initially known to us through a kind of non-linguistic encounter—through banging into it, or letting it bounce some photons to penetrate our retinas. This initial encounter is an encounter with the very world itself—the world as it intrinsically is. When we try to recapture what we learned in this encounter in language, however, we are frustrated by the fact that the sentences of our language merely relate things to other things. The sentences "This is brown" or "This is square" or "This is hard" tell us something about how our nervous system deals with emanations from the neighborhood of the object. Sentences like "It is located at the following space-time coordinates" are, even more obviously, sentences which tell us about what the essentialist mournfully calls "merely relational, merely accidental, properties."

Confronted with this impasse, the essentialist is tempted to turn for help to natural science. He is tempted to say that a sentence like "It is made up of the following sorts of elementary particles arranged in the following ways" gets us inside the object as it truly is. The last line of defense for essentialist philosophers is the belief that physical science gets us outside ourselves, outside our language and our needs and our purposes to something splendidly non-human and non-relational. Essentialists who retreat to this line argue that seventeenth-century corpuscularians like Hobbes and Boyle were right to distinguish between the features of things which are really "in" them and those which it is useful, for human purposes, to describe them as having.

To us anti-essentialists, descriptions of objects in terms of elementary particles are useful in many different ways—as many ways as particle physics can contribute either to technological advances or imaginative astrophysical redescriptions of the universe as a whole. But that sort of utility is their *only* virtue. To the essentialist philosophers, and to many natural scientists who otherwise do not concern themselves with philosophy, this pragmatic view of physics as the handmaiden of technology and of the poetic imagination is offensive. These people share a sense that particle physics—and more generally whatever scientific vocabulary could, in principle, serve to formulate explanations of any phenomenon whatever—is an example of a kind of truth which pragmatism does not recognize. This kind of truth is not a matter of the utility of a description for a human purpose, but rather of a transcendence of the merely human. Particle physics has, so to speak, become the last refuge of the Greek sense of wonder—the sense of an encounter with the almost Wholly Other.[5]

Why does particle physics seem to give the notion of "intrinsic nature" a new lease on life? I think the answer is that the vocabulary of this branch of physics seems to offer a special kind of mastery and self-assurance, in that it can ("in principle") explain the utility of all other descriptions, as well as its own.[6] An ideal psychophysics would treat human beings as themselves swirls of particles, and would provide explanations of why these organisms had developed certain linguistic habits—why they have described the world as they have. So it seems as if such an ideal physics could treat utility to human beings as itself something explicable, subsumable, capable of being distanced and being put in perspective. When we think of the universe in terms of the dispersion and interaction of particles, we seem to rise above human needs and look down upon them. We seem to become slightly more than human, for we seem to have distanced ourselves from our own humanity and seen ourselves within a non-human perspective, within the largest possible context.

For us anti-essentialists this temptation to think that we have eluded our human finitude by seeing ourselves under the aspect of elementary particles is just one more attempt to create a divinity—a god of power—and then to claim a share in the divine life. The trouble with all such attempts is that the need to be God is just one more human need. Or, to put the point less invidiously, the project of seeing all our needs from the point of view of someone without any such needs is just one more human project. Stoic absence of passion, Zen absence of will, Heideggerian *Gelassenheit,* and physics-as-the-absolute-conception-of-reality are, from this angle, just so many variations on a single project—the project of escaping from time and chance.[7]

We pan-relationalists, however, cannot afford to sneer at this project. For, in our strictly philosophical capacity as opposed to our political capacity, we cannot afford to sneer at *any* human project, any chosen form of human life, any description which aids. In particular, we should not allow ourselves to say what I have just said: that by taking this view of physical science we *seem* to see ourselves as more than human. For a pan-relationalist cannot invoke the appearance-reality distinction. We cannot say that our opponents' way of looking at physics gets physics wrong, mistakes its intrinsic nature, substitutes an accidental and inessential use of it for what it is in itself.

On our view, physical science no more has an intrinsic nature than does the number 17. Like 17, it is capable of being described in an infinity of ways, and none of these ways is the "inside" way. Seeing ourselves as participating in the divine life by describing ourselves under the aspect of eternity is not an illusion or a confusion—it is just one more attempt to satisfy one more human need. Seeing ourself as at last in touch, through physical science, with the ultimate nature of reality is also not an illusion or a confusion. It is one more human project which may, like all human projects, eclipse the possibility of other, incompatible, projects.

Nor can we pan-relationalists let ourselves get away with saying that our essentialist opponents mistakenly think that they have "eluded human finitude" by taking refuge in a secularized version of a theology of power. It is not as if human finitude is the ultimate truth of the matter, as if human beings are *intrinsically* finite. On our view, human beings are what they make themselves and one of the things they have wanted to make themselves is a divinity—what Sartre calls a "being in and for itself." We pan-relationalists cannot say, with Sartre, that this attempt is a "futile passion." The metaphysical systems of Aristotle and Spinoza, or Kant's fanatical pursuit of the unconditional, are not exercises in futility, any more than the anti-metaphysical systems of William James, Nietzsche, and Sartre himself. There is no inescapable truth which either metaphysicians or pragmatists are trying to evade or capture, for any candidate for truth can be escaped by a suitable choice of description and can be underwritten by another such choice.

What about the Sartrean proposition that "human beings are what they make themselves" which I have just put forward as pan-relationalist doctrine. Is that proposition true? Well, it is true in the same way that Peano's axioms for arithmetic are true. These axioms sum up the implications of the use of a certain vocabulary, the vocabulary of numbers. But suppose you have no interest in using that vocabulary. Suppose, for example, that you are willing to forego the advantages of counting and calculating. Suppose that, perhaps because of a morbid fear of technology, you are willing and eager to speak a language in which no mention of the number 17 occurs. For you, those axioms are not candidates for truth—they have no relevance to your projects.

So it is for the Sartrean proposition. This proposition sums up a certain view about what sorts of projects it is best to pursue. If, however, your own projects are religious or metaphysical—if you deeply need to feel safe within the everlasting arms of a god of power and are therefore willing to forego the advantages of the kinds of egalitarian politics and Romantic art whose implications Sartre sums up—then Sartre's proposition will not even strike you as a plausible truth-candidate. You may call it false if you like, but the falsity is not like the falsity of a candidate for truth which has been tested and found wanting. It is rather a matter of obvious *irrelevance*—obvious inability to be of use for your purposes. Putting a Sartrean description before a Spinozist is like putting a bicycle pump in the hands of a ditch digger, or a yardstick in the hands of a brain surgeon—it is not even a *candidate* for utility.[8]

Is there then no argument possible between Sartre and Spinoza, no communication between Peano and the anti-technologist? It makes all the difference here whether we are talking about "argument" or about "communication." You can have communication and disagreement without an argument having been joined. Indeed, you often do. That is what happens whenever we find ourselves unable to find common premises, when we have to agree to differ, when we begin to talk about "differences of taste." Communication requires no more than agreement to use the same tools to pursue shared needs. Argument requires agreement about which needs take priority over others. The language, and the common sense, which the Spinozist and the Sartrean share reflects the fact that both need food, sex, shelter, books, and quite a lot of other things—and that they go about getting those things in much the same ways. Their inability to *argue* fruitfully on philosophical questions reflects the fact that neither gives much weight to the particular needs which led the other to philosophize. Similarly, the inability of two painters to agree on how to paint reflects the fact that neither gives much weight to the needs which led the other to the easel. To say that such disagreements are "merely philosophical" or "merely artistic" is to say that, when they agree to put philosophy or painting aside, the participants can agree to collaborate on common projects.[9] To say that their philosophical or artistic disagreements are nevertheless profound and important is to say that neither considers those *other* projects central to their lives.

This way of putting things may seem to neglect the fact that Sartreans sometimes turn Spinozist, atheists Catholic, anti-essentialists essentialist, metaphysicians pragmatist, and vice versa. More generally, it seems to neglect the fact that people change their central projects, change those parts of their self-image which they had previously found most precious. The question is, however, whether this ever happens as a result of *argument*. Perhaps sometimes it does, but this is surely the exception. Such conversions are typically as much a surprise to the person herself as to her friends. The phrase "she has become a new person—you would not recognize her" typically means "she no longer sees the point or relevance or interest of the arguments which she once deployed on the other side."

Common sense, however, like Greek philosophy, thinks that conversions *should* come about by argument. Common sense hopes that these conversions will not be like suddenly falling in love with an utterly different sort of person but rather like gradually coming to recognize the shape of one's own mind. The Socratic assumption that desirable conversions are a matter of self-discovery rather than self-transformation necessitates the Platonic doctrine that every human mind has, in broad outlines, the same shape: the shape given by memory of the Forms. In latter philosophers, this becomes the belief in "reason," either as a faculty for penetrating through appearances to reality or as a set of elementary truths which lie deep within each of us, waiting for argument to bring them to light. To believe in reason, in either sense, is to believe that there is not only such a thing as human nature, but that this nature is not a matter of what we share with the other animals, but something unique. This unique ingredient in human beings makes us knowers rather than simply users, and thus makes us capable of being converted by argument rather than bowled over by irrational forces.

We anti-essentialists, of course, do not believe that there is such a faculty. Since nothing has an intrinsic nature, neither do human beings. But we are happy to admit that human beings are unique in a certain respect: they do stand in a set of relations to other objects which no other objects stand in to anything. Or, more exactly, we have to admit that normal, adult, properly socialized and trained human beings stand in a unique set of relations. These human beings are able to use language, and so they are able to describe things. As far as we know, nothing else is able to describe things. Numbers and physical forces can be greater than each other, but they do not describe each other as greater. *We* so describe them. Plants and the other animals can interact, but their success in these interactions is not a matter of their finding increasingly more profitable redescriptions of each other. Our success *is* a matter of finding such redescriptions.

Darwin made it hard for essentialists to think of the higher anthropoids as having suddenly acquired an extra added ingredient called "reason" or "intelligence," rather than simply more of the sort of cunning which the lower anthropoids had already manifested. This is why, since Darwin, essentialist philosophers have tended to talk less about "mind" and more about "language." Words like "sign," "symbol," "language," and "discourse" have become philosophical buzzwords in our century in the way in which "reason," "science," and "mind" were buzzwords in the previous century.[10] The development of symbolizing abilities is, indeed, susceptible to an evolutionary account in terms of increasing cunning. But essentialist philosophers have tended to forget that they substituted "language" for "mind" in order to accommodate Darwin, and have gone on to raise exactly the same problems about the former as their predecessors raised about the latter.[11]

As I suggested earlier in this lecture, these problems arise from thinking of language as a third thing, intruding between subject and object and forming a barrier to human knowledge of how things are in themselves. To keep faith with Darwin, however, we should think of the word "language" not as naming a thing with an intrinsic nature of its own, but as a way of abbreviating the kinds of complicated interactions with the rest of the universe which are unique to the higher anthropoids. These interactions are marked by the use of complex noises and marks to facilitate group activities, as tools for coordinating the activity of individuals.

The new relations in which these anthropoids stand to other objects are signalized not simply by the use of the mark X to direct the attention of the rest of the group to the object A, but by the use of several different marks to direct attention to A, corresponding to the several different purposes which A may serve. In philosophical jargon, one can say that behavior becomes properly linguistic only when organisms start using a semantical metalanguage and become capable of putting words in intensional contexts.[12] More plainly: it only becomes properly linguistic when we can say things like "It is also called 'Y', but for your purposes you should describe it as X" or "You have every reason to call it an X, but nevertheless it is not an X." For only at that point do we need to use specifically linguistic notions like "meaning," "truth," "reference," and "description." Only now does it become not only useful, but almost indispensable, to describe the anthropoids as "meaning A by X" or "believing falsely that all A's are B's."

Looking at language in this Darwinian way, as providing tools for coping with objects rather than representations of objects, and as providing different sets of tools for different purposes, obviously makes it hard to be an essentialist. For it becomes hard to take seriously the idea that one description of A can be more "objective" or "closer to the intrinsic nature of A" than another. The relation of tools to what they manipulate is simply a matter of utility for a particular purpose, not of "correspondence." A stomach-pump is no closer to human nature than a stethoscope, and a voltage tester is no closer to the essence of an electrical appliance than a screwdriver. Unless one believes, with Aristotle, that there is a difference between knowing and using, that there is a purpose called "knowing the truth" distinct from all other purposes, one will not think of one description of A as "more accurate" than another *sans phrase*. For accuracy, like utility, is a matter of adjusting the relation between an object and other objects, a matter of putting an object in a profitable context. It is a not a matter of getting the object right, in the Aristotelian sense of seeing it as it is, apart from its relations to other things.

An evolutionary description of the development of linguistic ability gives essentialist thinking no foothold, just as an Aristotelian account of human knowledge leaves no room for a Darwinian understanding of the growth of such knowledge. For example, that developed by Alvin Plantinga, who employed an Aristotelian account of knowledge. But, once again, you should notice that it would be inconsistent with my own pan-relationalism to try to convince you that the Darwinian way of thinking of language—and, by extension, the Deweyan, pragmatist way of thinking of truth—is the objectively true way. All I am entitled to say is that it is a useful way, useful for certain particular purposes. All I can claim to have done in this lecture is to offer you a redescription of the relation between human beings and the rest of the universe. Like every other redescription, this one has to be judged on the basis of its utility for a purpose.

So it seems appropriate to end this lecture by turning to this question: for what purpose does the anti-essentialist think that his description of knowledge and inquiry, of human culture, is a better tool than the Aristotelian, essentialist description? My answer has already been suggested several times, but it may be as well to make it explicit. Pragmatists think that there are two advantages to anti-essentialism. The first is that adopting it makes it impossible to formulate a lot of the traditional philosophical problems, and harder to incite the sort of culture wars in which philosophers like to take part. The second is that adopting it makes it easier to come to terms with Darwin.

I agree with Dewey that the function of philosophy is to mediate between old ways of speaking, developed to accomplish earlier tasks, with new ways of speaking, developed in response to new demands. As he put it,

> When it is acknowledged that under disguise of dealing with ultimate reality, philosophy has been occupied with the precious values embedded in social traditions, that it has sprung from a clash of social ends and from a conflict of inherited institutions with incompatible contemporary tendencies, it will be seen that the task of future philosophy is to clarify men's ideas as to the social and moral strifes of their own day.[13*]

The social and moral strife incited by the publication of Darwin's *Descent of Man* has been largely forgotten. But it seems to me that philosophy has still not caught up with Darwin—still not faced up to the challenge which he pre-

---

* Rorty wrote on his manuscript: "My favorite passage in Dewey."

sents. There is still, I think, a lot of work to be done in reconciling the precious values embedded in our traditions with what Darwin had to say about our relation to the other animals. Dewey and Davidson seem to me the philosophers who have done most to help us accomplish this reconciliation.

To see the work of these men in this light, it helps to compare what they have done with what Hume and Kant did. The latter philosophers faced the task of assimilating the New Science of the seventeenth century to the moral vocabulary which Europe inherited from, among other sources, the Stoics and the Christians. Hume's solution to the problem consisted in assimilating human reason to that of animals and assimilating human morality to the kind of benevolent interest in fellow members of the species which animals also display. Hume was a proto-pragmatist, in the sense that when he has finished with it the distinction between knowing reality and coping with reality has become very fuzzy indeed. But, notoriously, Hume's solution struck most readers—especially German readers—as a cure worse than the disease. They thought that human knowledge—and in particular claims to universal and necessary truth—had to be saved from Hume.

Kant offered an alternative solution, one which Hegel considered still far too skeptical and defeatist—far too Humean and proto-pragmatic. But philosophers less ambitious than Hegel have been, for the most part, willing to settle for some form of Kant's solution. Kant saved the claim to unconditionality, in the form of universality and necessity, by distinguishing between the transcendental phenomenal-world-creating scheme, and the empirical and merely phenomenal content which fills up that scheme. He immunized our traditional moral vocabulary, and in particular our claim to be under *unconditional* moral obligations, by sheltering it behind the wall which separates the moral and noumenal from the phenomenal and empirical. By creating this system, he earned the whole-hearted thanks of people who, like the protagonist of Fichte's *The Vocation of Man,* had been afraid that their self-image as moral agents could not survive corpuscularian mechanics.

Kant thus helped us hang on to the idea of something non-relational because unconditional. Universal and necessary a priori synthetic truths and unconditional moral commands were safe because the world of corpuscularian mechanics was not the real world. The real world was the world in which we, behind our own backs so to speak, constituted the phenomenal world—the same world in which we were non-empirical, non-pragmatic moral agents. Kant thereby helped us hang onto the idea that there was a great big difference between us and the other animals. For them, poor phenomenal things that they are, everything is relative and pragmatic. But we have a noumenal and transcendental side, a side which escapes relationality. So we may hope to know the truth, in a non-Baconian sense of "know," a sense in which knowing is quite different from using. We may hope to do the right, in a sense of right which is not reducible to the pursuit of pleasure or to the gratification of benevolent instincts.

Darwin, however, made it much harder to be a Kantian than it had previously been. Once people started experimenting with a picture of themselves as what Darwin's fervent admirer,* Nietzsche, called "clever animals," they found it very hard to think of themselves as having a transcendental or a noumenal side. Further, when Darwinian evolutionary theory was brought together with the suggestion, mooted by Frege and Peirce and anticipated by Herder and Humboldt, that it is *language*,[14] rather than consciousness or mind, which is the distinguishing feature of our species, Darwinian evolutionary theory made it possible to see all of human behavior—including that "higher" sort of behavior previously interpreted as fulfillment of the desire to know the unconditionally true and do the unconditionally right—as continuous with animal behavior. For the origin of language, unlike the origin of consciousness, or of a faculty called "reason" capable of grasping the intrinsic nature of things, is intelligible in naturalistic terms. We can give what Locke called a "plain, historical, account" of how animals came to talk. But we cannot give a plain historical account of how they stopped coping with reality and began representing it, much less of how they stopped being merely phenomenal beings and began to constitute the phenomenal world.

We can, of course, stick with Kant and insist that Darwin, like Newton, is merely a story about phenomena, and that transcendental stories have precedence over empirical stories. But the hundred-odd years spent absorbing

---

* The Spanish translator inserted the following note: "During the reading of this lecture, Rorty added nuance to this affirmation with the following commentary: "This is not entirely true. Nietzsche always speaks badly of Darwin. Although this does not prevent him from accepting without any problem many of the things that Darwin affirms. In any event, another case of typical Nietzschean ingratitude." See note 15 in the Spanish translation; English translation by ed.

and improving on Darwin's empirical story have, I suspect and hope, made us unable to take transcendental stories seriously. In the course of those years we have gradually substituted a making a better future—a utopian, democratic, society—for ourselves, for the attempt to see ourselves from outside of time and history. Pan-relationalism is one expression of that shift. The willingness to see philosophy as helping us to change ourselves rather than to know ourselves is another.

6

Against Depth

Pan-relationalists are typically described by their opponents as believing that many of the things which common sense thinks are found or discovered are really made or invented. So when our Platonist or Kantian opponents are tired of calling us "relativists" they call us "subjectivists" or "social constructionists." On their picture of the situation, we are claiming to have discovered that something which was supposed to come from outside us really comes from inside us. They think of us as saying that what was previously thought to be objective has turned out to be merely subjective—that things are somehow brought into being by language.

But we pan-relationalists must not accept this way of formulating the issue. For if we do, we shall be in serious trouble. If we leave the distinction between making and finding unquestioned, our opponents will be able to ask us an awkward question: viz., have we *discovered* the surprising fact that what was thought to be objective is actually subjective, or have we *invented* it? If we claim to have discovered it, if we say that it is an objective fact that truth is subjective, we are in danger of contradicting ourselves. If we say that we invented it, we seem to be being merely whimsical. Why should anybody take our invention seriously? If truths are merely convenient fictions, what about the truth of the claim that that is what they are? Is that too a convenient fiction? Convenient for what? For whom?

It is important that pan-relationalists be careful never to use the distinction between finding and making, discovery and invention, except in some

There does not appear to be a previous English publication of this lecture.

concrete, causal, context. For example, pan-relationalists can cheerfully admit that bank accounts were made by human beings and giraffes were not, so in that sense the former but not the latter are social constructions. We can do so because in this case "found or made?" is a straightforward empirical question about causal relations between human beings and various other things. But we cannot ask whether giraffehood is "in the world" or something imposed on the world by us. We have to carry through on Quine's dismissal of the distinction between factual and linguistic questions and on Davidson's dismissal of that between scheme and content. This means getting rid of the distinction between "inside us" and "outside us."

It also means insisting that there is no way for language to swing free from the world, or conversely. There is no space for such swinging because the pan-relationist conception of things is, so to speak, two-dimensional. No relation between things is higher or deeper than any other, and linguistic descriptions of the world are just more such relations. There is no dimension in which we can move in order to get above, or below, language. There is neither a God's-eye view, nor a Ground of Being, nor a Way the World Is independent of how it is described. Because pan-relationalists cannot use the notion of intrinsic properties lurking below merely relational properties, all metaphors of depth look suspect to them. Nor, of course, can we retain metaphors of higher, purer, isolated things getting stained with relational accretions when they descend into, or are exemplified by, other realms of being. All metaphors of verticality must be eschewed.

Pan-relationalists live on a darkling two-dimensional plane, where there is neither certitude, nor peace, nor a comforting distinction between a fixed *ordo essendi* and a transitory historical *ordo cognoscendi*. The pan-relationalist view squashes these two orders into one, by refusing to admit that we can come between language and its object. The question of whether this plane will always be as dark as it is now, and as swept with confused alarms, is not a philosophical but an empirical one. It is not a question about the human condition—a topic about which pan-relationalists have nothing to say—but an empirical question about what the future holds. Perhaps someday the sunlit democratic vistas which Whitman glimpsed will cease to darken as we approach them; perhaps they never will.

The pan-relationalists' distrust of vertical metaphors originates in the realization that one does not conduct two activities, first finding that a property is exemplified and then producing a predicate to signify that property. Nor do we first dream up a predicate and then wonder whether it signifies a property. To say that one cannot get between language and its object is to say that we cannot separate talking about a property from using a predicate. This means that there is no place for properties to exist except, so to speak, on the same plane of existence as predicates. There cannot be deep properties, or deep questions. There can only be predicates whose use is hard to teach, and questions of which it is hard to see the point.

One way to produce the effect of a third dimension is to over-dramatize the distinction between arduous and easy uses of predicates. Some predicates take a lot of work to give a use to—for example, "transubstantiated," "Proustian," and "rigidly designated." Others come, and their use is conveyed, easily and naturally—for example, "hard," "soft," "hip," and "square." The language-game played with "transubstantiated" took a lot of work to get under way, whereas those played who worked with "soft" and "square" did not take much work. But the difficulty of instituting and communicating a practice is not an indication of anything save itself; it is not a sign that the new practice takes us to a plane of existence which we had not occupied previously. In particular, it does not support the assumption, shared by Locke, Quine, and Kripke, that physical science delves deeper than ordinary language.

Another way essentialists produce the effect of depth is to capitalize on Socrates's unfortunate suggestion that even familiar, common-sense terms like "just" and "pious" need analysis and definition—that beneath the use of these terms there lurks something which, if displayed, might help us correct that use. Socrates did not make a similar suggestion about "hard" and "soft," nor about the Greek equivalents of "hip" and "square." He stuck to terms of socio-political importance, and managed to convince Plato that philosophy could have such importance only if there were indeed something deep to be discovered, something like the intrinsic nature of justice. Philosophers like Habermas still invoke the memory of Socrates when they argue that unless there is something deep for philosophers to discover—something like the transcendental conditions of communication—then social criticism amounts to no more than "irrational expression of preference."

Nietzsche's claim that Socrates is the "vortex and turning-point of Western civilization" has a lot to it. For Socrates, or at least Socrates as interpreted by Plato, told us that knowledge of something deep and unfamiliar would let us escape from the darkling plane of historical contingency. "'Virtue is knowledge; all sins arise from ignorance; only the virtuous are happy'—these three basic formulations of optimism," Nietzsche said, "spell the death of tragedy." From the point of view I am advocating in these lectures, the problem with these formulations is not that they killed tragedy among the Greeks, but that they divert the optimism of the moderns. They divert it from its proper concern—utopian politics—to the possibility of escaping from politics by moving out of practice into theory.

A contemporary Nietzschean, Bernard Williams, agrees that Socratism was a turning-point, and that our sense of ourselves changed radically when Plato and Aristotle replaced unpredictable fate and moody Olympians by something more stable and knowable. In *Shame and Necessity* he says that what separates Plato and Aristotle from Sophocles and Thucydides is that the former believe that "beyond some things that human beings have themselves shaped, there is [something] that is intrinsically shaped to human interests, in particular to human beings' ethical interests."[1] Plato, noting that there was nothing very stable and reliable in human social practice, produced new objects of knowledge which purported to be both relevant to such practices and to transcend them, and thus could only be known by means which swung free of such practices. Such objects could only be found on the heights or in the depths. After Plato and Aristotle, the universe became three-dimensional and theoretical knowledge became the access to this additional dimension. Access to such a dimension then came to be regarded as the distinctive human ability.

Metaphors of verticality tend to flop back and forth unpredictably between height and depth. In analytic philosophy nowadays, height is out of fashion, but depth is in. The initial thrust of analytic philosophy was to eschew both height and depth by affecting a brisk, practical tone—the tone of people clearing away rubbish and setting things straight. But depth staged a comeback when the backlash against verificationism gained momentum. It took the form of resistance to the idea that we can collapse the *ordines cognoscendi et essendi* into one other. Writers such as Nagel, Kripke, Cavell, and Stroud—and now, alas, even Putnam—are helping to make the term "deep problem" respectable.

Pan-relationalism has no room for the notion of an *ordo essendi,* because it has no room for the notion of an intrinsic nature of things, apart from how they are described. The classical pragmatists were on the right pan-relationalist track in arguing that the traditional problems of philosophy were verbal, in the sense that they could be solved by redescription, by employing different linguistic tools. The verificationism of the first, logical positivist, stage of analytic philosophy was also on the right track. Verificationism was an early attempt to substitute use for meaning, to substitute a description of our practices for an attempt to look beneath those practices.

Logical positivism, and, more generally, pre-Quinean analytic philosophy, went wrong not in being verificationist but in being analytic: in believing that there was such a thing as "the correct analysis" of a concept. That notion of "correct analysis" is one of the successors of Socrates's unhappy notion of "correct definition." Philosophers who were quite happy to deny that there was such a thing as *the* correct description of a spatio-temporal object were unfazed by the idea that there was one correct analysis of concept. They thought concepts were somehow different enough from such objects as to make possible a non-empirical activity called "conceptual analysis."

Their practice embodied an unpragmatic and unessentialist view of concepts, one which suggests, as Socrates had, that our use of a term is not self-correcting, but is an attempt to live up to a fixed external standard. Quine helped break down the analysis-description distinction, and the later Wittgenstein helped us realize that there are at least as many analyses of a concept as there are uses to which the corresponding word can be put, and no criterion for correctness of analysis which is neutral between these various uses. The so-called "paradox of analysis"—the argument just insofar as an analysis had a surprising result it was bound to be incorrect—was never resolved. It died when the practice of giving analyses died, largely as a result of "Two Dogmas of Empiricism" and *Philosophical Investigations*.

The practice of giving analyses satisfied the needs of many early analytic philosophers for depth. Russell, who had given up on logic once he ceased to believe that it gave the one true key to the secrets of the universe, wrote an acerbic and disdainful review of *Philosophical Investigations*. In it he accused Wittgenstein of having lost all sense of the urgency and importance of philosophical work. Russell was thought to be a bad loser at the time, in the first flush of Wittgensteinian enthusiasm, but a few decades after the publication of the *Investigations* philosophers began to wonder if Russell had not had a point. For it dawned on analytic philosophers that, if Wittgenstein were right, the image of the philosopher would have to change in thoroughly disconcerting ways.

In particular, the distinction between philosophy and culture criticism—between, for example, the *Philosophische Untersuchungen* and the *Vermischte Bemerkungen* (which was translated into English as "Culture and Value")—would not, if Wittgenstein was on the right track, be all that great. Dewey would have sympathized with attempts to fuzz up this distinction but the sense of professionalism which Carnap and Quine had imbued in their students made it hard for them to put up with the thought that they might be in the same business as professors of literature. One result of analytic philosophers' reluctance to follow Wittgenstein's and Dewey's leads was, as Putnam has said, that "analytic philosophy has recently become the most prometaphysical movement on the world philosophical scene."[2]

Among contemporary analytic philosophers, Thomas Nagel is both the best defender of verticality and the fiercest critic of the later Wittgenstein. Nagel sums up Wittgenstein's later work as "it makes sense to say that someone is or is not using a concept correctly only against the background of the possibility of agreement and identifiable disagreement in judgments employing the concept." Nagel regards this as a disastrous view, because accepting it means that "what there is and what is true" is limited to what we "could ever discover or conceive of or describe in some extension of human language."[3]

Nagel thinks that "It is necessary to combine the recognition of our contingency, our finitude, and our containment in the world with an ambition of transcendence, however limited may be our success in achieving it."[4] To give up that ambition by succumbing to what Nagel calls "deflationary metaphilosophical theories like positivism and pragmatism" is, he says, "a rebellion against the philosophical impulse itself."[5] Unlike Nietzsche, Heidegger, and Dewey, who think of the yearning for verticality as a datable historical development, Nagel thinks that the sources of philosophy, including this impulse, are "preverbal and often precultural."[6] For Nagel, philosophy is vertical or nothing.

I cited, in an earlier lecture, Dewey's conception of philosophy as a matter of reconciling older, and frequently datable, linguistic innovations with newer ones—for example, reconciling Aristotelian descriptions of knowledge with Newtonian descriptions of the object of knowledge, or Christian descriptions of human brotherhood with Darwin's account of the descent of man. For

Dewey, the philosophical ambition to transcend should be replaced by the political hope to reconcile.

On a Deweyan conception, to be a philosopher is to be something like a repairman—somebody who updates old tools in order to adapt them to new uses. Nagel's conception of philosophy's role is more dramatic; he regards it as "philosophically fundamental" to "try to climb outside of our own minds." "Philosophy," he says, "is the childhood of the intellect, and a culture that tries to skip it will never grow up."[7] For Dewey, there is no such thing as the intellect; there are only cultures with problems. He sees Platonic-Aristotelian metaphors of verticality as having been useful in earlier stages of European culture, and harmful in later ones. Dewey has a story to tell about the matura-tion of European thought, but no story to tell about the human condition, or about the nature of the human intellect.

Nagel brings out the connection between his dislike of verificationism and his need to get outside his own mind when he says

> Only a dogmatic verificationist would deny the possibility of forming objective concepts that reach beyond our current capacity to apply them. The aim of reaching a conception of the world which does not put us at the center in any way requires the formation of such concepts. We are supported in this aim by a kind of intellectual optimism: the belief that we possess an open-ended capacity for understanding what we have not yet conceived, and that it can be called into operation by detaching from our present understanding and trying to reach a higher-order view which explains it as part of the world. But we must also admit that the world probably reaches beyond our capacity to understand it, no matter how far we travel, and this admission, which is stronger than the mere denial of verificationism, can be expressed only in general concepts whose extension is not limited to what we could in principle know about.[8]

Nagel's paradigm of the use of a higher-order view to explain a lower-order view as part of the world is Locke's use of corpuscularian physics to explain our use of the vocabulary of colors. Intellectual optimism, in his sense, is the hope that we shall get more and more "objective" explanations of how we be-have and talk. In contrast, Deweyans regard what Locke and physiological optics accomplished not as a vertical progression from lower to higher orders, or from the inside view to an outside view, but as the development of one more tool for the improvement of man's estate. So when confronted with Nagel's claim that we must go beyond intellectual optimism to humility, to the realization that no conceivable higher-order view taken by humans will exhaust the world, Deweyans have to see this claim as itself one more tool—one more sketch of a language-game which human beings may find it useful to play. But of course Nagel will view this way of taking his suggestion as one more way of putting human beings in the center—one more version of the deflationary impulse which led to verificationism.

What seems to me most interesting about the opposition between Nagel on the one hand and Dewey and Wittgenstein on the other is that it is not going to be resolved by argument, or by the production of new evidence. It is an admirable example of the ability of competing philosophers to spin cocoons around themselves by providing comprehensive redescriptions of what both rival philosophers and they themselves are doing—redescriptions so comprehensive as to form self-sustaining linguistic practices, practices which can offer a redescription of everything but an answer to nothing.

The wide and intense interest aroused by Nagel's work seems to me due to the fact that he has appreciated, better than anyone else, the radically pragmatist and pan-relationalist implications of the later Wittgenstein's thought. Unlike such less subtle "realist" philosophers as John Searle, Nagel realizes that the issue between himself and his opponents is beyond the reach of argument—that these opponents do not differ from him because they are stupid, but because they are playing a different language-game, one Nagel cannot imagine playing. One of the few points on which Nagel and I agree is that each of us can redescribe everything the other says in ways to which there is no argumentative reply. All that either of us can hope is a conversion experience, an overcoming of what is at present a psychological impossibility.

Consider Nagel's remark that

> If Wittgenstein is right, then my claim to have formed a significant thought about what is entirely beyond the reach of our minds clearly won't stand up ... But though I have no alternative, I find it completely impossible to believe Wittgenstein's view—psychologically impossible."[9]

The best that Nagel can do to explain what it is like to be psychologically unable to believe Wittgenstein's view is to outline the Platonist view he himself cannot help believing. He paraphrases Wittgenstein's remarks on rule-following as the claim that "*nothing* in my mind determines the infinite application of any of my concepts. We simply do apply them, unhesitatingly, in certain ways, and correct others who do not," and then goes on to say:

> It seems to me that to accept this as the final story is to acknowledge that all thought is an illusion. If our thoughts do not have infinite reach in a much stronger sense than this, then even the most mundane of them is not what it pretends to be. It is as if a natural Platonism makes the attempt to view the world in any other way look phony. In sum, the Wittgensteinian attack on transcendent thoughts depends on a position so radical that it also undermines the weaker transcendent pretensions of even the least philosophical of thoughts. I can't imagine what it would be like to believe it, as opposed to subscribing to it verbally.[10]

But Nagel would grant that people like Wittgenstein, Dewey, and I cannot only believe it, but honestly cannot imagine how Nagel could believe that the least philosophical of thoughts has transcendent pretensions.

When Nagel says that the view advocated by pragmatists like me "shows a lack of humility . . . an attempt to cut the universe down to size,"[11] he is providing further evidence for my analogy between losing the sense of Sin and giving up the correspondence theory of truth. But of course my production of this analogy is further evidence for his view that pragmatists are unable to see past culture to the unchanging nature of the human intellect—unable to see the difference between an historical process such as secularization and a set of intuitions which are defining of human existence.

I hope I have made clear why I take Nagel to be the clearest-headed and most consistent opponent of pragmatism, pan-relationalism, and every other view I hold dear on the contemporary philosophical scene. Now to strengthen my claim that Nagel has shown us the limits of philosophical argument by reviewing a couple of sample controversies within contemporary philosophy—controversies in which we again and again encounter arguments which produce no conviction in, nor admit of refutation by, the philosophers on the other side. Both are controversies in which, predictably, Nagel and I are on opposite sides.

The two examples I shall offer are: (1) the controversy that swirls around Daniel Dennett's claim that there are no such things as qualia or "raw feels"; (2) the controversy between Barry Stroud and Michael Williams about whether skepticism about the existence of the external world is natural or artificial—whether such skepticism is a product of ineliminable transcultural intuitions or a product of a dispensable, datable, Cartesian language-game. I shall try to show that each of these can usefully be viewed as a controversy between pan-relationalists and essentialists, and also that it is immensely unlikely that these could be resolved by anything like argument or evidence. Each is the sort of controversy where something like a Kuhnian conversion-experience has to occur before anybody can change sides.

1. Qualia

There is an obvious relationship between pan-relationalism and a view which Nagel finds incredible—Daniel Dennett's claim that we do not need to worry what it is like to be this or that, and that there are no such things as qualia. Dennett's arguments against qualia are verificationist, in the sense that he is not willing to say that we should attribute raw feels to anything unless doing so can make a difference to the causal explanation of the thing's behavior. If, for all we male brunettes will ever know, red-headed female humans happen to be qualialess, though charming, zombies, then (Dennett argues, in the spirit of William James) the presence of raw feels seems to be a difference that makes no difference. Dennett thinks this is common sense, and Nagel thinks it is dogmatic verificationism. Dennett is, in my jargon, a pan-relationalist because he is a pragmatist.[12]

The most effective argument in *favor* of qualia is probably Frank Jackson's story of Mary the Color Scientist—the history of a woman blind from birth who acquires all imaginable "physical" information about the perception of color, and whose sight is thereafter restored. Jackson claims that at the moment when she can see she learns something that she didn't know before—namely what blue, red, etc., *are like*. Dennett replies to Jackson by putting the following words in Mary's mouth:

You have to remember that I know *everything*—absolutely everything—
that could ever be known about the physical causes and effects of color
vision . . . I had already written down, in exquisite detail, what physical
impression a yellow object or a blue object . . . would make on my nervous system. So I already knew exactly what *thoughts* I would have [in-
cluding the thought "this is a blue object they are holding up before my
eyes"]. I was not in the slightest surprised by my experience of blue . . .
I realize how *hard it is for you to imagine* that I could know so much
about my reactive dispositions that the way I was affected came as no
surprise. [But] it's hard for anyone to imagine the consequences of
someone knowing absolutely everything physical about anything.[13]

Anybody who teaches a class in philosophy of mind will tell you that when
Jackson's and Dennett's stories about Mary are put before a class, the class
will divide—often fairly evenly—into people who find Dennett's response
pretty convincing and those who find it utterly unconvincing.

As Dennett says, he and Jackson are operating competing intuition pumps.
Jackson's pump sucks up all the essentialist intuitions which tell you that an
experience of blue is what it is and no other thing—that it is something utterly
distinct from the disposition to say "that's blue." Dennett's sucks up all the
intuitions that might incline you to verificationism and pan-relationalism—all
those which suggest that to know all about the causes and effects of an event is
to know all there is about the event itself, and that to know all about the inferential connections between a sentence and all other sentences is to know all
about the reference of the referring expressions in the first sentence. An example of the intuitions which incline you in this direction is Dennett's claim
that "If some creature's life depended on lumping together the moon, blue
cheese, and bicycles, you can be pretty sure that Mother Nature would find a
way for it to 'see' these as 'intuitively just the same thing.'"[14]

From the essentialist point of view, the one shared by Jackson and Nagel,
Dennett's pump sucks in genuine intuitions and the other sucks in only philosophical fantasies. From the pan-relationalist point of view, both pumps
suck in the same sort of thing—namely dispositions to linguistic response.
Pan-relationalists think that what their opponents call an "intuition" is just
a linguistic response made instantly and unreflectively. So they think that
philosophical controversy arises when two language-games—typically one

old one and one new one—are playable by the same person, and are such that two unreflective responses, each produced by familiarity with one of those two games, clash with one another. The antinomies around which philosophical discussion cluster are not tensions built into the human mind but merely reflections of the inability to decide whether to use an old tool or a new one. The inability to have an argument which amounts to more than manning one or another intuition pump results from the fact that either tool will serve most of our purposes equally well.

To reinforce my point, let me cite one more argument in favor of qualia, this one by Peter Bieri. Bieri's article, "Why Is Consciousness Puzzling?" appears in a volume of papers edited by Thomas Metzinger called *Conscious Experience*. Most of the articles in this volume are schizophrenic: they start off from the Nagel-Jackson-Searle-McGinn intuition that raw feels are simply *given* to us, in their full ineffable ipseity, and cannot be described away. But they then proceed, in a rush of scientific optimism, to explore the possibility of effing the ineffable by developing a "unified science of consciousness." Metzinger's introduction to the volume combines fervent expressions of Nagelian faith with confidence that further research in neuroscience will resolve what he calls "the problem of qualia." "Many researchers in the neurosciences," Metzinger says, "are now quick to admit [this] is indeed a truly deep problem."[15] But of course if this deep problem *were* resolved by neuroscientific means, then Mary the neuroscientist would have all the more reason not to be surprised when her sight was restored. Success in solving this problem would help eliminate the intuitions which were pumped up to create it in order to propound it.

In a section of his article called "Can the question be dropped?" Bieri examines the Dennett-like suggestion that "A phenomenon, a state of affairs is puzzling only against the background of certain expectations regarding explanation and understanding. And these expectations can, like others, be justified or unjustified." Continuing in the same pragmatist vein, he asks "Could we not content ourselves with what we have already got—covariance, dependence, determination [of reports of conscious experience with neural states]?"

"The answer," Bieri replies firmly, is "no." Unless we can get beyond covariance to "an understanding of the way in which the material or functional properties of the brain, or both, make the emergence of sensing necessary," he says, "we do not understand how sensing and experiencing can be causally efficacious in our behavior." Bieri is quite willing to grant to Dennett that "as regards causation and control of our behavior, consciousness . . . seems redundant. It might as well be absent—our trajectory through the world would be exactly the same." But, Bieri continues, in words which Nagel might have written, "if that were true, it would be a pervasive *illusion* that we . . . control our behavior from the inside when it is a doing and not a mere happening."[16] Like Nagel, Bieri sees his opponents' view as flying in the face of common sense, but his only argument for this claim is that he thinks commonsense views have presuppositions which are invisible to those opponents. Here we confront the same problem as I discussed yesterday in connection with Habermas and Apel: how can you convince people that they are presupposing what they do not believe?

Dennett's response to Bieri's line of argument, we might infer from his book on the problem of free will,[17] would be to say that the very idea of "the inside" is one which Hume showed us how to get along without. This reminds us that the question of the compatibility of free will with determinism is another of those issues which divides philosophers into squads manning competing intuition pumps, but which is no closer to resolution than it was when Hume raised it. The inside-vs-outside contrast is indispensable to Nagel's philosophical vocabulary: "the internal-external tension," he says, "pervades human life."[18] But that distinction has no place whatever in any game which Dennett would wish to play. (Nor in any that Davidson would play. Davidson sees what he calls "the myth of subjectivity" as engendered precisely by the attempt to cut through the relational network of cause and effect and isolate something on the inside which can vary independently from everything on the outside; the inner, he suggests, is merely the non-relational.[19] Once this attempt is dropped, Davidson thinks, the inside-outside distinction fades away, and compatibilism becomes "intuitively" plausible.)

Bieri's argument gives me an occasion to hark back to my claim, at the beginning of this lecture, that pan-relationalists, in order to get rid of the objective-subjective and found-made distinctions, have to get rid of the inside-vs.-outside distinction. I paired this with the claim that they will have to get rid of the idea that there is a dimension in which language and world can swing free of one another. The connection between my two claims is that the Cartesian notion of mental events as capable of varying independently of physical events—the notion which creates the intuition that freedom and determinism are incompatible—became sublated, when Cartesian dualism became unpopular, into the claim that language and world, scheme and content, could vary independently. The linguistic turn put language in place of mind or noumenal reality as something that escaped from the web of relations which bound everything else together. This move encouraged the hope to which I referred earlier—that there might be an activity called conceptual analysis which was different in kind from a description of the use of words.

As I see it, the structural similarity between the mind-body problem, the free-will problem, and the problem of whether language can ever describe the world as it is in itself consists in this: in each case, the propounder of the problem points to something which is not part of the familiar causal network, something which escapes the network of relations in which we had hoped everything might be caught. In each case, the pan-relationalist says that there is nothing there, and that dust is being kicked up so that philosophers may then claim to have glimpsed a deep problem concealed by that dust. In each case their essentialist opponents say that their anti-dualist, pragmatist, pan-relationalist opponent is handicapped by blinkered two-dimensional vision, and that this causes him to mistake a plain, straightforward fact for a mere linguistic contrivance. These opponents are glad that they themselves find it "psychologically impossible" to acquire this sort of vision.

My own view, as I suggested at the beginning of this lecture, is that it is pointless to debate whether the disputed entity was found or made. All that can be debated is whether the language-game in which the problem is propounded is one we should play. But of course putting the matter in that way begs all the questions against Nagel and my other opponents. There is no metaphilosophical escape route from the dialectical impasse, because both sides have equally comprehensive metaphilosophies at their disposal. I shall return to this point after taking up my second example of such an impasse.

2. Stroud and Williams on Skepticism*

In his book *The Significance of Philosophical Scepticism*, Barry Stroud criticizes those who say that skepticism about the external world is produced by

---

* The following section draws on Richard Rorty, "Comments on Michael Williams' *Unnatural Doubts*" (read at the APA Central Division Meeting, April 28, 1995), *Journal of Philosophical Research* 22 (1997), 1–10.

an obsolete Cartesian theory of mental functioning, a theory which creates
the pseudo-problem of "the veil of ideas." He constructs an argument for
skepticism which mentions neither minds nor ideas. This argument depends
solely on the intuition that "we must know that we are not dreaming if we
are to know anything about the world around us."[20]

Stroud also criticizes the pragmatist suggestion that the only sort of reality
from which Descartes's argument cuts us off is some weird sort of noumenal,
ineffable reality—that that argument leaves our knowledge of the world of
common sense intact. Stroud sums up this line of argument as "The inac-
cessible 'reality' denied to us is . . . simply an artefact of the philosopher's
investigation and not something that otherwise should concern us."[21] Stroud
insists that the skeptic does not use "know" and "real" and "word" in any new-
fangled philosophical way, and concludes that

> Without a demonstration that Descartes's philosophical investigation
> differs from our ordinary assessments in some way that prevents its neg-
> ative conclusion from having the kind of significance similar conclu-
> sions are rightly taken to have in ordinary life, we can derive no conso-
> lation from the ungrounded idea that the reality from which he shows
> our knowledge is excluded does not or should not concern us anyway.
> (37–38)

Skepticism, Stroud says, appeals to "something deep in our nature" (39)—
not something extraneous, introduced by philosophical trickery. "The sources
of Descartes's requirement . . . illuminate something about our actual conception of knowledge."[22]

In his reply to Stroud in *Unnatural Doubts: Epistemological Realism and
the Basis of Scepticism,* Michael Williams claims to provide just the demonstration Stroud does not think is available: a demonstration that there is a
big difference between what non-philosophers are doing and what Descartes
is doing.

Williams thinks that the clue to the difference between what ordinary
people do and what Descartes does lies in "the context-sensitivity of both
sceptical doubts and everyday certainties."[23] Once we realize that the skeptic
has created a *new* context of inquiry by inventing a topic called "our epistemic situation," we can say, with Williams, that the skeptic has indeed dis-

covered that "knowledge is impossible under the conditions of philosophical reflection." But we can comfort ourselves with the thought that this discovery does nothing to show that "under the conditions of philosophical reflection, knowledge is generally impossible."[24]

Williams claims that the sceptic is taking "epistemological realism"—the doctrine that there is something called "human knowledge" to be investigated—for granted. He takes this topic to a philosopher's invention, and the effect of depth to be a product of the puzzlement produced in the plain man by that invention's novelty. As he says, "the deep demands of our ordinary ways of thinking only come to the surface in the context of his [the skeptic's] extraordinary investigation into the status of human knowledge in general."[25] Williams argues that we do not have an "actual conception of knowledge" to be illuminated, and that nobody except the skeptic needs such terms as "human knowledge" or "our epistemic position" or "our view of reality." Williams does not doubt that the skeptic's extraordinary investigation creates a context—a context in which skeptical doubts make sense, and indeed are irrefutable. But he urges that Stroud and his ilk owe us an argument about why this context needs to be created.

Williams makes a very helpful distinction between theoretical diagnoses of skepticism and therapeutic diagnoses. Therapeutic diagnoses claim that skepticism somehow does not make sense, because it is somehow based on a misuse of words. This therapeutic strategy cannot be used by pan-relationalists, who think that anything has a sense if you give it one. So Williams discards this strategy and says that he will "never accuse the sceptic of incoherence."[26] Rather, he will "grant that [the skeptic's problems] are fully genuine, but only given certain theoretical ideas about knowledge and justification." This means that we must abandon hope for a "definitive refutation" of the skeptic,[27] and be content with criticism of the skeptic's "theory of the relation of philosophical reflection to ordinary life."[28] This criticism consists in pointing out that philosophical reflection of the Cartesian sort does not make us context-free, but simply creates a new, seemingly pointless, context. Near the end of his book, Williams sums up by saying

> I have never denied that the sceptic is conditionally correct, in the sense that, by the standards he insists on applying, we never know anything about the world. My point has always been that these standards . . . are

not built into the human condition, but into a particular intellectual project.[29]

Williams's originality is shown by the fact that he neither attempts therapy, nor falls back on what he calls "a bluff pragmatism"—the sort of pragmatism which would argue that "we don't have to respond to scepticism because it makes no difference whether we do or not."[30] Rather, he admits that it will make a difference whether or not we work within the context of philosophical doubt, but insists that Stroud has not provided a reason for working within that context.

Williams notes that many philosophers see the context within which Stroud works as created by what Williams calls "the objectivity requirement": "the requirement that the knowledge we want to explain is knowledge of an objective world, a world that is the way it is independently of how it appears to us to be or what we are inclined to believe about it."[31] Such philosophers, as he says, typically "see the objectivity requirement as the deep source of sceptical problems."[32] Williams is, I think, strikingly original in pointing out that it is only the "fatal interaction" of the objectivity requirement with "the totality condition" that gives rise to such problems. The totality condition is the condition that all our knowledge be examined at once.

Williams's alternative to epistemological realism—to the Cartesian assumption that "human knowledge" or "our knowledge of the external world" is a suitable topic of assessment—is what he calls "contextualism." This is the doctrine that "the epistemic status of a proposition is liable to shift with situational, disciplinary and other contextually variable factors" and that, "independently of all such influences, a proposition has no epistemic status whatsoever."[33] A contextualist denies what the epistemological realist asserts: that every belief, by virtue of its content, has "an inalienable epistemic character which it carries with it wherever it goes and which determines where its justification must finally be sought."[34]

Williams sums up the issue between contextualism and epistemological realism by saying that contextualism is "not offered as a question-begging direct answer to an undeniably compelling request for understanding, but as a challenge to justify the presumption that there is something to understand."[35] The skeptic creates this presumption by assuming that "experiential knowledge is generally prior to knowledge of the world." But, Williams points out, the only reason for so taking it is that otherwise there would be no way to go about assessing our knowledge of the world. As he says "the sceptic's foundationalism, together with the [epistemological] realism it embodies, is a brute metaphysical commitment."[36]

Williams has, I think, succeeded in showing that you do not have to agree with Stroud when he says that "it must be shown or explained *how* it is possible for us to know things about the world, given that the sense-experiences we get are compatible with our merely dreaming."[37] You will agree with him only if you are already a foundationalist. You will only see his problem as urgent if you have already partitioned your beliefs into beliefs about the external world and experiential beliefs, and assumed that the former must be inferred from the latter. But you will only partition them in this way if you have already come to believe that there is what Descartes called "a natural order of reasons,"[38] and therefore a *context-free epistemic status which is intrinsic to the content of a belief.*[39] Williams has thus shown that it is not enough to criticize epistemological foundationalism, and to substitute a coherentist epistemology for a foundationalist one. One only gets to the bottom of the issue if one asks why one might think that there is a discipline called epistemology, or a topic called "human knowledge."

But although Williams has convinced me, he has not convinced Stroud, and I doubt very much that his book will have much impact on philosophers who join Stroud in finding skepticism *deep*—philosophers like Stanley Cavell, Thompson Clarke, and, of course, Nagel. These philosophers find the existence of a topic called "human knowledge" as obvious as Nagel, Searle, McGinn, and Jackson find the existence of a topic called "conscious experience" (defined either by ostension or, begging the question, as "what zombies lack"). Such philosophers think the context-free character of Cartesian epistemological inquiry is an advantage, just as they think that prescinding what it is like to see blue from the disposition to call an object blue is an advantage. For they believe that both moves help get a deep and important problem into focus.

De-contextualization as a means of focusing is, of course, a contradiction in terms for us pan-relationalists. For we think that only by being placed in a specific set of relationships—placed in a specific context—can a topic be made thinkable. From our point of view, what is most significant about Williams's criticism of Stroud is his point that epistemology creates a new context, and his admission that you can give any question, no matter how silly it looks at first, a sense by creating a language-game in which the question has a home.[40]

This admission, which pan-relationalists have to make, contrasts with attempts, by Cavell, Cora Diamond, James Conant, and others, to resurrect Wittgenstein's notion of "nonsense." Pan-relationalists do not have much use for this notion, nor for that of "deep confusion," which they think no better than "deep problem." They regard the use of the sense-nonsense distinction, still deployed in *Philosophical Investigations*, as an unfortunate relic of Wittgenstein's Tractarian salad days.

Conant builds upon Putnam's recent claim that "metaphysical realism"—the doctrine that language and thought can vary so independently that, even at the end of inquiry, the one may have no representational relation to the other—is *unintelligible*. He quotes Putnam as saying

> If we agree that if it is *unintelligible* to say 'We sometimes succeed in comparing our language and thought with reality as it is in itself,' then we should realize that it is also unintelligible to say 'It is *impossible* to stand outside and compare our thought and language with the world.'[41]

Putnam's view, as paraphrased by Conant, is that if one says the latter, as he himself did in the past, one is "already succumbing to the decisive move in the philosophical conjuring trick."[42] Putnam thinks that I am still deceived by this trick, and says

> Rorty moves from a conclusion about the unintelligibility of metaphysical realism . . . to a skepticism about the possibility of representation *tout court*. We are left with the conclusion that there is no metaphysically innocent way to say that our words *do* "represent things outside of ourselves."[43]

Conant notes that I prefer "useless" to "unintelligible" as a stick with which to beat proponents' views whom Putnam and I both criticize—Bernard Williams's notion of "the absolute conception of reality," for example. But Conant thinks this is a bad choice of weapons. He gives two reasons for this view.

The first is that I do not give a clear answer to the question "useless for what purpose." The second is more complex, and goes like this:

> If what the metaphysical realist's vocabulary brought to light (contrary to his original intentions) was that we really cannot do something which we would like to do (and which it does make sense to think we might be able to do), it is not evident that the distastefulness of this insight would, in and of itself, constitute a sufficient reason for rejecting the vocabulary which made this insight available . . . Our simply finding a discovery inconvenient or oppressive is not generally considered an intellectually defensible reason for wishing no longer to attend to it. Its "lacking in utility" (whatever that means) might be such a reason. But when Rorty turns to the task of giving principled reasons for being suspicious of metaphysical realism, considerations of utility do not seem to be what is at issue . . . Rorty now wants a way of dismissing metaphysical realism that does not even commit him to the claim that it is in some way "confused." He now just wants to be able to conclude—through a vague appeal to what helps us "cope better"—that, since the vocabulary of the metaphysical realist forces us into a skeptical problematic . . . we are better off chucking that vocabulary altogether.[44]

Conant is quite right that I do not want to claim that metaphysical realism (or skepticism about the external world, or the doctrine of qualia) is "in some way 'confused.'" I think this word should be restricted to cases in which our interlocutor seems unable to make his view coherent, even to himself—an inability betokened by repeated failure to know how to reply to fairly simple questions, constant equivocation between senses of terms which seem widely diverse, bewildered inability to understand objections, etc. This sort of situation is sometimes encountered when dealing with children or victims of mental disturbance.

This sort of inability is not evinced by Bernard Williams, Stroud, Nagel, and many other philosophers who verge on metaphysical realism. They are smooth and fluent in the linguistic moves they make, and in their handling of questions and objections. It would be strange to say that they are "confused." Nor do I want to say that I find their views unintelligible. I can talk their funny little language-games if I want to, and sometimes do so for pedagogic purposes. But I do want to say that I think it would be a bad idea for us to play those games.

I have restated Michael Williams's criticism of Descartes and Stroud at some length because he seems to me to take exactly the right metaphilosophical stance. He finds his opponents' views fully intelligible, and has no theoretical, but only practical, objections to their becoming prevalent. It would miss Williams's point to say, with Conant, that, since Descartes's and Stroud's view is *fully intelligible,* it cannot be dismissed as merely inconvenient or oppressive.

Conant goes from "metaphysical realism is intelligible" to "the metaphysical realist has made a discovery which it would be intellectually discreditable to dismiss merely because it is found inconvenient or oppressive." But everything we find intelligible counts as a "discovery." Astrology, for example, is a readily learnable and enjoyably playable language game, but many people think it would be well to "chuck it altogether." They think so because they believe that it has no place in the world of modern astronomy, modern medicine, modern psychiatry, and the like.

I should like to chuck the appearance-reality distinction, the essence-accident distinction, the notions of "in itself" and of "correspondence to reality," and the vertical metaphors which are used by these distinctions, because I think they have no place in the culture Whitman and Dewey hoped to build—a culture in which hope for the human future takes the place of knowledge of high or deep matters. When I say "useless" I mean useless for the construction and maintenance of that culture. That is why I offer big swooshy historical generalizations about the connections between the sense of Sin with the Platonic-Aristotelian conception of knowledge. It is why I applaud Dewey for making politics prior to philosophy and asking "what sort of views on traditional philosophical topics are suited for the utopian American democracy that is to come? what sort of language games would it be best for the intellectuals of that utopia to play?"

As I see it, the idea that we philosophers can uncover subtle, deep unintelligibility, or deep conceptual confusion, is a revival of the bad pre-Quinean notion that philosophers can do something rather arcane called "conceptual analysis." I think that Wittgenstein never quite rid himself of the latter notion, even though my favorite passages of *Philosophical Investigations* show why it is not a useful one. I had thought that Putnam had freed himself from it, and I am puzzled to find him now moving in the direction of Cavell, a philosopher who specializes in depth, and who cultivates exactly those bits of Wittgenstein which I think should be allowed to wither away.

There is, however, another, quite separate, question raised by Putnam's criticism of me in "The Question of Realism," and by Conant's glosses on that essay. This is the *practical* question of whether my anti-representationalism throws out a innocent ordinary sense of "represent," one which is worth hanging onto, along with a pernicious philosophical sense. That seems to me a good question, because it goes to the real issue: what are the best tactics to use if one wants to cleanse our culture of metaphors of verticality (or, as Derrida puts it, "deconstruct the metaphysics of presence")? Unlike Cavell, but like Putnam at an earlier stage of his career, I should like to nudge our culture in a direction in which no one can even remember why they cared about Other Minds and The External World—not because they have found their earlier ruminations unintelligible, but because they seem so pointless.

But it may be that Putnam and Conant are right when they suggest that my methods and my rhetoric, and specifically my frenetic anti-representationalism, are counter-productive. A similar suggestion has been made by John McDowell, and so I shall come back to this question when I take up McDowell's views in our final meeting.

7

Ethics without Universal Obligations

In earlier lectures I suggested that we think of pragmatism as an attempt to alter our self-image so as to make it consistent with the Darwinian claim that we differ from other animals simply in the complexity of our behavior.* To adopt this image of ourselves as exceptionally clever animals is to set aside the Greek way of distinguishing ourselves from the brutes. Plato and Aristotle suggested that the other animals lived in a world of sensory appearance, that their lives consisted in adjusting to the changes of these appearances, and that they were thus incapable of *knowing*, for knowledge consists in penetrating behind appearance to reality. We humans can do something quite different from adjusting to changing conditions, for we can know; we can accurately represent the intrinsic and unchanging natures of the things around us.

Pragmatists offer an account of inquiry—both in physics and ethics—as the search for adjustment, and in particular for the kind of adjustment to our fellow humans which we call "the search for justification and agreement."

This lecture was first published in English with a different title, as Richard Rorty, "Ethics without Principles," in Rorty, *Philosophy and Social Hope*, 72–90 (New York: Penguin, 1999) (hereafter *PSH*). It was published with two other lectures as Part 2 of that volume, "Hope in Place of Knowledge: A Version of Pragmatism," 23–90. "Hope in Place of Knowledge" is the title that Rorty had given to the original lectures, which were delivered in Vienna and Paris in 1993. They were published first in German as Rorty, *Hoffnung statt Erkenntnis* (Vienna: Passagen, 1994), and in French as Rorty, *L'espoir au lieu de savoir* (Paris: Albin Michel, 1995).
*In *PSH*, this paragraph begins: "I have been suggesting that we think of pragmatism as an attempt to alter our self-image so as to make it consistent with the Darwinian claim that we differ from other animals simply in the complexity of our behaviour" (72).

I have been arguing that we should substitute the latter search for the traditional quest for truth. Such a substitution would let us think of knowing as just a more complex means of adjusting, and would thereby let us see our faculties as continuous with those of the brutes.

I have also portrayed pragmatism as a generalized form of anti-essentialism—as an attempt to break down the distinction between intrinsic and extrinsic features of things. By thinking of everything as relational through and through, pragmatists attempt to get rid of the contrast between reality and appearance—between the way things are in themselves and the way they appear to us, or the way we represent them, or the way we talk about them. In particular, they insist that we can only talk about things under more or less optional descriptions of them, descriptions dictated by our own human needs, and that this is not a spiritual or epistemological disaster. Pragmatists hope to make it impossible for the skeptic to raise the question, "Is our knowledge of things adequate to the way things really are?" They substitute for this traditional question the *practical* question: are our ways of describing things, or relating them to other things so as to cope with them better by making them fulfill our needs more adequately, as good as possible? Or can we do better? Can our future be made better than our present?*

In this lecture I shall take up the distinction between morality and prudence. This distinction is traditionally drawn by opposing unconditional and categorical obligations to conditional and hypothetical ones. Obviously, pragmatists are going to have doubts about the suggestion that anything is unconditional. For they doubt that anything, or could be, nonrelational. So they need to reinterpret the distinctions between morality and prudence, morality and expediency, and morality and self-interest in ways which dispense with the notion of unconditional obligation.

Dewey suggested that we reconstruct the distinction between prudence and morality in terms of the distinction between routine and non-routine social relationships. He saw "prudence" as a member of the same family of

---

* The three paragraphs preceding this note were not translated into Spanish. The seventh Girona lecture begins with the next paragraph. There are no marks on the manuscript indicating that nearly a page and a half should be deleted. However, the translator, Joan Vergés Gifra, who was present at the delivery of the lecture in Girona, believes Rorty may have begun with "In this lecture . . ." and thus surmised Rorty meant to delete the first three paragraphs.

concepts as "habit" and "custom." All three words describe familiar and relatively uncontroversial ways in which individuals and groups adjust to the stresses and strains of their non-human and human environments. It is obviously prudent both to keep an eye out for poisonous snakes in the grass and to trust strangers less than members of one's family. "Prudence," "expediency," and "efficiency" are all terms which describe such routine and uncontroversial adjustments to circumstance.

Morality and law, on the other hand, begin when controversy arises. We invent both when we can no longer just do what comes naturally, when routine is no longer good enough, when habit and custom no longer suffice. These will no longer suffice when the individual's needs begin to clash with those of her family, or her family's with those of the neighbors', or when economic strain begins to split her community into warring classes, or when that community must come to terms with an alien community. On Dewey's account, the prudence-morality distinction is, like that between custom and law, a distinction of degree—the degree of need for conscious deliberation and explicit formulation of precepts—rather than a distinction of kind. There is no distinction of kind, for pragmatists like Dewey, between what is useful and what is right. For, as Dewey said, "Right is only an abstract name for the multitude of concrete demands in action which others impress upon us, and of which we are obliged, if we would live, to take some account."[1] The utilitarians were right when they coalesced the moral and the useful. (But they were wrong insofar as they tried to reduce utility simply to getting pleasure and avoiding pain. Dewey agrees with Aristotle that human happiness cannot be reduced to the accumulation of pleasures.)

From Kant's point of view, however, Aristotle, Mill, and Dewey are equally blind to the true nature of morality. To identify moral obligation with the need to adjust one's behavior to the needs of other human beings is, for Kantians, either vicious or simple-minded. Dewey seems to Kantians to have confused duty with self-interest, the intrinsic authority of the moral law with the banausic need to bargain with opponents whom one cannot overcome.

Dewey was well aware of this Kantian criticism. Here is one of the passages in which he attempted to answer it:

> Morals, it is said, imply the subordination of fact to ideal consideration,
> while the view presented [Dewey's own view] makes morals secondary to

bare fact, which is equal to depriving them of dignity and jurisdiction . . .
The criticism rests upon a false separation. It argues in effect that either
ideal standards antecede customs and confer their moral quality upon
them, or that in being subsequent to custom[s] and evolved from them,
they are mere accidental by-products. But how does the case stand with
language? . . . Language grew out of unintelligent babblings, instinc-
tive motions called gestures, and the pressure of circumstance. But
nevertheless language once called into existence is language and operates as language.[2]

The point of Dewey's analogy between language and morality is that there
was no decisive moment at which language stopped being a series of reactions to the behavior of other humans and started to represent reality. Similarly, there was no point at which practical reasoning stopped being prudential and became specifically moral, no point at which it stopped being merely
useful and started being authoritative.

Dewey's reply to those who, like Kant, think of morality as stemming from
a specifically human faculty called "reason," and of prudence as something
shared with the brutes, is that the *only* thing that is specifically human is language. But the history of language is a seamless story of gradually increasing
complexity. The story of how we got from Neanderthal grunts and nudges to
German philosophical treatises is no more discontinuous than the story of
how we got from the amoebae to the anthropoids. The two stories are parts
of one larger story. Cultural evolution takes over from biological evolution
without a break. From an evolutionary point of view, there is no difference
between the grunts and the treatises save complexity. Yet the difference between the language-using and the mute animals, and the difference between
cultures which do not engage in conscious, collective, moral deliberation and
cultures which do, are as important and obvious as ever, even though they
are differences of degree. On Dewey's view, philosophers who have sharply
distinguished reason from experience, or morality from prudence, have tried
to turn an important difference of degree into a difference of metaphysical
kind. They have thereby constructed problems for themselves which are as
insoluble as they are artificial.

Dewey saw Kant, in his moral philosophy, as taking "the doctrine that
the essence of reason is complete universality (and hence necessity and

immutability) with the seriousness becoming the professor of logic."[3] He interpreted Kant's attempt to get advice about what to do out of the mere idea of universalizability as offering not an impossible disregard of consequences but merely "a broad impartial view of consequences." All that the categorical imperative does, Dewey said, is to commend "the habit of asking how we should be willing to be treated in a similar case."[4] The attempt to do more, to get "ready-made rules available at a moment's notice for settling any kind of moral difficulty," seemed to Dewey to have been "born of timidity and nourished by love of authoritative prestige." Only such a tendency to sado-masochism, Dewey thought, could have "led to the idea that absence of immutably fixed and universally applicable ready-made principles is equivalent to moral chaos."[5]

So much for the standard Deweyan criticism of the Kantian way of viewing the distinction between morality and prudence. I want now to turn to another distinction, that between reason and sentiment, thinking and feeling. Doing so will let me relate Dewey's work to that of the contemporary American moral philosopher Annette Baier. Baier, one of the leading feminist philosophers in the United States, takes David Hume as her model. She praises Hume as the "woman's moral philosopher" because of his willingness to take sentiment, and indeed sentimentality, as central to the moral consciousness. She also praises him for "de-intellectualizing and de-sanctifying the moral endeavor . . . presenting it as the human equivalent of various social controls in animal or insect populations."[6] Though Baier rarely mentions Dewey, and Dewey rarely discusses Hume's moral philosophy at any length, these three militantly anti-Kantian philosophers are on the same side of most arguments. All three share the same distrust of the notion of "moral obligation." Dewey, Baier, and Hume might all agree with Nietzsche that the pre-Socratic Greeks were free from the "timidity," the fear of having to make hard choices, which led Plato to search for immutable moral truth. All three see the temporal circumstances of human life as difficult enough without sado-masochistically adding immutable, unconditional obligations.

Baier has proposed that we substitute the notion of "appropriate trust" for that of "obligation" as our central moral concept. She has said that

> there is no room for moral theory as something which is more philo-
> sophical and less committed than moral deliberation, and which is not

simply an account of our customs and styles of justification, criticism, protest, revolt, conversion, and resolution.[7]

In words that echo some of Dewey's, Baier says that "the villain . . . is the rationalist, law-fixated tradition in moral philosophy,"[8] a tradition which assumes that "behind every moral intuition lies a universal rule."[9] That tradition assumes that Hume's attempt to think of moral progress as a progress of sentiments "fails to account for moral obligation." But, on Baier's view as on Dewey's, there is nothing to account for: moral obligation does not have a nature, or a source, different from tradition, habit, and custom. Morality is simply a new and controversial custom. The special obligation we feel when we use the term "moral" is simply the special need we feel to act in a relatively unfamiliar, untried way—a way which may have unpredictable and dangerous consequences. Our sense that prudence is unheroic and morality heroic is merely the recognition that testing out the relatively untried is more dangerous, more risky, than doing what comes naturally.

Baier and Dewey agree that the central flaw in much traditional moral philosophy has been the myth of the self as non-relational, as capable of existing independently of any concern for others, as a cold psychopath needing to be constrained to take account of other people's needs. This is the picture of the self which philosophers since Plato have interpreted in terms of the division between "reason" and "the passions"—a division which Hume unfortunately perpetuated in his notorious inversion of Plato: his claim that "reason is, and should be, the slave of the passions." Ever since Plato, the West has construed the reason-passion distinction as paralleling the distinction between the universal and the individual, as well as that between unselfish and selfish actions. The religious, Platonic, and Kantian traditions have thus saddled us with a distinction between the true self and the false self, the self which hears the call of conscience and the self which is merely "self-interested." The latter self is merely prudential, and not yet moral.

Baier and Dewey both argue that this notion of the self as a cold, self-interested, calculating psychopath should be set aside. If we really were such selves, the question "Why should I be moral?" would be forever unanswerable. Only when we masochistically picture ourselves as such selves do we feel the need to punish ourselves by quailing before divine commands, or before Kant's tribunal of pure practical reason. But if we follow the pragmatists' advice to see everything as constituted by its relations to everything else, it will be easy to detect the fallacy which Dewey described as "transforming the (truistic) fact of acting *as* a self into the fiction of acting always *for* self."[10] We shall commit this fallacy, and continue to think of the self as a psychopath in need of restraint, as long as we accept what Dewey called the "belief in the fixity and simplicity of the self." Dewey associated this belief with the theologians' "dogma of the unity and ready-made completeness of the soul."[11] But he might equally well have associated it with the argument of Plato's *Phaedo,* or with Kant's doctrine that the moral self is a non-empirical self.

If we put such notions of unity and ready-made completeness to one side, we can say, with Dewey, that "selfhood (except as it has encased itself in a shell of routine) is in process of making, and that any self is capable of including within itself a number of inconsistent selves, of unharmonized dispositions."[12] This notion of multiple inconsistent selves is, as Donald Davidson has shown, a good way of naturalizing and demystifying the Freudian notion of the unconscious.[13] But the most important link between Freud and Dewey is the one which Baier emphasizes: the role of the family, and in particular of maternal love, in creating non-psychopaths—human selves who find concern for other human beings entirely natural. Baier says, in words which Dewey might have written, that "the secular equivalent of faith in God . . . is faith in the human community and its evolving procedures—in the prospects for many-handed cognitive ambitions and moral hopes."[14] But she sees that faith as rooted in the faith most of us have in our parents and siblings. The trust which holds a family together is Baier's model for the secular faith which may hold together modern, post-traditional societies.

Freud helped us see that we get psychopaths—people whose self-conception involves no relations to others—only when parental love, and the trust which such love creates in the child, are absent. To see the point Baier wants us to appreciate, consider the question: Do I have a moral obligation to my mother? My wife? My children? "Morality" and "obligation" seem inapposite terms. For doing what one is obliged to do contrasts with doing what comes naturally, and for most people responding to the needs of family members is the most natural thing in the world. Such responses come naturally because most of us define ourselves, at least in part, by our relations to members of our family. Our needs and theirs largely overlap; we are not happy if they are not. We would not wish to be well fed while our children go hungry; that would be unnatural. Would it also be immoral? It is a bit strange to say so. One would only employ this term if one encountered a parent who was also a pathological egoist, a mother or father whose sense of self has nothing to do with her or his children—the sort of person envisaged by decision theory, someone whose identity is constituted by "preference rankings" rather than by fellow feeling.

By contrast, I may feel a specifically *moral* obligation to deprive both my children and myself of a portion of the available food because there are starving people outside our door. The word "moral" is appropriate here because the demand is less *natural* than the demand to feed my children. It is less closely connected with my sense of who I am. But the desire to feed the hungry stranger may of course *become* as tightly woven into my self-conception as the desire to feed my family. Moral development in the individual, and moral progress in the human species as a whole, is a matter of remarking human selves so as to enlarge the variety of the relationships which constitute those selves. The ideal limit of this process of enlargement is the self envisaged by Christian and Buddhist accounts of sainthood—an ideal self to whom the hunger and suffering of *any* human being (and even, perhaps, that of any other animal) is intensely painful.

Should this progress ever be completed, the term "morality" would drop out of the language. For there would no longer be any way, nor any need, to contrast doing what comes naturally with doing what is moral. We should all have what Kant called a "holy will." The term "moral obligation" becomes increasingly less appropriate to the degree to which we identify with those whom we help: the degree to which we mention them when telling ourselves stories about who we are, the degree to which their story is also our story.[15] It comes fairly naturally to share what one has with an old friend, or a near neighbor, or a close business associate, who has been left destitute by a sudden disaster. It comes less naturally to share with a casual acquaintance, or a complete stranger, who is in the same unfortunate situation. In a world in which hunger is common, it does not come naturally to take food from one's childrens' mouths in order to feed a hungry stranger and her children. But if the stranger and her children are on your doorstep, you may well feel obliged to do just that. The terms "moral" and "obligation" become even more appropriate when it is a matter of depriving your children of something they want in order to send money to the victims of a famine in a country you have never seen, to people whom you might well find repellent if you ever encountered them: people whom you might not want as friends, might not want your children to marry, people whose *only* claim on your attention is that you have been told that they are hungry. But Christianity taught the West to look forward to a world in which there are no such people, a world in which all men and women are brothers and sisters. In that world, there would never be any occasion to speak of "obligation."

When moral philosophers in the Kantian tradition put sentiment on a par with prejudice, and tell us that "from a strictly moral point of view," there is no difference between one's own hungry child and a randomly selected hungry child on the other side of the world, they are contrasting this so-called "moral point of view" with a point of view they call "mere self-interest." The idea behind this way of speaking is that morality and obligation starts where self-interest stops. The problem with this way of speaking, Dewey insisted, is that the boundaries of the self are fuzzy and flexible. So philosophers in this tradition try to obscure this fuzziness by defining those boundaries. They do so by saying that the self is constituted by a preference ranking—one which divides people up according to whom one would prefer to be fed first, for example. Then they either contrast moral obligation with preference, or else "subjectivize" feelings of moral obligation by taking them as just further preferences.

There are difficulties with both of these alternatives. If you contrast moral obligation with preference, you have trouble with the question of moral motivation: what sense does it make, after all, to say that a person acts against her own preferences? On the other hand, if you no longer distinguish between morality and self-interest, and say that what we call "morality" is simply the self-interest of those who have been acculturated in a certain way, then you will be accused of "emotivism," of having failed to appreciate Kant's distinction between dignity and value. One way leads to the question Plato tried to answer: "Why should I be moral?" The other way leads to the question, "Is there any difference between a preference for feeding hungry strangers over letting them starve and a preference for vanilla over chocolate ice cream?" More generally, one way seems to lead to a dualistic metaphysics to splitting the human self, and possibly the universe as a whole, into higher and lower segments. The other seems to lead to a wholesale abnegation of our aspirations to something "higher" than mere animality.

Pragmatists are often accused of just such an abnegation. They are lumped with reductionists, behaviorists, sensualists, nihilists, and other dubious characters. I think that the pragmatist's best defense against this sort of charge is to say that she too has a conception of our difference from the animals. But hers does not involve a sharp difference—a difference between the infinite and the finite—of the sort illustrated by Kant's distinction between dignity and value, between the unconditioned and the conditioned, the non-relational and the relational. Rather, the pragmatist sees our difference as a much greater degree of flexibility—in particular, a much greater flexibility in the boundaries of selfhood, in the sheer quantity of relationships which can go to constitute a human self. She sees the ideal of human brotherhood and sisterhood not as the imposition of something non-empirical on the empirical, nor of something non-natural on the natural, but as the culmination of a process of adjustment which is also a process of remaking the human species.*

From this point of view, moral progress is not a matter of an increase of rationality—a gradual diminution of the influence of prejudice and superstition, permitting us to see our moral duty more clearly. Nor is it what Dewey called an increase of intelligence, increasing skill at inventing courses of action which simultaneously satisfy many conflicting demands. People can be very intelligent, in this sense, without having wide sympathies. It is neither irrational or unintelligent to draw the limits of one's moral community at a national, or racial, or gender, border. But it is undesirable—morally undesirable. So it is best to think of moral progress as a matter of increasing *sensitivity,* increasing responsiveness to the needs of a larger and larger variety of people and things. Just as the pragmatists see scientific progress not as the gradual attenuation of a veil of appearance which hides the intrinsic nature of reality from us, but as the increasing ability to respond to the concerns of ever larger groups of people—especially the people who carry out ever more acute observations and perform ever more refined experiments—so they see moral progress as a matter of being able to respond to the needs of ever more inclusive groups of people.

I want to pursue this analogy between science and morals a bit further.† I said in earlier lectures that pragmatists do not think of scientific, or any other

---

* In *PSH* this last sentence reads differently: "is also a process of recreating human beings." See *PSH,* 81.

† In *PSH,* this paragraph begins, "Let me pursue this analogy between science and morals a bit further" (81).

inquiry, as aimed at truth, but rather at better justificatory ability—better ability to deal with doubts about what we are saying, either by shoring up what we have previously said or by deciding to say something slightly different. The trouble with aiming at truth is that you would not know when you had reached it, even if you do in fact reach it. But you *can* aim at assuaging ever more doubt. Analogously, you cannot aim at "doing what is right" because you will never know whether you have hit the mark. Long after you are dead, better informed and more sophisticated people may judge your action to have been a tragic mistake, just as they may judge your scientific beliefs to have presupposed an obsolete cosmology. But you *can* aim at ever more sensitivity to pain, and ever greater satisfaction of ever more various needs. Pragmatists think the idea of something non-human luring us human beings on should be replaced with the idea of getting more and more human beings into our community—of taking the needs and interests and views of more and more diverse human beings into account. Justificatory ability is, on the pragmatist view, its own reward. There is no need to worry about whether we will be rewarded with a sort of immaterial medal labeled "Truth" or "Moral Goodness."[16]

The idea of a "God's eye view" to which science continually approximates is of a piece with the idea of "the moral law" to which social custom, in periods of moral progress, continually approximates. The ideas of "discovering the intrinsic nature of physical reality" and of "clarifying our unconditional moral obligations" are equally distasteful to pragmatists, because both presuppose the existence of something non-relational, something exempt from the vicissitudes of time and history, something unaffected by changing human interests and needs. Both ideas are to be replaced, pragmatists think, by metaphors of width rather than of height or depth. Scientific progress is a matter of integrating more and more data into a coherent web of belief—data from microscopes and telescopes with data obtained by the naked eye, data forced into the open by experiment with data which has always been lying about. It is not a matter of penetrating appearance until one comes upon reality. Moral progress is a matter of wider and wider sympathy. It is not a matter of rising above the sentimental to the rational. Nor is it a matter of appealing from lower and corrupt local courts to a higher court which administers an ahistorical, non-local, transcultural moral law.

This switch from metaphors of vertical distance to metaphors of horizontal extent ties in with the pragmatists' insistence on replacing traditional distinctions of kind with distinctions in degree of complexity. Pragmatists substitute the idea of a maximally efficient explanation of a maximally wide range of data for that of the theory which cuts reality at the joints. They substitute the idea of a maximally warm, sensitive, and sympathetic human being for the Kantian idea of a Good Will. But though maximality cannot be aimed at, you can aim at explaining more data or being concerned about more people. You cannot aim at being at the end of inquiry, in either physics or ethics. That would be like aiming at being at the end of biological evolution— at being not merely the latest heir of all the ages but the being in which the ages were destined to culminate. Analogously, you cannot aim at moral perfection, but you can aim at taking more people's needs into account than you did previously.

So far in this lecture I have been suggesting in rather general terms why the pragmatist wants to get rid of the notion of "unconditional moral obligation." In the hope of greater concreteness and vividness, I turn now to another example of unconditionality: the notion of unconditional human rights. Such rights are said to form the fixed boundaries of political and moral deliberation. In American jurisprudence as it is interpreted by, for example, Ronald Dworkin, rights "trump" every consideration of social expediency and efficiency.[17] In much political discussion, it is taken for granted that the rights which the US courts have interpreted the US Constitution to bestow, and those universal human rights enumerated in the Helsinki Declaration, are beyond discussion. They are the unmoved movers of much of contemporary politics.

From a pragmatist point of view, the notion of "inalienable human rights" is no better and no worse a slogan than that of "obedience to the will of God." Either slogan, when invoked as an unmoved mover, is simply a way of saying that our spade is turned—that we have exhausted our argumentative resources. Talk of the will of God or of the rights of man, like talk of the "the honor of the family" or of "the fatherland in danger" are not suitable targets of philosophical analysis and criticism. It is fruitless to look behind them. None of these notions should be analyzed, for they are all ways of saying "Here I stand: I can do no other." They are not reasons for action so much as announcements that one has thought the issue through and come to a decision.

Traditional philosophy, the kind which sees morals as resting on metaphysics, presses such notions too hard when it asks questions like "But *is*

there a God?" or "Do human beings really *have* these rights?"* Such questions presuppose that moral progress is at least in part a matter of increasing
moral knowledge, knowledge about something independent of our social
practices: something like the will of God or the nature of humanity. This
metaphysical suggestion is vulnerable to Nietzschean suggestions that both
God and human rights are superstitions—contrivances put forward by the
weak to protect themselves against the strong. Whereas metaphysicians reply
to Nietzsche by asserting that there is a "rational basis" for belief in God or
in human rights, pragmatists reply by saying that there is nothing wrong with
contrivances. The pragmatist can cheerfully agree with Nietzsche that the
idea of human brotherhood would only have occurred to the weak—to the
people being shoved around by the brave, strong, happy warriors whom
Nietzsche idolizes. But for pragmatists this fact no more counts against the
idea of human rights than Socrates's ugliness counts against his account of
the nature of love, or than Freud's little private neuroses count against *his*
account of love, or than Newton's theological and alchemical concerns count
against his mechanics, or than Heidegger's bad moral character counts against
his philosophical achievement. Once you drop the distinction between reason
and passion, you will no longer discriminate against a good idea because of
its dubious origins. You will classify ideas according to their relative utility
rather than by their sources.

Pragmatists think that the quarrel between rationalist metaphysicians and
Nietzsche is without interest.[18] They grant to Nietzsche that reference to
human rights is merely a convenient way of summarizing certain aspects of
our real or proposed practices. Analogously, to say that the intrinsic nature
of reality consists of atoms and the void is, for a pragmatist, a way of saying
that *our* most successful scientific explanations interpret macro-structural
change as a result of micro-structural change. To say that God wills us to wel-
come the stranger within our gates is to say that hospitality is one of the
virtues upon which *our* community most prides itself. To say that respect for
human rights demanded our intervention to save the Jews from the Nazis,
or the Bosnian Muslims from the Serbs, is to say that a failure to intervene

---

*In *PSH,* this paragraph reads differently: "Philosophers who see morals as resting on metaphysics, press such notions too hard when they ask the question: 'But *is* there a God? or, 'Do
human beings really *have* these rights?'" (84).

would make *us* uncomfortable with ourselves, in the way in which knowledge that our children or our neighbors are hungry while we have plenty on the table makes us unable to continue eating. To speak of human rights is to explain our actions by identifying ourselves with a community of like-minded persons—those who find it natural to act in a certain way.

Claims of the sort I have just made—claims which have the form "To say such-and-such is to say so-and-so"—are often interpreted in terms of the reality-appearance distinction. Metaphysically inclined thinkers, obsessed by the distinction between knowledge and opinion or between reason and passion, interpret such claims as "irrationalist" and "emotivist." But pragmatists do not intend these as claims about what is *really* going on—claims that what appeared to be a fact is actually a value, or what appeared to be a cognition is actually an emotion. Rather, these claims are practical recommendations about what to talk about, suggestions about the terms in which controversy on moral questions is best conducted. On the subject of atoms, the pragmatist thinks that we should not debate the issue of whether unobservable microstructure is a reality or just a convenient fiction. On the subject of human rights, the pragmatist thinks that we should not debate whether human rights have been there all the time, even when nobody recognized them, or are just the social construction of a civilization influenced by Christian doctrines of the brotherhood of man and by the ideals of the French Revolution.*

In one sense of the term "social construction," human rights are social constructions, but then so are neutrinos and giraffes. In that sense, to be a social construction is simply to be the intentional object of a certain set of sentences—sentences used in some societies and not in others.† All that it takes to be an object is to be talked about in a reasonably coherent way, but not everybody needs to talk in all ways—nor, therefore, about all objects. Once we give up the idea that the point of discourse is to represent reality accurately, we shall have no interest in distinguishing social constructs from

---

* The version in *PSH* ends with "Christian doctrines of the brotherhood of man" (85).

† In *PSH* this paragraph begins differently: "*Of course,* they are social constructions. So are atoms, and so is everything else. For, as I suggested in chapter 3, to be a social construction is simply to be the intentional object of a certain set of sentences—sentences used in some societies and not in others." (85) Chapter 3 here refers to "A World without Substances or Essences," pp. 47–71, the second of a three-lecture series Rorty gave in Vienna and Paris in 1993.

other things. We shall confine ourselves to debating the utility of alternative social constructs.

The only other sense of "social construction" that I can think of is the one I referred to earlier: the sense in which bank accounts are social constructions but giraffes are not. Here the criterion is simply causal. The causal factors which produced giraffes did not include human societies, but those which produced bank accounts did. This sense has no application to the question about human rights, for even the most fervent moral realist has no causal story to tell about how those rights came into being.*

To debate the utility of the set of social constructs we call "human rights" is to debate the question of whether the language-games played by inclusivist societies are better than those played by exclusivist societies. There is no way to pass judgment on those language-games without passing judgment on the societies as wholes. So instead of debating the ontological status of human rights we should debate the question of whether communities which encourage tolerance of harmless deviance should be preferred to those communities whose social cohesion depends on conformity, on keeping outsiders at a distance and on eliminating people who try to corrupt the youth.† The best single mark of our progress toward a full-fledged human rights culture may be the extent to which we stop interfering with our children's marriage plans because of the national origin, the religion, the race, or the wealth of the intended partner, or because the marriage will be homosexual rather than heterosexual.

Those who wish to supply rational, philosophical foundations for a human rights culture say that what human beings have in common outweighs such adventitious factors as race or religion. But they have trouble spelling out what this commonality consists in. It is not enough to say that we all share a common susceptibility to pain, for there is nothing distinctively human about pain. If pain were all that mattered, it would be as important to pro-

---

* This entire paragraph has been omitted from *PSH*. See p. 86.
† In *PSH* this paragraph begins differently: "To debate the utility of the set of social constructs we call 'human rights' is to debate the question of whether inclusivist societies are better than exclusivist ones. That is to debate the question of whether communities which encourage tolerance of harmless deviance should be preferred to those communities whose social cohesion depends on conformity, on keeping outsiders at a distance and on eliminating people who try to corrupt the youth" (86).

tect the rabbits from the foxes as to protect the Jews from the Nazis. If one accepts a naturalistic, Darwinian account of human origins, it is not helpful to say that we all have reason in common, for on this account to be rational is simply to be able to use language. But there are many languages, and most of them are exclusionist. The language of human rights is no more or less characteristic of our species than languages which insist on racial or religious purity.[19]

Pragmatists suggest that we simply give up the philosophical search for commonality. They think that moral progress might be accelerated if we focused instead on our ability to make the particular little things that divide us seem unimportant—not by comparing them with the one big thing that unites us but by comparing them with other little things. We pragmatists think of moral progress as more like sewing together a very large, elaborate, polychrome quilt, than like getting a clearer vision of something true and deep. Here as elsewhere, we prefer metaphors of breadth and extent to metaphors of height and depth. Convinced that there is no subtle human essence which philosophy might grasp, we do not try to replace superficiality with depth, nor to rise above the particular in order to grasp the universal. Rather, we should like to minimize one difference at a time—the difference between Christians and Muslims in a particular village in Bosnia, the difference between blacks and whites in a particular town in Alabama, the difference between gays and straights in a particular Catholic congregation in Quebec. The hope is to sew such groups together with a thousand little stitches—to invoke a thousand little commonalities between their members, rather than by specifying one great big one, their common humanity.

This picture of moral progress makes us resist Kant's suggestion that morality is a matter of reason. We pragmatists are more sympathetic to Hume's suggestion that it is a matter of sentiment. If we were limited to these two candidates, we should side with Hume. But we would prefer to reject the choice, and to set aside the old Greek faculty psychology once and for all.* We recommend dropping the distinction between two separately functioning sources of beliefs and desires. Instead of working within the confines of this distinction, which constantly threatens us with the picture of a division between a true and real self and a false and apparent self, we can once again

---

* In *PSH* "the old Greek" is missing. See *PSH,* 87.

resort to the distinction with which I began my first lecture: the distinction between the present and the future.

More specifically, we can see both intellectual and moral progress not as a matter of getting closer to the True or the Good or the Right, but as an increase in imaginative power. Imagination is the cutting edge of cultural evolution, the power which—given peace and prosperity—constantly operates so as to make the human future richer than the human past. Imagination is the source both of new scientific pictures of the physical universe and of new conceptions of possible communities. It is what Newton and Christ, Freud and Marx, had in common—the ability to redescribe the familiar in unfamiliar terms.

Such redescription was practiced by the early Christians when they explained that the distinction between Jew and Greek was not as important as had been thought. It is being practiced by contemporary feminists, whose descriptions of sexual behavior and marital arrangements seem as strange to many men (and, for that matter, many women) as St. Paul's indifference to traditional Judaic distinctions seemed to the scribes and the Pharisees. It is what the Founding Fathers of the United States attempted when they asked people to think of themselves not so much as Pennsylvania Quakers or Catholic Marylanders but as citizens of a tolerant, pluralistic, federal republic. It is being attempted by those passionate advocates of European unity who hope that their grandchildren will think of themselves as European first and French or German second. But an equally good example of such redescription is Democritus's and Lucretius's suggestion that we try thinking of the world as rebounding atoms, or Copernicus's suggestion that we try thinking of the sun as at rest.

I said in an earlier lecture that pragmatism tries to substitute hope for knowledge. I hope that this lecture has helped make clear what I meant.* The difference between the Greek conception of human nature and the post-Darwinian, Deweyan, conception is the difference between closure and openness—between the security of the unchanging and the Whitmanesque and Whiteheadian romance of throwing oneself into the process of unpredictable change. This apotheosis of the future, this willingness to substitute

---

* In *PSH* the beginning of this paragraph reads differently: "I hope that what I have been saying has helped make clear what I meant by urging that we substitute hope for knowledge" (88).

imagination for certainty and curiosity for pride, breaks down the Greek distinction between contemplation and action. Dewey saw that distinction as the great incubus from which intellectual life in the West needed to escape.[20] His pragmatism was, as Hilary Putnam has said, an "insistence on the supremacy of the agent point of view."[21] In these lectures I have been interpreting this supremacy as the priority of the hope of inventing new ways of being human over the need for stability, security, and order.

8

Justice as a Larger Loyalty

All of us would expect help if, pursued by the police, we asked our family to hide us. Most of us would extend such help even when we know our child or our parent to be guilty of a sordid crime. Many of us would be willing to perjure ourselves in order to supply such a child or parent with a false alibi. But if an innocent person is wrongly convicted as a result of our perjury, most of us will be torn by a conflict between loyalty and justice.

Such a conflict will be felt, however, only to the extent to which we can identify with the innocent person whom we have harmed. If the person is a neighbor, the conflict will probably be intense. If a stranger, especially one of a different race, class, or nation, it may be considerably weaker. There has to be *some* sense that he or she is "one of us" before we start being tormented by the question of whether we did the right thing when we committed perjury. So it may be equally appropriate to describe us as torn between conflicting loyalties—loyalty to our family and to a group large enough to include the victim of our perjury—rather than between loyalty and justice.

Our loyalty to such larger groups will, however, weaken, or even vanish altogether, when things get really tough. Then people whom we once thought of as like ourselves will be excluded. Sharing food with impoverished people down the street is natural and right in normal times, but perhaps not in a famine, when doing so amounts to disloyalty to one's family. The tougher

This lecture appeared in English as Rorty, "Justice as a Larger Loyalty," in *Philosophical Papers*, vol. 4: *Philosophy as Cultural Politics*, 42–55 (Cambridge: Cambridge University Press, 2007) (hereafter *PCP*).

things get, the more ties of loyalty to those near at hand tighten, and the more those to everyone else slacken.

Consider another example of expanding and contracting loyalties: our attitude toward other species. Most of us nowadays are at least half-convinced that the vegetarians have a point, and that animals do have some sort of rights. But suppose that the cows, or the kangaroos, turn out to be carriers of a newly mutated virus which, though harmless to them, is invariably fatal to humans. I suspect that we would then shrug off accusations of "speciesism" and participate in the necessary massacre. The idea of justice between species will suddenly become irrelevant because things have gotten very tough indeed, and our loyalty to our own species must come first. Loyalty to a larger community—that of all living creatures on our home planet—would, under such circumstances, quickly fade away.

As a final example, consider the tough situation created by the accelerating export of jobs from the First World to the Third. There is likely to be a continuing decline in the average real income of most American families. Much of this decline can plausibly be attributed to the fact that you can hire a factory worker in Thailand for a tenth of what you would have to pay in Ohio. It has become the conventional wisdom of the rich that US and European labor is overpriced on the world market. When American business people are told that they are being disloyal to the United States by leaving whole cities in our Rust Belt without work or hope, they sometimes reply that they place justice over loyalty.[1] They argue that the needs of humanity as a whole take moral precedence of those of their fellow citizens, and override national loyalties. Justice requires that they act as citizens of the world.

Consider now the plausible hypothesis that democratic institutions and freedoms are viable only when supported by an economic affluence which is achievable regionally but impossible globally. If this hypothesis is correct, democracy and freedom in the First World will not be able to survive a thorough-going globalization of the labor market. So the rich democracies face a choice between perpetuating their own democratic institutions and traditions and dealing justly with the Third World. Doing justice to the Third World would require exporting capital and jobs until everything is leveled out—until an honest day's work, in a ditch or at a computer, earns no higher a wage in Cincinnati or Paris than in a small town in Botswana. But then, it can plausibly be argued, there will be no money to support free public libraries, competing newspapers and networks, widely available liberal arts education, and all the other institutions which are necessary to produce enlightened public opinion, and thus to keep governments more or less democratic.

What, on this hypothesis, is the right thing for the rich democracies to do? Be loyal to themselves and each other? Keep free societies going for a third of mankind at the expense of the remaining two-thirds? Or sacrifice the blessings of political liberty for the sake of egalitarian economic justice?

These questions parallel those confronted by the parents of a large family after a nuclear holocaust. Do they share the food supply they have stored in the basement with their neighbors, even though the stores will then only last a day or two? Or do they fend off those neighbors with guns? Both moral dilemmas bring up the same question: should we contract the circle for the sake of loyalty, or expand it for the sake of justice?

I have no idea of the right answer to these questions, neither about the right thing for these parents to do, nor about the right thing for the First World to do. I have posed them simply to get a more abstract, and merely philosophical, question into focus. That question is: should we describe such moral dilemmas as these as conflicts between loyalty and justice, or rather, as I have suggested we might, between loyalties to smaller groups and loyalties to larger groups?

This amounts to asking: Would it be a good idea to treat "justice" as the name for loyalty to a certain very large group, the name for our largest current loyalty, rather than the name of something distinct from loyalty? Could we replace the notion of "justice" with that of loyalty to that group—for example, one's fellow citizens, or the human species, or all living things? Would anything be lost by this replacement?

Moral philosophers who remain loyal to Kant are likely to think that a *lot* would be lost. Kantians typically insist that justice springs from reason, and loyalty from sentiment. Only reason, they say, can impose universal and unconditional moral obligations, and our obligation to be just is of this sort. It is on another level from the sort of affectional relations which create loyalty. Jürgen Habermas is the most prominent contemporary philosopher to insist on this Kantian way of looking at things: the thinker least willing to blur either the line between reason and sentiment, or the line between universal validity and historical consensus. But contemporary philosophers who depart from Kant, either in the direction of Hume (like Annette Baier) or in the direction of Hegel (like Charles Taylor) or in that of Aristotle (like Alasdair MacIntyre) are not so sure.

Michael Walzer is at the other extreme from Habermas. He is wary of terms like "reason" and "universal moral obligation." The heart of his new book, *Thick and Thin*, is the claim that we should reject the intuition which Kant took as central: the intuition that "men and women everywhere begin with some common idea or principle or set of ideas and principles, which they then work up in many different ways." Walzer thinks that this picture of morality "start[ing] thin" and "thicken[ing] with age" should be inverted. He says that

> Morality is thick from the beginning, culturally integrated, fully reso-
> nant, and it reveals itself thinly only on special occasions, when moral
> language is turned to specific purposes.[2]

Walzer's inversion suggests, though it does not entail, the neo-Humean picture of morality sketched by Annette Baier in her book *Moral Prejudices*. On Baier's account, as I was saying this morning, morality starts out not as an obligation, but as a relation of reciprocal trust among a closely knit group, such as a family or clan.* To behave morally is to do what comes naturally in one's dealing with your parents and children, or your fellow clan members. It amounts to respecting the trust they place in you. Obligation, as opposed to trust, enters the picture only when your loyalty to a smaller group conflicts with your loyalty to a larger group.[3]

When, for example, the families confederate into tribes, or the tribes into nations, you may feel obliged to do what does not come naturally: to leave your parents in the lurch by going off to fight in the wars, or to rule against your own village in your capacity as a federal administrator or judge. What Kant would describe as the resulting conflict between moral obligation and sentiment, or between reason and sentiment, is, on a non-Kantian account of the matter, a conflict between one set of loyalties and another set of loyalties. The idea of a *universal* moral obligation to respect human dignity gets replaced by the idea of loyalty to a very large group—the human species. The idea that moral obligation extends beyond that species to an even larger group

---

* "This morning" refers to Lecture 7 in this volume.

becomes the idea of loyalty to all those who, like yourself, can experience pain—even the cows and the kangaroos—or perhaps even to all living things, even the trees.

This non-Kantian view of morality can be rephrased as the claim that one's moral identity is determined by the group or groups with which one identifies—the group or groups to which one cannot be disloyal and still like oneself. Moral dilemmas are not, in this view, the result of a conflict between reason and sentiment but between alternative selves, alternative self-descriptions, alternative ways of giving a meaning to one's life. Non-Kantians do not think that we have a central, true self by virtue of our membership in the human species—a self which responds to the call of reason. They can, instead, agree with Daniel Dennett that a self is a center of narrative gravity. In non-traditional societies, most people have several such narratives at their disposal, and thus several different moral identities. It is this plurality of identities which accounts for the number and variety of moral dilemmas, moral philosophers, and psychological novels in such societies.

Walzer's contrast between thick and thin morality is, among other things, a contrast between the detailed and concrete stories you can tell about yourself as a member of a smaller group and the relatively abstract and sketchy story you can tell about yourself as a citizen of the world. You know more about your family than about your village, more about your village than about your nation, more about your nation than about humanity as a whole, more about being human than about simply being a living creature. You are in a better position to decide what differences between individuals are morally relevant when dealing with those whom you can describe thickly, and in a worse position when dealing with those whom you can only describe thinly. This is why, as groups get larger, law has to replace custom, and abstract principles have to replace *phronesis*. So Kantians are wrong to see *phronesis* as a thickening up of thin abstract principles. Plato and Kant were misled by the fact that abstract principles are designed to trump parochial loyalties into thinking that the principles are somehow prior to the loyalties—that the thin is somehow prior to the thick.

Walzer's thick-thin distinction can be aligned with Rawls's contrast between a shared *concept* of justice and various conflicting *conceptions* of justice. Rawls sets out that contrast as follows:

the concept of justice, applied to an institution, means, say, that the institution makes no arbitrary distinctions between persons in assigning basic rights and duties, and that its rules establish a proper balance between competing claims . . . [A] conception includes, besides this, principles and criteria for deciding which distinctions are arbitrary and when a balance between competing claims is proper. People can agree on the meaning of the concept of justice and still be at odds, since they affirm different principles and standards for deciding these matters.[4]

Phrased in Rawls's terms, Walzer's point is that thick, "fully resonant" *conceptions* of justice, complete with distinctions between the people who matter most and the people who matter less, come first. The thin concept, and its maxim "do not make arbitrary distinctions between moral subjects," is articulated only on special occasions. On those occasions, the thin concept can often be turned against any of the thick conceptions from which it emerged, in the form of critical questions about whether it may not be merely arbitrary to think that certain people matter more than others.

Neither Rawls nor Walzer think, however, that unpacking the thin concept of justice will, by itself, resolve such critical questions by supplying a criterion of arbitrariness. They do not think that we can do what Kant hoped to do—derive solutions to moral dilemmas from the analysis of moral concepts. To put the point in the terminology I am suggesting: we cannot resolve conflicting loyalties by turning away from them all toward something categorically distinct from loyalty: the universal moral obligation to act justly. So we have to drop the Kantian idea that the moral law starts off pure but is always in danger of being contaminated by irrational feelings which introduce arbitrary discriminations among persons. We have to substitute the Hegelian-Marxist idea that the so-called moral law is, at best, a handy abbreviation for a concrete web of social practices. This means dropping Habermas's claim that his "discourse ethics" articulates a transcendental presupposition of the use of language, and accepting his critics' claim that it articulates only the customs of contemporary liberal societies.[5]

Now I want to raise the question of whether to describe the various moral dilemmas with which I began as conflicts between loyalty and justice, or rather as conflicting loyalties to particular groups, in a more concrete form. Consider the question of whether the demands for reform made on the rest of the world by Western liberal societies are made in the name of something not merely Western—something like morality, or humanity, or rationality—or are simply expressions of loyalty to local, Western conceptions of justice.

Habermas would say that they are the former. I would say that they are the latter, but are none the worse for that. I think it is better not to say that the liberal West is better informed about rationality and justice, and instead to say that, in making demands on non-liberal societies, it is simply being true to itself.

In a recent paper called "The Law of Peoples," Rawls discusses the question of whether the conception of justice which he has developed in his books is something peculiarly Western and liberal, or rather something universal. He would like to be able to claim universality. He says that it is important to avoid "historicism," and believes that he can do this if he can show that the conception of justice suited to a liberal society can be extended beyond such societies through formulating what he calls "the law of peoples."[6] He outlines, in that paper, an extension of the constructivist procedure proposed in his *A Theory of Justice*—an extension which, by continuing to separate the right from the good, lets us encompass liberal and non-liberal societies under the same law.

As Rawls develops this constructivist proposal, however, it emerges that this law applies only to *reasonable* peoples, in a quite specific sense of the term "reasonable." The conditions which non-liberal societies must honor in order to be "accepted by liberal societies as members in good standing of a society of peoples"[7] include the following: "its system of law must be guided by a common good conception of justice . . . that takes impartially into account what it sees not unreasonably as the fundamental interests of all members of society."[8]

Rawls takes the fulfillment of that condition to rule out violation of basic human rights.[9] These rights include "at least certain minimum rights to means of subsistence and security (the right to life), to liberty (freedom from slavery, serfdom, and forced occupations) and (personal) property, as well as to formal equality as expressed by the rules of natural justice (for example, that similar cases be treated similarly)."[10] When Rawls spells out what he means by saying that the admissible non-liberal societies must not have unreasonable philosophical or religious doctrines, he glosses "unreasonable" by saying that these societies must "admit a measure of liberty of conscience and freedom of thought, even if these freedoms are not in general equal for all members of society." Rawls's notion of what is reasonable, in short, confines membership of the society of peoples to societies whose institutions encompass most of the hard-won achievements of the West in the two centuries since the Enlightenment.

It seems to me that Rawls cannot both reject historicism and invoke this notion of reasonableness. For the effect of that invocation is to build most of the West's recent decisions about which distinctions between persons are arbitrary into the conception of justice which is implicit in the law of peoples. The differences between different *conceptions* of justice, remember, are differences between what features of people are seen as relevant to the adjudication of their competing claims. There is obviously enough wriggle room in phrases like "similar cases should be treated similarly" to allow for arguments that believers and infidels, men and women, blacks and whites, gays and straights should be treated as relevantly *dis*similar. So there is room to argue that discrimination on the basis of such differences is *not* arbitrary. If we are going to exclude from the society of peoples societies in which infidel homosexuals are not permitted to engage in certain occupations, those societies can quite reasonably say that we are, in excluding them, appealing not to something universal, but to very recent developments in Europe and America.

I agree with Habermas when he says that

> What Rawls in fact prejudges with the concept of an 'overlapping consensus' is the distinction between modern and premodern forms of consciousness, between 'reasonable' and 'dogmatic' world interpretations.

But I disagree with Habermas, as I think Walzer also would, when he goes on to say that Rawls

> can defend the primacy of the right over the good with the concept of an overlapping consensus only if it is true that postmetaphysical worldviews that have become reflexive under modern conditions are epistemically superior to dogmatically fixed, fundamentalistic worldviews—indeed, only if such a distinction can be made with absolute clarity.

Habermas's point is that Rawls needs an argument from trans-culturally valid premises for the superiority of the liberal West. Without such an argument, he says, "the disqualification of 'unreasonable' doctrines that cannot be brought into harmony with the proposed 'political' concept of justice is inadmissible."[11]

Such passages make clear why Habermas and Walzer are at opposite poles. Walzer is taking for granted that there can be no such thing as a non-question-begging demonstration of the epistemic superiority of the Western idea of reasonableness. There is, for Walzer, no tribunal of trans-cultural reason before which to try the question of superiority. Walzer is presupposing what Habermas calls "a strong contextualism for which there is no single 'rationality.'" On this conception, Habermas continues, "individual 'rationalities' are correlated with different cultures, worldviews, traditions, or forms of life. Each of them is viewed as internally interwoven with a particular understanding of the world."[12]

I think that Rawls's constructivist approach to the law of peoples can work if he adopts what Habermas calls a "strong contextualism." Doing so would mean giving up the attempt to escape historicism, as well as the attempt to supply a universalistic argument for the West's most recent views about which differences between persons are arbitrary. The strength of Walzer's *Thick and Thin* seems to me to be its explicitness about the need to do this. The weakness of Rawls's account of what he is doing lies in an ambiguity between two senses of universalism. When Rawls says that "a constructivist liberal doctrine is universal in its reach, once it is extended to . . . a law of peoples,"[13] he is not saying that it is universal in its validity. Universal reach is a notion which sits well with constructivism, but universal validity is not. It is the latter that Habermas requires. That is why Habermas thinks that we need really heavy philosophical weaponry, modeled on Kant's—why he insists that only transcendental presuppositions of any possible communicative practice will do the job.[14] To be faithful to his own constructivism, I think, Rawls has to agree with Walzer that this job does not need to be done.

Rawls and Habermas often invoke, and Walzer almost never invokes, the notion of "reason." In Habermas, this notion is always bound up with that of context-free validity. In Rawls, things are more complicated. Rawls distinguishes the reasonable from the rational, using the latter to mean simply the sort of means-end rationality which is employed in engineering, or in working out a Hobbesian *modus vivendi*. But he often invokes a third notion, that of "practical reason," as when he says that the authority of a constructivist lib-

eral doctrine "rests on the principles and conceptions of practical reason."[15]*
Rawls's use of this Kantian term may make it sound as if he agreed with Kant
and Habermas that there is a universally distributed human faculty called
practical reason (existing prior to, and working quite independently of, the
recent history of the West)—a faculty which tells us what counts as an arbitrary distinction between persons and what does not. Such a faculty would
do the job Habermas thinks needs doing: detecting trans-cultural moral
validity.

But this cannot, I think, be what Rawls intends. For he also says that his
own constructivism differs from all philosophical views which appeal to a
source of authority, and in which "the universality of the doctrine is the direct consequence of its source of authority." As examples of sources of authority, he cites "(human) reason, or an independent realm of moral values,
or some other proposed basis of universal validity."[16] So I think we have to
construe his phrase "the principles and conceptions of practical reason" as
referring to *whatever* principles and conceptions are in fact arrived at in the
course of creating a community.

Rawls emphasizes that creating a community is not the same thing as
working out a *modus vivendi*—a task which requires only means-end rationality, not practical reason. A principle or conception belongs to practical
reason, in Rawls's sense, if it emerged in the course of people starting thick
and getting thin, thereby developing an overlapping consensus and setting
up a more inclusive moral community. It would not so belong if it had emerged
under the threat of force. Practical reason for Rawls is, so to speak, a matter

---

* Rorty is quoting from the first version of Rawls's essay "The Law of Peoples," in *On Human
Rights: The Oxford Amnesty Lectures, 1993,* ed. Steven Shute and Susan Hurley (New York: Basic
Books, 1993). The passage in question reads: "Its authority rests on the principles and conceptions of practical reason, but always on these as suitably adjusted to apply to different subjects as
they arise in sequence; and always assuming as well that these principles are endorsed on due
reflection by the reasonable agents to whom the corresponding principles apply" (46). However,
in a later book, Rawls reverses himself. See John Rawls, *The Law of Peoples, with the Idea of
Public Reason Revisited* (Cambridge, MA: Harvard University Press, 1990), 86, where Rawls
writes: "12.2. *No Deduction from Practical Reason* . . . at no point are we deducing the principles
of right and justice, or the decency, or the principles of rationality, from a conception of practical reason in the background." It is very plausible that Rawls was persuaded, and thus reversed
himself, over Rorty's objections, as they are elaborated below.

of procedure rather than of substance—of how we agree on what to do rather than of what we agree on.

This definition of practical reason suggests that there may be only a verbal difference between Rawls's and Habermas's positions. For Habermas's own attempt to substitute "communicative reason" for "subject-centered reason" is itself a move toward substituting "how" for "what." The first sort of reason is a source of truth, truth somehow coeval with the human mind. The second sort of reason is not a source of anything, but simply the activity of justifying claims by offering arguments rather than threats. Like Rawls, Habermas focuses on the difference between persuasion and force, rather than, as Plato and Kant did, on the difference between two parts of the human person—the good rational part and the dubious passionate or sensual part. Both would like to de-emphasize the notion of the *authority* of reason—the idea of reason as a faculty which issues decrees—and substitute the notion of rationality as what is present whenever people communicate, whenever they try to justify their claims to one another, rather than threatening each other.

The similarities between Rawls and Habermas seem even greater in the light of Rawls's endorsement of Thomas Scanlon's answer to the "fundamental question why anyone should care about morality at all," namely that "we have a basic desire to be able to justify our actions to others on grounds that they could not reasonably reject—reasonably, that is, given the desire to find principles that others similarly motivated could not reasonably reject."[17] This suggests that the two philosophers might agree on the following claim: the only notion of rationality we need, at least in moral and social philosophy, is that of a situation in which people do not say "your own current interests dictate that you agree to our proposal" but rather "your own central beliefs, the ones which are central to your own moral identity, suggest that you should agree to our proposal."

This notion of rationality can be delimited using Walzer's terminology by saying that rationality is found wherever people envisage the possibility of getting from different thicks to the same thin. To appeal to interests rather than beliefs is to urge a *modus vivendi*. Such an appeal is exemplified by the speech of the Athenian ambassadors to the unfortunate Melians, as reported by Thucydides. To appeal to your enduring beliefs as well as to your current interests is to suggest that what gives you your *present* moral identity—your thick and resonant complex of beliefs—may make it possible for you to develop a new, supplementary moral identity.[18] It is to suggest that what makes you loyal to a smaller group may give you reason to cooperate in constructing a larger group, a group to which you may in time become equally loyal, or perhaps even more loyal. The difference between the absence and the presence of rationality, on this account, is the difference between a threat and an offer—the offer of a new moral identity and thus a new and larger loyalty, a loyalty to a group formed by an unforced agreement between smaller groups.

In the hope of minimizing the contrast between Habermas and Rawls still further, and of rapprochement between both and Walzer, I want to suggest a way of thinking of rationality which might help to resolve the problem I posed earlier: the problem of whether justice and loyalty are different sorts of things, or whether the demands of justice are simply the demands of a larger loyalty. I said that question seemed to boil down to the question of whether justice and loyalty had different sources—reason and sentiment respectively. If the latter distinction disappears, the former one will not seem particularly useful. But if by rationality we mean simply the sort of activity which Walzer thinks of as a thinning-out process—the sort that, with luck, achieves the formulation and utilization of an overlapping consensus, then the idea that justice has a different source than loyalty no longer seems plausible.[19]

For, on this account of rationality, being rational and acquiring a larger loyalty are two descriptions of the same activity. This is because *any* unforced agreement between individuals and groups about what to do creates a form of community, and will, with luck, be the initial stage in expanding the circles of those whom each party to the agreement had previously taken to be "people like ourselves." The opposition between rational argument and fellow feeling thus begins to dissolve. For fellow feeling may, and often does, arise from the realization that the people whom one thought one might have to go to war with, use force on, are, in Rawls's sense, "reasonable." They are, it turns out, enough like us to see the point of compromising differences in order to live in peace, and of abiding by the agreement that has been hammered out. They are, to some degree at least, trustworthy.

From this point of view, Habermas' distinction between a strategic use of language and a genuinely communicative use of language begins to look like a difference between positions on a spectrum—a spectrum of degrees of trust. Baier's suggestion that we take trust rather than obligation to be our fundamental moral concept would thus produce a blurring of the line between rhetorical manipulation and genuine validity-seeking argument—a line which I think Habermas draws too sharply. If we cease to think of reason as a source of authority, and think of it simply as the process of reaching agreement by persuasion, then the standard Platonic and Kantian dichotomy of reason and feeling begins to fade away. That dichotomy can be replaced by a continuum of degrees of overlap of beliefs and desires.[20] When people whose beliefs and desires do not overlap very much disagree, they tend to think of each other as crazy, or, more politely, as irrational. When there is considerable overlap, on the other hand, they may agree to differ, and regard each other as the sort of people one can live with—and eventually, perhaps, the sort one can be friends with, intermarry with, and so on.[21]

To advise people to be rational is, on the view I am offering, simply to suggest that somewhere among their shared beliefs and desires there may be enough resources to permit agreement on how to co-exist without violence. To conclude that somebody is irredeemably *irrational* is not to realize that she is not making proper use of her God-given faculties. It is rather to realize that she does not seem to share enough relevant beliefs and desires with us to make possible fruitful conversation about the issue in dispute. So, we reluctantly conclude, we have to give up on the attempt to get her to enlarge her moral identity, and settle for working out a *modus vivendi*—one which may involve the threat, or even the use, of force.

A stronger, more Kantian notion of rationality would be invoked if one said that being rational guarantees a peaceful resolution of conflicts—that if people are willing to reason together long enough, what Habermas calls "the force of the better argument" will lead them to concur.[22] This stronger notion strikes me as pretty useless. I see no point in saying that it is more rational to prefer one's neighbors to one's family in the event of a nuclear holocaust, or more rational to prefer leveling off incomes around the world to preserving the institutions of liberal Western societies. To use the word "rational" to commend one's chosen solution to such dilemmas, or to use the term "yielding to the force of the better argument" to characterize one's way of making up one's mind, is to pay oneself an empty compliment.

More generally, the idea of "the better argument" makes sense only if one can identify a natural, trans-cultural relation of relevance which connects propositions with one another so as to form something like Descartes's "natural order of reasons." Without such a natural order, one can only evaluate arguments by their efficacy in producing agreement among particular persons or groups. But the required notion of natural, intrinsic relevance— relevance dictated not by the needs of any given community, but by human reason as such—seems no more plausible or useful than that of a God whose Will can be appealed to in order to resolve conflicts between communities. It is, I think, merely a secularized version of that earlier notion.

Non-Western societies in the past were rightly skeptical of Western conquerors who explained that they were invading in obedience to divine commands. More recently, they have been skeptical of Westerners who suggest that they should adopt Western ways in order to become more rational. (This suggestion has been abbreviated by Ian Hacking as "Me rational, you Jane.") On the account of rationality I am recommending, both forms of skepticism are equally justified. But this is not to deny that these societies *should* adopt recent Western ways by, for example, abandoning slavery, practicing religious toleration, educating women, permitting mixed marriages, tolerating homosexuality and conscientious objection to war, and so on. As a loyal Westerner, I think they should indeed do all these things. I agree with Rawls about what it takes to count as reasonable, and about what kind of societies we Westerners should accept as members of a global moral community.

But I think that the rhetoric we Westerners use in trying to get everybody to be more like us would be improved if we were more frankly ethnocentric, and less professedly universalist. It would be better to say: Here is what we in the West look like as a result of ceasing to hold slaves, beginning to educate women, separating church and state, and so on. Here is what happened after we started treating certain distinctions between people as arbitrary rather than fraught with moral significance. If you would try treating them that way, you might like the results. Saying that sort of thing seems preferable to saying: Look at how much better we are at knowing what differences between persons are arbitrary and which not—how much more *rational* we are.

If we Westerners could get rid of the notion of universal moral obligations created by membership in the species, and substitute the idea of building a community of trust between ourselves and others, we might be in a better position to persuade non-Westerners of the advantages of joining in that community. We might be better able to construct the sort of global moral community which Rawls describes in "The Law of Peoples." In making this suggestion, I am urging, as I have on earlier occasions, that we need to peel apart Enlightenment liberalism from Enlightenment rationalism.

I think that discarding the residual rationalism which we inherit from the Enlightenment is advisable for many reasons. Some of these are theoretical and of interest only to philosophy professors, such as the apparent incompatibility of the correspondence theory of truth with a naturalistic account of the origin of human minds.[23] Others are more practical. One practical reason is that getting rid of rationalistic rhetoric would permit the West to approach the non-West in the role of someone with an instructive story to tell, rather than in the role of someone purporting to be making better use of a universal human capacity.

9

Is There Anything Worth Saving in Empiricism?

In earlier lectures I said that the American pragmatist tradition founded by Peirce, James, and Dewey is continued in the work of Sellars, Quine, Putnam, and Davidson. In these last two lectures I want to focus more narrowly on the work of Sellars and Davidson, and to relate their work to that of two other philosophers—Robert Brandom and John McDowell—who have been greatly influenced by them.

Robert Brandom's *Making It Explicit* and John McDowell's *Mind and World* were both published in 1994. These two path-breaking books are being widely discussed by Anglophone philosophers. One reason for this is that both help bring out the overlap between the views of two great critics of empiricism—Sellars and Davidson, philosophers who never discussed one another's work.

Though they share indebtedness to Sellars and Davidson, the two books differ dramatically. Brandom helps us to tell a story about our knowledge of objects which makes almost no reference to experience. He does not so much criticize empiricism as assume that Sellars has disposed of it. The term "experience" does not occur in the admirably complete index to Brandom's 700-page book; it is simply not one of his words. By contrast, McDowell's book tries to defend empiricism against Sellars and Davidson—conceding most of

This lecture was published in English with a different title as Rorty, "Robert Brandom on Social Practices and Representations," in *Philosophical Papers*, vol. 3: *Truth and Progress*, 122–137 (Cambridge: Cambridge University Press, 1998).

their premises but dissenting from their conclusions. Brandom can be read as carrying through on "the linguistic turn" by restating pragmatism in a form which makes James's and Dewey's talk of experience entirely obsolete. McDowell can be read as arguing that pragmatists should not be allowed to banish the term "experience" from philosophy, because the price of such disappearance is much greater than Sellars, Davidson, or Brandom realize.

The possibility of such disappearance raises the question of the place of British empiricism in the history of philosophy. The American pragmatists have usually been viewed as belonging to the same empiricist tradition to which the so-called "logical empiricism" of Russell, Carnap, and Ayer also belongs. Their version of empiricism has seemed, to many historians of philosophy, to differ from others simply by being less atomistic in its description of the perceptual given. Yet carrying through on the anti-dualist and pan-relationalist impulses which gave rise to James's and Dewey's critiques of Hume's and Mill's psychological atomism seems, in the light of Sellars and Davidson, to lead to a much more radical view—one which is no longer a version of empiricism at all.

Looked back upon in the light of the work of these two men, British empiricism may well seem a mere unfortunate distraction, a parochial and unimportant movement whose only impact on contemporary philosophy has been to provide piles of rubbish for us to sweep away. Those who have been convinced by Sellars and Davidson are led to wonder whether the epistemologico-metaphysical efforts of Locke, Berkeley, and Hume leave us with no residue (except perhaps for the proto-pragmatism which Berkeley formulated in response to Locke's unhappy distinction between primary and secondary qualities). Sellars and Davidson can be read as saying that Aristotle's slogan, constantly cited by the empiricists, "Nothing in the intellect which was not previously in the senses," was a wildly misleading way of describing the relation between the objects of knowledge and our knowledge of them.

McDowell, however, though agreeing that this slogan was misleading, thinks that we are now in danger of tossing the baby out with the bath. We need to recapture the insight which motivated the empiricists. He disagrees with Brandom's implicit suggestion that we simply forget about sense-impressions, and other putative mental contents which cannot be identified with judgments. The controversy between McDowell and Brandom is exciting wide interest among Anglophone philosophers because it is forcing them to ask whether we still have any use for the notion of "perceptual experience." Brandom thinks that this notion was never of much use, and that its place can be taken by that of "non-inferential judgments caused by changes in the physiological condition of sense-organs." McDowell thinks that such a replacement would deprive us of an important empiricist insight—one which Locke and Aristotle shared, though both formulated it very badly indeed.

Brandom carries through on Sellars's criticism of "the Myth of the Given" by showing how the notion of "accurate representation of objective reality" can be constructed out of material provided by our grasp of the notion of "making correct inferential connections between assertions." He carries through on the "linguistic turn" by showing that if we understand how organisms came to use a logical and semantical vocabulary, we do not need to give any further explanation of how they came to have minds. For to possess beliefs and desires, on Brandom's view, is simply to play a language game which deploys such a vocabulary.

McDowell demurs from Brandom's conclusions while accepting many of his premises. He does not agree that we can reconstruct the notion of representation out of that of inference, and thinks that Brandom's "inferentialist" account of concepts does not work. For McDowell, it is equally important to accept Sellars's point that something without conceptual structure cannot justify a belief and to insist, *pace* Sellars, that mental events which are not judgments can justify beliefs. So he pumps new life into the notion of "perceptual experience" by arguing that such experience *is* conceptually structured, but is nonetheless distinct from the belief which may result from it.

McDowell's book is daring and original. Reading it side by side with Brandom's permits one to grasp the present situation in Anglophone philosophy of mind and language. One way of describing that situation is to say that whereas Sellars and Davidson use Kantian arguments to overcome the Humean dogmas retained by Russell and Ayer, Brandom and McDowell supplement Kantian arguments with Hegelian ones. Most Anglophone philosophers still do not take Hegel seriously, but the rise of what Brandom and McDowell refer to as their "Pittsburgh School of neo-Hegelians" may force them to. For this school holds that analytic philosophy still needs to pass over from its Kantian to its Hegelian moment.

I shall begin my discussion of Brandom and McDowell by citing some of the Sellarsian and Davidsonian doctrines which I and other admirers of these two men have found most inspiring.

Sellars is perhaps best known for a doctrine he called "psychological nominalism," formulated as follows:

> *all* awareness of *sorts, resemblances, facts,* etc., in short, all awareness of abstract entities—indeed, all awareness even of particulars—is a linguistic affair . . . [Not] even the awareness of such sorts, resemblances and facts as pertain to so-called immediate experience is presupposed by the process of acquiring the use of language.[1]

Sellars's discussion of awareness in "Empiricism and the Philosophy of Mind" follows the same lines as Wittgenstein's discussion of sensation in his *Philosophical Investigations.* Wittgenstein says, when talking about private sensations, that "a nothing would be as good as a something about which nothing can be said." Sellars's version of this slogan is that a difference which cannot be expressed in behavior is not a difference that makes a difference. The pragmatism he shares with Wittgenstein can be summed up as I did in my discussion of "pan-relationalism" on Wednesday: if you find people talking about something like "sentience" or "consciousness" or "qualia" which seems not to tie up with anything else, to be capable of varying even when everything stays the same, to be merely externally related to everything else, forget about it. Or, at least, do not regard it as a topic on which philosophers need to shed light.

Sellars's psychological nominalism paves the way for his claim that if you have semantical talk you have all the intentional talk you need. For, as Sellars says, "the categories of intentionality are, at bottom, semantical categories pertaining to overt verbal performances."[2] The force of this claim is that if you understand how we started using a meta-linguistic vocabulary to comment on and criticize our overt verbal performances, you understand how intentionality came to exist. You can see intentionality, the ability to have beliefs and desires, and rationality, the self-conscious attempt to make those beliefs and desires more coherent, as emerging over the course of time, just as we see an ability to stand on two legs, and to pick up sticks, as emerging over the course of time. If you accept what Sellars says in the passages I have quoted, you can not only link cultural to biological evolution in the way Dewey hoped to link it, but do so far more perspicuously and convincingly than Dewey did.

The trick here is not to try, as Carnap once did, to give necessary and sufficient conditions for sentences like "The word 'red' refers, in English, to this color" or "That Spanish sentence is about the union of Leon and Castille" by describing how these sentences are used by the relevant sets of speakers. There is no reductionist impulse at work in Sellars, but there is a therapeutic impulse. The therapy consists in saying: imagine how a term like "refers to" or "is about" came to be used, and you will thereby know all you need to know about how reference, aboutness, and intentionality came into the world. The analogy here is with a term like "money": imagine how a barter economy transformed itself into one in which legal currency and commercial credit were in use, and you will know all you need to know both about how money came into existence and about what money is. No mystery remains for philosophers to puzzle about. The illusion of *depth* vanishes—an illusion which was caused, in this case, by the idea that only things that can be experienced through the senses are unproblematic.

The effect of focusing on intentionality rather than consciousness is to deflect attention from non-sentential sense-impressions—the sort of thing which might cause a squawk of "Red!" in a parrot or a human—to beliefs and desires, the sort of thing expressed in complete sentences. Focusing on consciousness leads to the question which intrigues Nagel and other defenders of the idea of "qualia": the question of how machines which respond differentially to a range of stimuli differ from animals which do the same. For Nagel, there is a thing called "consciousness" which such machines, and zombies, lack, and which animals such as ourselves possess. For Sellars, it is not clear that the machines lack anything except behavioral flexibility and complexity.

To put this point another way, almost all philosophers, from Aristotle through Locke to Hegel and Dewey have assumed that there was a sort of quasi-intentionality called "sentience" present in non-human animals, and that sentience was something more than merely an ability to respond differentially. Those who denied this, as Descartes did in his suggestion that non-human animals might be just complex machines, are thought to be insufficiently sympathetic to the situation of dogs—creatures which have feelings but no language. The most common objection to Sellars's psychological nominalism is that babies and dogs are aware of pain—and therefore have some sort of proto-consciousness—even though their awareness can obviously not be a "linguistic affair." Philosophers like Nagel and Searle still dismiss psychological nominalism on this ground alone: that he failed to make a place for sentience.

As I shall be saying this afternoon, McDowell wishes to revive the notion of sentience, even though he accepts psychological nominalism. But almost the only passage in Brandom's book at which sentience is mentioned reads as follows:

> Described in the language of physiology, our sensing may be virtually indistinguishable from that of nondiscursive creatures. But we not only sense, we also perceive. That is, our differential response to sensory stimulation includes noninferential acknowledgement of propositionally contentful doxastic commitments . . . Our mammalian cousins, primate ancestors, and neonatal offspring—who are sentient and purposive but not discursive creatures—are interpretable as perceiving and acting *only in a derivative sense.* [emphasis added] An interpreter can make sense of what they do by attributing propositionally contentful intentional states to them, but the interpreter's grasp of those contents and of the significance of those states derives from mastery of the richer practices of giving and asking for reasons.[3]

On Brandom's and Sellars's view, the difference between complex animals like dogs or complex machines like computers, on the one hand, and simple animals like amoebae or simple machines like thermostats, on the other, is simply that it pays to describe the former, but not the latter, as having beliefs and desires. We can predict and explain the behavior of dogs and computers on the basis of such descriptions better than we can without them. So we do what Daniel Dennett calls "taking the intentional stance" toward these more complexly behaving entities. There is not much point in adopting the intentional stance toward amoebae and thermostats, though we can do so if we like.

For pragmatists, the question which looms large for Thomas Nagel and John Searle, "Yes, but do computers really *have* beliefs and desires?," does not arise. For the question of the utility of a vocabulary is not distinct from the question of the real possession of properties signified by the descriptive terms

of that vocabulary. Pragmatists agree with Wittgenstein that there is no way
to come between language and its object. Philosophy cannot answer the question: Is our vocabulary in accord with the way the world is? It can only answer the question: Can we perspicuously relate the various vocabularies we
use to one another, and thereby dissolve the philosophical problems which
seem to arise at the places where we switch over from one vocabulary into
another?

I read Sellars and Brandom as pragmatists, because I treat psychological
nominalism as a version of the pragmatist doctrine that truth is a matter of
the utility of a belief rather than of a relation between pieces of the world and
pieces of language. If our awareness of things is always a linguistic affair, if
Sellars is right that we cannot check our language against our non-linguistic
awareness, then philosophy can never be anything more than a discussion
of the utility and compatibility of beliefs—and, more particularly, of the
various vocabularies in which those beliefs are formulated. There is no authority outside of convenience for human purposes which can be appealed
to in order to legitimize the use of a vocabulary. We have no duties to anything non-human.

Brandom puts this point by saying that philosophy's job is to make our
practices, linguistic and other, explicit, rather than to judge these practices
in the light of norms which lie outside them. He takes Wittgenstein's infinite-
regress argument against the possibility of appealing to such outside norms
as fundamental to his metaphilosophical position. "Pragmatic theories of
norms are distinguished from platonist theories, in treating as fundamental
norms *implicit* in *practices* rather than norms *explicit* in *principles*."[4] There
is no way for human beings to get beyond their own practices except by
dreaming up better practices, and no way to judge these new practices better
except by reference to their various advantages for various human purposes.
To say that philosophy's task is to make human practices explicit rather than
to legitimize them by reference to something beyond them is to say that there
is no authority beyond utility for these purposes to which we can appeal.

So much, for the moment, for Sellars and psychological nominalism. I turn
now to Davidson. Davidson's most pregnant and striking philosophical doctrine is his claim that most of our beliefs, most of the beliefs of any language
user, must be true. This is also his most controversial doctrine, but I choose it
because I think that expounding it is a good way of bringing out Davidson's

central contribution to the philosophy of mind and language: his insistence that the idea of "accurate representation of reality" is as dispensable a notion as "sentience" or "experience" or "consciousness."

As I read him, Davidson does for the very idea of representation what Sellars does for the very idea of experience. Just as Sellars gets rid of the question "What is the relation between experience and knowledge?" by replacing experiences with non-inferentially acquired beliefs, so Davidson gets rid of the question "How do we know that our knowledge represents the world accurately?" by replacing beliefs viewed as representations with beliefs viewed as states attributed to persons in order to explain their behavior. Both of these therapeutic moves are recommendations for changes in philosophers' linguistic practices, suggestions that we shall lose nothing except our grip on traditional philosophical problems by making these changes.

In an essay called "A Coherence Theory of Truth and Knowledge," Davidson says that

> a correct understanding of the speech, beliefs, desires, intentions and other propositional attitudes of a person leads to the conclusion that most of a person's beliefs must be true, and so there is a legitimate presumption that any one of them, if it coheres with most of the rest, is true.[5]

He sums this up as the doctrine that "belief is in its nature veridical."

If one understands true beliefs as accurate representations of something which would be as it is even if never represented adequately in any human language, then this claim will seem paradoxical. But if one takes beliefs to be states ascribed to an organism or a machine in order to explain and predict its behavior, then one will find oneself agreeing with Davidson that

> we can't in general first identify beliefs and meanings and then ask what causes them. The causality plays an indispensable role in determining the content of what we say and believe. This is a fact we can be led to recognize by taking up, as we have, the interpreter's point of view.[6]

Taking up that point of view amounts to being interested in what people believe not because we want to measure their beliefs against what they purport to represent, but because we want to deal with these people's behavior. Dealing with that behavior may mean disregarding those people's beliefs as insufficiently coherent with our own, and thereupon treating them as we treat the uninformed and uneducated. Or it may mean blending ours and theirs in the course of instructive conversation. Or, in the most interesting case, it may mean being converted by those with whom we have been conversing to a new *Weltanschauung,* a fairly radical change in one's goals.

Davidson's coherentism amounts to the claim that the decision between these alternatives is never a matter of comparing these people's beliefs with non-beliefs, thereby testing for accuracy of representation. It is always a matter of seeing how much coherence between new and old candidates for belief is possible.

Putting this point in Brandom's preferred terms of "social practices," decisions about truth and falsity are always a matter of rendering practices more coherent or of developing new practices. They never require us to check practices against a norm which is not implicit in some alternative practice, real or imagined. Davidson agrees with Sellars that the search for truth cannot lead us beyond our own practices into what Sellars called "an archē beyond discourse." It can only be a search for a discourse which works better than previous discourses, a discourse which is linked with those previous discourses by the fact that most of the beliefs had by any participant in discourse must be true.[7]

Brandom would like to fill in the details of Davidson's argument that a grasp of the distinction between true and false belief "can emerge only in the context of interpretation, which alone forces us to the idea of an objective, public truth."[8] He agrees with Davidson that interpretation comes first and objectivity later—that the distinction between intersubjective agreement and objective truth is itself only one of the devices we use in order to improve our social practices. But he thinks that Davidsonians need to be more tolerant of notions such as "representation" and "correspondence to reality."

Brandom's attitude toward these notions is analogous to McDowell's attitude toward the notion of "experience." Just as McDowell thinks that one can be a psychological nominalist and still find something true and important in empiricism, so Brandom thinks that one can be a good pragmatist and a good Davidsonian and still find something true in the correspondence theory of truth, and in the distinction between reality and appearance. This is the burden of chapter 8 of his book, which is titled "Ascribing Propositional Attitudes: The Social Route from Reasoning to Representing."

Brandom is, in this respect, to Davidson as McDowell is to Sellars. Each thinks that a distinguished precursor was unfortunately tempted to throw the baby out with the bath. Brandom wants to recuperate "representation" and McDowell wants to recuperate "perceptual experience." It is natural, therefore, that both Brandom and McDowell have doubts about my own version of pragmatism—a version which delights in throwing out as much of the philosophical tradition as possible, and urges that philosophers perform their social function only when they change intuitions, as opposed to reconciling them. In the eyes of both Brandom and McDowell, I am a sort of aging *enfant terrible*, making the appropriation of Sellars and Davidson unnecessarily difficult by recasting the views of each in unnecessarily counterintuitive ways.

In what follows, I shall first summarize Brandom's treatment of objectivity and of representation. Then I shall discuss the relative advantages of abandoning and preserving the notion of "representation."

Davidson's view of representation is simple and dismissive. He says that "Beliefs are true or false, but they represent nothing. It is good to be rid of representations, and with them the correspondence theory of truth, for it is thinking there are representations that engenders thoughts of relativism."[9] Brandom's view is more complex. He writes as follows:

> The chief task [of chapter 8] is to explain the *representational* dimension of thought and talk . . . [The] representationalist order of explanation, dominant since the seventeenth century, presents propositional contentfulness in representational terms from the outset . . . This approach is objectionable if it is pretended that an account in these terms gives one an independent grip on what is expressed by the declarative use of sentences—as though one could understand the notions of states of affairs or truth conditions in *advance* of understanding claiming or judging. The representational semantic tradition embodies an undeniable insight: whatever is propositionally contentful does necessarily have such a representational aspect; nothing that did not would be recognizable as expressing a proposition.[10]

To grasp what Brandom is saying, it is important to realize that he does not think that to call a belief true is to describe a property the belief has. A fortiori, it is not to impute the property of corresponding to reality. Brandom thinks that "the classical metaphysics of truth properties misconstrues what one is doing in endorsing the claim as *describing* it in a special way."[11] For Brandom, to call one's conversational partner's claim "true" is simply to endorse it, not to say something about its relation to non-linguistic reality. So Brandom can heartily agree with Davidson that most of our beliefs must be true, if that simply means that translation and conversation require that interlocutors endorse most of each other's beliefs (not to mention their own).

This is a thoroughly pragmatist approach to ascriptions of truth. But Brandom thinks this approach is compatible with saying that "objects and the world of facts that comprises them are what they are regardless of what anyone takes them to be."[12] This latter claim seems to be at odds with my claim, in earlier lectures, that pragmatists are pan-relationalists who do not believe that there is a way the world is in itself. For Brandom thinks that "thought and talk give us a perspectival grip on a nonperspectival world."[13] For Nietzsche, Dewey, and Nelson Goodman there are perspectives all the way down, but for Brandom there seems to be something more.

It seems that way, but the appearance may be illusory. Brandom never suggests that inquiry will someday converge to this non-perspectival world. On the contrary, he insists that any and every grip on it will be perspectival, determined by some historically contingent set of human needs and interests. Brandom is not saying that there is, *pace* Goodman, a Way the World Is. He is saying that something like the idea of such a way is essential to our linguistic practices. He is, as he says, reconstruing

> objectivity as consisting in a kind of perspectival *form,* rather than in a nonperspectival . . . *content.* What is shared by all discursive perspectives is *that* there is a difference between what is objectively correct in the way of concept application and what is merely taken to be so, not *what* it is—the structure, not the content.[14]

Like Davidson—and unlike Peirce, Putnam, and Habermas—Brandom is not committed to defining "true" in epistemic terms. He does, in other words, define by reference to "what is taken true by all the members of a community, or by the experts in a community, or what will always be taken true by them, or what would be taken true by them under some ideal conditions for inquiry."[15] As he goes on to say, "there is no bird's-eye view above the fray of competing claims from which those that deserve to prevail can be identified, *nor from which even necessary and sufficient conditions for such deserts can be formulated.*"[16] Brandom is not defining the word "true" but rather agreeing with Davidson that one should not attempt such a definition.

When I first read Brandom's book, it seemed to me that Brandom was abandoning hard-won ground by making the notions of "representation," "fact," and "making true" respectable. This was because I had gotten accustomed to Davidson's repudiation of all these notions. I no longer am sure about this, and now I am inclined to say that Brandom and Davidson pretty much agree on all the issues, and are simply employing different rhetorical strategies to make pretty much the same points. But rhetoric matters, especially if, as I do, one sees the pragmatist tradition not just as clearing up little messes left behind by the great dead philosophers, but as taking part in a world-historical change in the self-image of European and American civilization.

Consider the question of whether there are such things as facts—what Strawson sneeringly called "sentence-shaped bits of reality"—which make true sentences true. Davidson thinks that one of the great contributions of Tarski was to show how we could avoid the notion of facts. He thinks that there is no need to talk of any sort of truth-maker, and that doing so is highly misleading. Brandom thinks that doing so is harmless, and cheerfully says things that would make Davidson's hair stand on end. For example:

the nonlinguistic facts could be largely what they are, even if our discursive practices were quite different (or absent entirely), for what claims are true does not depend on anyone's claiming of them. But our discursive practices could not be what they are if the nonlinguistic facts were different.[17]

Again, Davidson thinks that one good reason never to talk about representation is that doing so encourages talk of relativism, and thus attempts to defeat relativism by cultivating what philosophers like Michael Devitt and

Crispin Wright call "our realist intuitions"—our sense that we are committed to getting something out there, something which exists independently of our human needs and interests, *right*. Brandom, in an as yet unpublished reply to my doubts about his book, says that "a central enterprise of [his] book is an anti-relativist one: to offer an account of what it is to be committed to the correctness of our claims answering to how things actually *are*, rather than to anyone or everyone *takes* them to be." He goes on to say that "our use of *de re* ascriptions of propositional attitudes" expresses our

> nonrelativist commitments to one way of talking being a *better* way of talking about what there really is—[as when we say things like] 'Ptolemy claimed *of* the orbital trajectories of the planets that they were the result of the motion of crystalline spheres.'

I think that Davidson's response to the passages I have just quoted from Brandom would run something like this: Certainly we should not think of our claims answering to how anyone or everyone takes things to be, but neither should we take them to answer to how things really are. The alternative is to take them as *about* things, but not as *answering to* anything, either objects or opinions. Aboutness is all you need for intentionality. Answering to things is what the infelicitous notion of representing adds to the harmless notion of aboutness: it is what differentiates good inferentialists like you and me from the representationalist bad guys. For as long as our beliefs are said to be answerable to something, we shall want to be told more about how this answering works, and the history of epistemology suggests that there is nothing to be said. Aboutness, like truth, is indefinable, and none the worse for that. But "answering" and "representing" are metaphors which cry out for further definition, for literalization.

Whether or not this would be Davidson's response, it is mine. It seems to me that when Brandom says he is offering us a non-relativist view is he doing the same sort of thing that Kant did when he said that he was not a skeptic but an empirical realist. A lot of his readers, including Hegel, decided that a transcendental idealist was just what they had been accustomed to calling a skeptic. Brandom says he is not a relativist, even though the objectivity he believes in is "a kind of perspectival form, rather than a nonperspectival content." But Brandom's readers who are accustomed to use "relativist" as a term of abuse are going to insist that being a relativist consists precisely in denying the existence of non-perspectival content. The shift from "about X" to "answering to X" is the same sort of shift as Kant makes from "non-illusory" to "empirically real"; this shift did not give critics the full-blooded notion of reality they were demanding.

Brandom wants to get from the invidious comparison made in such *de re* ascriptions as "She believes *of* a cow that it is a deer," to the traditional distinction between subjective appearance and objective reality. It seems to me that all that such invidious comparisons give one is a distinction between better and worse tools for handling the situation at hand—the cow, the planets, or whatever. They do not give us a distinction between more and less accurate descriptions of what the thing really is, in the sense of what it is all by itself, apart from the utilities of human tools for human purposes. But only the latter sense of "what it really is" is going to satisfy people who worry about relativism. What Brandom calls "the fundamental distinction of *social* perspectives between commitments one *attributes* to another and those one *undertakes* oneself" gives me a distinction between your bad tools and my better ones. But I doubt that it gives us a distinction between my representing reality accurately and your representing it inaccurately.

I can restate my doubts by considering Brandom's description of "intellectual progress" as "making more and more true claims about the things that are really out there to be talked and thought about." I see intellectual progress as developing better and better tools for better and better purposes—better, of course, by our lights. Philosophers like Searle, who find Kuhn's description of scientific progress intolerable, insist that we are only making genuine intellectual progress if we are getting us closer and closer to the way things are in themselves. Brandom's perspectivalism prevents him from using the phrase "in themselves," but his term "more and more true claims about the things that are really out there" flirts with something like the "bird's-eye view above the fray of competing claims" which he has already repudiated.

To sum up, my hunch is that Brandom, like Kant, is trying too hard to compromise an uncompromisable dispute, and so falls between two stools. When he says that "concern with getting things right is built into any practices that generate disposition-transcendent conceptual norms," aggressive realists like Searle are going to read "getting things right" in one way, while sympathetic pragmatists like me are going to read them in another way. It is hard to pour new wine into old bottles without getting the customers confused.

I want to interpret the claim that Copernicus got right what Ptolemy got mostly wrong, or that Saint Paul got right what Aristotle got mostly wrong, as claims about the greater suitability of the former figures for the purposes I want to serve. But people who worry about realism vs. anti-realism—as I do not, but as the vast majority of Anglophone philosophers do—will feel cheated if they think that that is *all* that Brandom has in mind.

One way of putting the issue is to revert to the words I put in Davidson's mouth earlier, and to say that one should just stop answering altogether, thus avoiding the choice between answering to people and answering to non-people. As long as the latter choice is posed, one will count as a defender of objectivity merely by virtue of denying, as Brandom does, that truth can be identified with what people believe under certain conditions. But when Brandom then goes on to say that he identifies truth with answering to non-people, realists like Searle will ask him how he knows that he is giving the right answers.

The choice is between dropping the notions of "answering" and "representing" (though not those of "of" and "about") and keeping them. My argument for dropping them is that they preserve an image of the relation between people and non-people which, in these lectures, I have been calling "authoritarian" and denouncing. I see both Brandom's identification of calling an assertion "true" with endorsing it and Davidson's refusal to define "true" as tools for persuading us to abandon this authoritarian image. But I see Brandom's persistence in using the terms "getting right," "really is" and "making true" as tools which will fall into authoritarian hands and be used for reactionary purposes.

In the controversy between the authoritarians and the anti-authoritarians, Brandom's heart is certainly in the right place. This is clear from his insistence that reality has no norms of its own to offer, apart from those which we develop. But his rhetoric will not convey the state of his heart to those who still hanker after answerability.

I shall conclude with some remarks on a neologism which Brandom invents in order to legitimize his use of the word "fact." This is the word "claimable." I quote from another unpublished paper of his, "Vocabularies of Pragmatism":[18]

For we should distinguish between two senses of 'claim'; on the one hand there is the act of claim*ing*, and on the other there is what is claim*ed*. I want to say that facts are true claims in the sense of what is claimed (indeed, of what is claimable), rather than in the sense of true claimings. With this distinction on board, there is nothing wrong with saying that facts *make* claims true—for they make claimings true. This sense of 'makes' should not be puzzling: it is inferential. "John's remark that [p] is true because it is a fact that *p*" just tells us that the first clause follows from the second.[19]

Consider an argument that what makes opium put people to sleep is its dormitive power. The sense of "makes" here should not be puzzling, it is inferential. "The doctor's remark that opium puts people to sleep because it has a dormitive power" just tells us that the first clause follows from the second.

It seems to me that the notion of a claimable is as useless for explanatory purposes as that of dormitive power. Unless we are given some details about how the opium's dormitive power does the trick, what it consists in, we shall not find the term "dormitive power" useful. It is not rendered useful just because clauses referring to it can be given an inferential role. I find the notion of "claimable" useless, except to encourage a rhetoric which suggests that human inquiry is "answerable" to something, a rhetoric which seems to me better avoided.

Brandom points out that to deny the existence of facts and truths about protons long before the term "proton" appeared in language leads to paradox. This is because it seems reasonable to infer from

(1) There were photons five million years ago and then to
(2) It was the case then that there were photons and then to
(3) It is true that it was the case then that there were photons and then to
(4) It was true then that there were photons.

It seems reasonable, but of course philosophers have, paradoxically, denied it. Heidegger notoriously said that "before Newton, Newton's laws were neither true nor false." Brandom quotes me as having said, "Since truth is a property of sentience, since sentences are dependent for their existence upon vocabularies, and since vocabularies are made by human beings, so are truths."

Paradox, however, is sometimes a small price to pay for progress, as the examples of Copernicus, Kant, and Freud may suggest. Further, it is a price Brandom himself is willing to pay, at least in the eyes of Searle, Nagel, and others, when he follows Sellars in casting sentience to the winds and denying that dogs and babies have beliefs "except in a derivative sense." I am not sure that the paradox of which Heidegger and I are guilty is all that much more paradoxical than the one which many people think Sellars and Brandom are guilty of when they assert that all awareness is a linguistic affair.

I am willing to say that facts make beliefs true in a derivative sense of "make"—namely, the inferential sense. The force of saying that this sense is derivative and metaphorical is to decline responsibility for giving further details about how the making gets done. Analogously, the force of saying that babies and dogs have beliefs only in a derivative and metaphorical sense is to decline responsibility for explaining how they differ from thermostats. Reference to such derivative senses should, however, be avoided where possible— if only because employing them will seem a cop-out to one's philosophical critics.

David Lewis once said that philosophy is a matter of gathering together our intuitions and then finding the way to keep as many of them as possible. I think that it is a matter of treating both intuitions and accusations of paradox as the voice of the past, and as possible impediments to the creation of a better future. Of course the voice of the past must always be heeded, since rhetorical effectiveness depends upon a decent respect for the opinions of mankind. But intellectual and moral progress would be impossible unless people sometimes, in exceptional cases, can be persuaded to turn a deaf ear to ancestral voices.

10

McDowell's Version of Empiricism

Or: On the Very Idea of Human Answerability to the World

I shall begin by summarizing some of the most prominent features of John McDowell's *Mind and World*, a task made easier by the new introduction which he has written for that book, and from which I shall be borrowing heavily.

McDowell's central notion is that of "answerability to the world." He says that

> to make sense of a mental state's or episode's being directed towards the world, in the way in which, say, a belief or judgment is, we need to put the state or episode in a normative context. A belief or judgment to the effect that things are thus and so . . . must be a posture or stance that is *correctly or incorrectly* adopted according to whether or not things are indeed thus and so . . . This relation between mind and world is normative, then, in this sense: thinking that aims at judgement, or at the fixation of belief, is answerable to the world—to how things are—for whether or not it is correctly executed.[1]

Before going on, let me note that McDowell here does something that critics of the correspondence theory of truth have always complained about: he treats perceptual judgments as a model for all judgments. To say that "This is red," is "directed toward the world," or "answerable to the world" is

This lecture appeared in English as Rorty, "The Very Idea of Human Answerability to the World: John McDowell's Version of Empiricism," in Rorty, *Philosophical Papers*, vol. 3: *Truth and Progress*, 138–152 (Cambridge: Cambridge University Press, 1998) (hereafter *TP*).

intuitively plausible. But such phrases seem less applicable if one's paradigm of a belief is, "We ought to love one another," or "There are many transfinite cardinals," or "Proust was only an effete petit-bourgeois."

Another way of making the same point is to remark that there are vast areas of culture in which "a belief or judgment that things are thus and so" is indeed "a posture or stance that is *correctly or incorrectly* adopted," but in which it would be strange to say that it is "*correctly or incorrectly* adopted according to whether things are indeed thus and so." The addition of this latter phrase may go unnoticed if one's paradigm of a belief or judgment is one of Newton's laws, but it will seem pointless when one is describing beliefs such as, "Blake is a better role model for poets than Byron," or "Heidegger's philosophy was better than his politics." In art, morals, and politics we want to judge correctly, but talk of "world-directedness" and of things "indeed being thus and so" sounds hollow.[2]

This point recalls one of the differences between the sort of Anglophone philosophy which harks back to Bacon and Locke, and philosophical traditions which regard Anglophone empiricism as a notable example of cultural lag. When Anglophone philosophers think of a cultural achievement, a triumph of the human intellect, they typically think first of modern physical science, the saga that links Newton to Murray Gell-Mann. Non-Anglophone philosophers may as easily think first of the European novel from Cervantes to Nabokov, or of socialist politics from Fourier to Helmut Schmidt. For these philosophers are more inclined than their Anglophone colleagues to follow Nietzsche's advice, and to "look at science through the optic of art, and at art through that of life."

Philosophers who take this advice will find Brandom's book more attractive than McDowell's. For Brandom is content to think of normativity, of the possibility of correctness and incorrectness, in terms of human beings' answerability to one another. As I was suggesting at the end of my lecture this morning, Brandom could probably say everything he needs to say about objectivity, about the possibility that any given judgment we make, no matter how unanimously, could be wrong, without talking about "answerability to the world" or "world-directedness." Brandom's account of objectivity works just as well for mathematics as for physics. It is as applicable to literary criticism as to chemistry.

The primacy of perception and of natural science becomes explicit when McDowell goes on to say*

> Even if we take it that answerability to how things are includes more than answerability to the empirical world, it nevertheless seems right to say this: since our cognitive predicament is that we confront the world by way of sensible intuition (to put it in Kantian terms), our reflection on the very idea of thought's directedness at how things are must begin with answerability to the empirical world.[3]

When discussing literature or politics, it is a bit strained to say that we are in a cognitive predicament. It is even more strained to say that this predicament is caused by the need to confront the world by way of sensible intuition.

McDowell's choice of Kantian terms is a choice of visual metaphors, metaphors which Kant used to lament our lack of the faculty of intellectual intuition which Aristotle had described, over-optimistically, in *De Anima*. It is also a choice of natural science as the paradigm of rational inquiry, a Kantian choice which Hegel explicitly repudiates. When one switches from Kant to Hegel, the philosopher whom Sellars described as "the great foe of immediacy," these metaphors lose much of their appeal. So it is not surprising that it is among Anglophone philosophers, who read far more Kant than they do Hegel, that these metaphors should remain most prevalent.

From a Sellarsian, Davidsonian, Brandomian, or Hegelian viewpoint, there is no clear need for what McDowell describes as

> 'a minimal empiricism': the idea that experience must constitute a tribunal, mediating the way our thinking is answerable to how things are, as it must be if we are to make sense of it as thinking at all.[4]

For Sellars, Davidson, and Brandom, we are constantly interacting with things as well as with persons, and one of the ways in which we interact with both is through their effects upon our sensory organs. But none of these three philosophers need the notion of experience as a mediating tribunal. They can be con-

---

* In *TP*, this sentence reads: "The centrality of perception and of natural science to this treatment of the topic of answerability becomes explicit when McDowell goes on to say . . ." (139).

tent with an account of the world as exerting control on our inquiries in a merely causal way, rather than as exerting what McDowell calls *"rational* control." What McDowell says of Davidson is true of Sellars and Brandom as well: all three think "a merely causal, not rational, linkage between thinking and independent reality will do, as an interpretation of the idea that empirical content requires friction against something external to thinking."[5] That such an account will *not* do is the first, and largely unargued, premise of McDowell's book.

McDowell is a devoted reader of Sellars, Davidson, and Brandom and is fully aware of the possibility of what he calls "a frame of mind . . . that makes it hard to see how experience *could* function as a tribunal, delivering verdicts on our thinking."[6] He sees these three philosophers as so infatuated with the need to repudiate the Myth of the Given—to avoid the British Empiricists' traditional confusion of causation with justification—as to be willing to give up world-directedness and rational answerability to the world.

McDowell develops his account of how these three demythologizing philosophers fell into error by distinguishing between the "logical space of nature" and "the logical space of reasons." The former he defines as "the logical space in which the natural sciences function, as we have been enabled to conceive them by a well-charted, and in itself admirable, development of modern thought."[7] He uses the term "the realm of law" as a synonym for "the logical space of nature," and often states the problem raised by abandoning the Myth of the Given as that of understanding the relation between the realm of law and the realm of reason.

As McDowell sees it, Sellars and Davidson are so impressed by nature as described by physics—the realm of law as the realm of atoms and void—that they feel impelled to give an account of experience which "disqualifies it from intelligibly constituting a tribunal." "For these purposes," McDowell says

> Sellars and Davidson are interchangeable. Sellars's attack on the Given corresponds . . . to Davidson's attack on what he calls "the third dogma of empiricism"—the dualism of conceptual scheme and empirical "content."[8]

Sellars and Davidson both think that adopting psychological nominalism, and thereby avoiding a confusion between justification and causation, entails claiming that only a belief can justify a belief. This means drawing a sharp line between experience as cause of the occurrence of a justification, and experience as itself justificatory. It means reinterpreting "experience" as the ability to acquire beliefs non-inferentially as a result of neurologically describable causal transactions with the world.

One can restate this reinterpretation of "experience" as the claim that human beings' only "confrontation" with the world is the sort which computers also have. Computers are programmed to respond to certain causal transactions with input devices by entering certain program states. We humans program ourselves to respond to causal transactions between the higher brain centers and the sense organs with dispositions to make assertions. There is no epistemologically interesting difference between a machine's program state and our dispositions, and both may equally well be called "beliefs" or "judgments." There is no more or less intentionality, world-directedness, or rationality in the one case than in the other. We can describe both ourselves and machines in normative programming terms, or in non-normative hardware terms. No problem arises, in either case, about the interface between software and hardware, the intentional and the non-intentional, the space of reasons and the space of laws.

McDowell regards Sellars, Davidson, and Brandom as "renouncing empiricism" because they renounce the idea of experience as a tribunal. Brandom and Sellars agree with Davidson that, as McDowell puts it, "we cannot take experience to be epistemologically significant without falling into the Myth of the Given."[9] But McDowell thinks that this renunciation of empiricism simply will not work. He thinks that doing so will "leave the [traditional] philosophical questions still looking as if they *ought* to be good ones" so that "the result is continuing philosophical discomfort, not an exorcism of philosophy."[10]

Like me, McDowell regards himself as a therapeutic philosopher. He hopes, as I do, to create a "frame of mind in which we would no longer seem to be faced with problems that call on philosophy to bring subject and object back together."[11] We both want to "achieve an intellectual right to shrug our shoulders at sceptical questions,"[12] and to "disown an obligation to try to answer the characteristic questions of modern philosophy."[13]

But McDowell believes, as I do not, that "a real insight is operative in seeming to be faced with that obligation."[14] So he thinks that empiricism, expelled with a pitchfork, will return again through the window. He thinks that we can "trace some distinctive anxieties of modern philosophy to a tension between two forces": the "attractiveness of a minimal empiricism on the one hand" and the fact that all awareness is a linguistic affair" on the other.[15] In McDowell's picture, the linguistic turn in philosophy helped us see that nothing was part of the process of justification which does not have a linguistic shape. It did not, however, take away the need to "make sense of the world-directedness of empirical thinking." "So long as the attractions of empiricism are not explained away," he says, the incoherence of the Myth of the Given will be "a source of continuing philosophical discomfort."[16]

In my picture, the linguistic turn in philosophy, the turn which made it possible for Sellars to envisage his doctrine of psychological nominalism, was a turn away from the very idea of human answerability to the world. I agree with Heidegger that there is a straight line between the Cartesian quest for certainty and the Nietzschean will to power. So I think that modern European philosophy amounts to an attempt by human beings to wrest power from God—or, more placidly put, to dispense with the idea of human answerability to something non-human. It involves what Heidegger lamented as "forgetfulness of Being." Like Nietzsche and Derrida, I think of such forgetfulness as a thoroughly good thing, and of what Heidegger called the "humanism" of modern philosophy as an equally good thing. I regard the need for world-directedness as a relic of the need for authoritative guidance, the need against which Nietzsche and his fellow pragmatists revolted.

I suspect that our differing accounts of the genesis and development of modern philosophy provide the most fruitful locus for debate between McDowell and myself. But before returning to these accounts, and to our differing metaphilosophical strategies, I need to sketch McDowell's own bold and ingenious resolution of the dilemma he believes to be posed by Sellars's and Davidson's anti-empiricist polemic. To do so, I shall discuss three notions which are central to McDowell's thinking: (1) "bald naturalism"; (2) "second nature"; (3) "rational freedom."

Bald Naturalism

McDowell sees, as I have already noted, a sharp dichotomy between the realm of nature and that of law. Bald naturalists are philosophers who deny this sharp dichotomy; they are people with reductionist instincts, such as Quine. Quine would like to think that the language of physics has some sort of priority, and that everything which does not fit into that language must be regarded as a concession to practical convenience rather than as part of an account of how things really are.

McDowell sometimes rephrases his nature-law dichotomy as a dichotomy between two kinds of intelligibility, as in the following passage:

> The modern scientific revolution made possible a newly clear concep-
> tion of the distinctive kind of intelligibility that the natural sciences
> allow us to find in things ... We must sharply distinguish natural-
> scientific intelligibility from the kind of intelligibility something ac-
> quires when we situate it in the logical space of reasons. That is a way of
> affirming the dichotomy of logical spaces, as bald naturalism refuses to.[17]

In his picture, people like Quine (and sometimes even Sellars) are so impressed with natural science that they think that the first sort of intelligibility is the only genuine sort.

I think that it is important, when discussing the achievements of the scientific revolution, to make a distinction which McDowell does not make: a
distinction between particle physics, together with those microstructural
parts of natural science which can easily be linked up with particle physics,
and all the rest of natural science. Particle physics, unfortunately, fascinates
many contemporary philosophers, just as corpuscularian mechanics fascinated John Locke. Quine once said that the reason that the indeterminacy of
translation was distinct from the indeterminacy of theory was that the differences in psychological explanation, unlike those in biological explanation,
made no difference to the motion of the elementary particles. David Lewis
thinks that all objects in the universe are gerrymandered artifacts except
these elementary particles. Sellars himself was all too inclined to describe
nature in Democritean terms as "atoms and void," and to invent pseudo-
problems about how to reconcile the "scientific" with the "manifest" image
of human beings.

To guard against this simple-minded and reductionistic way of thinking
of non-human nature, it is useful to remember that the form of intelligibility
shared by Newton's primitive corpuscularianism and contemporary particle
physics has no counterpart in, for example, the geology of plate tectonics, nor
in Darwin's and Mendel's accounts of heredity and evolution. What we get

in those areas of natural science are narratives, natural histories, rather than the subsumption of events under laws.

So I think that McDowell should not accept the bald naturalists' view that there is a "distinctive form of intelligibility" found in the natural sciences, and that it consists in relating events by laws. It would be better to say that what Davidson calls "strict laws" are the exception in natural science—nice if you can get them, but hardly essential to scientific explanation.[18] It would be better to treat "natural science" as a name of an assortment of useful gimmicks, rather than of a natural kind. It would be even better to stop using terms like "forms of intelligibility," for one might then avoid worrying, as McDowell worries, about whether "what we experience is [or is] not external to the realm of the kind of intelligibility which is proper to meaning."[19]

If you are fascinated by the kind of natural science that does give you nice strict laws, you will be inclined to over-dramatize the contrast between nature and reason by saying, as McDowell does, that the "logical space of reasons" is *sui generis*. I would argue that it is no more or less *sui generis* than the logical space of political argument, or biological explanation, or soccer, or carpentry. *All* language-games are *sui generis*. That is: that they are irreducible to one another, where the test of "reducibility" is something like the discovery of material conditionals relating statements made in one game to statements made in another. But this sense of *"sui generis"*—the sense in which baseball is *sui generis*, over against soccer, jai alai, basketball, chess, and poker—is philosophically sterile.

If we are trying to give philosophy Wittgensteinian peace, we should do what Dewey did: try to make all the traditional philosophical "dichotomies" look like over-dramatizations of the banal fact that different tools serve different purposes. We should treat the fact that you cannot use Intentional talk and Particle talk simultaneously as philosophically sterile as the fact that you cannot play baseball and jai alai simultaneously. We should not allow this fact to make us wonder, as McDowell wonders, how to "bring understanding and sensibility, reason and nature, back together."[20]

To sum up, McDowell thinks that we need to keep a big reason-nature, law-reason dichotomy in place, as bald naturalists do not. I think that both the bald naturalists and McDowell make too much of a fuss about this dichotomy, and use it to engender pseudo-problems. One reason they make too much of a fuss is that both talk about intelligibility rather than convenience.

Quine thinks that particle physics gives us the one true paradigm of intelligibility. McDowell thinks that we have two such paradigms. I think we would do better to rid ourselves of the notion of "intelligibility" altogether.[21] We should substitute the notion of techniques of problem-solving. Democritus, Newton, and Dalton solved some problems with particles and laws. Darwin, Gibbon, and Hegel solved others with narratives. Carpenters solve others with hammers and nails, and soldiers still others with guns. Philosophers' problems are about how to prevent the words used by some of these problem-solvers from getting in the way of other words used by other problem-solvers. These problems are not posed by dichotomies between realms of being, but by cultural imperialists, people with monotheistic delusions of grandeur, such as Quine and Fichte.

Second Nature

If, like McDowell, you are concerned with the question of whether there is rational as opposed to merely causal control of human inquiry by the world, you will want to concentrate on the interface between the space of reasons and the space of nature, and to find something which can be described as in both. To make room for something of that sort, you will need to say, as McDowell does, that "we need not equate the very idea of nature with the idea of instantiations of concepts that belong in the logical space . . . in which the natural-scientific kind of intelligibility is brought to light."[22]

"Human beings," McDowell goes on to say, "acquire a second nature in part by being initiated into conceptual capacities, whose interrelations belong in the logical space of reasons." Elsewhere he uses the analogy of being initiated into a moral community, and thereby acquiring a moral character. The acquisition of a moral character and the acquisition of the ability to have perceptual experiences are both examples of "initiation into conceptual capacities."[23] Further,

> Such initiation is a normal part of what it is for a human being to come to maturity, and that is why, although the structure of the space of reasons is alien to the layout of nature conceived as the realm of law, it does not take on the remoteness from the human that rampant platonism envisages. If we generalize the way Aristotle conceives the molding of ethical character, we arrive at the notion of having one's eyes opened to reasons at large by acquiring a second nature. I cannot

think of a good short English expression for this, but it is what figures in German philosophy as *Bildung*.[24]

Having one's eyes opened to reasons gives one the ability to be rationally controlled by the world, and thereby the ability to be in world-directed states and to have judgments which are answerable to the world. It also gives you rational freedom. All these endowments become unintelligible, McDowell thinks, if we describe encounters with the world through our sensory apparatus in the terms used by Sellars, Davidson, and Brandom.

For the latter three philosophers, *Bildung* is a matter of intra-human relationships—the acquisition of the ability to interact with other human beings by asking for and giving reasons. The more *gebildet* you are, the more complex and interesting kinds of reasons you can ask for and give. But at no point do these three philosophers describe the *world* as a sort of conversational partner, offering you candidates for belief, nominations you are free to accept or decline. The world thrusts beliefs on you, by causal interaction between the program you have internalized in the course of becoming *gebildet* and the state of your sense-organs. So for these philosophers it is not felicitous to describe *Bildung* as opening your eyes to reasons for belief offered you by the non-human world.

By contrast, for McDowell the idea that the world is a sort of conversational partner is all-important. He wants to conceive of experience as "openness to the world," or "openness to reality"[25] in the same sense of openness in which a conversable person is open to new ideas. It is essential for him to describe perceptual illusions (the Müller-Lyer illusion, the woman with her head in a black bag whom the unwary take to be headless, etc.) *not* as causing us to have true or false beliefs depending on our programming, but as presenting us with candidates for belief which we are free to accept or reject depending on our degree of intellectual sophistication.

McDowell likes to talk about the world doing you favors, showing you a kindness, vouchsafing facts. He says, for example, that

the particular facts that the world does us the favor of vouchsafing to us, in the various relevant modes of cognition, actually shape the space of reasons as we find it. The effect is a sort of coalescence between the idea of the space of reasons as we find it and the idea of the world as we encounter it.

Of course we are fallible in our judgments as to the shape of the space of reasons as we find it, or—what comes to the same thing—as to the shape of the world as we find it. That is to say that we are vulnerable to the world's playing us false; and when the world does not play us false we are indebted to it.[26]

Brandom, Sellars, and Davidson can all agree that the space of reasons as we find it is also, by and large, the shape of the world. Because most of our beliefs must be true, we can make no sense of the idea that a great gulf might separate the way the world is and the way we describe it. Unlike McDowell, however, they think that the world shapes the space of reasons not by "vouch-safing facts" to us but by exercising brute causal pressure on us. Just as the brute pressure of the environment led to successive stages of biological evolution, so it led to the successive stages of cultural evolution.

These three philosophers and McDowell agree that if you cannot use words you do not have conceptual capacities. To have a conceptual capacity just *is* being able to use a word. But the first three assume that, since babies, dogs, trees, and rocks do not use words, there is no reason to think of the non-human world as a conversational partner. But for McDowell things are not so simple. He says that "conceptual capacities . . . can be operative not only in judgments . . . but already in the transactions in nature that are constituted by the world's impacts on the receptive capacities of a suitable subject."[27] McDowell agrees that the rocks and trees do not talk, but they do not *just* cause us to make judgments either. He thinks of a perceptual appearance as a request to you by the world to make a judgment, but as not yet itself a judgment, even though it has the conceptual form of a judgment.

So the rocks and trees offer us reasons to believe by, so to speak, borrowing our ability to use words—an ability they did not have before humans developed language. McDowell's "impressions" are neither physiological states which produce non-inferential beliefs nor those non-inferential beliefs themselves, but something in between the two—the ingredients of *second* nature. McDowell says that

Once we remember second nature, we see that operations of nature can include circumstances whose descriptions place them in the logical space of reasons, *sui generis* though that logical space is. This makes it possible to accommodate impressions in nature without posing a threat to empiricism. From the thesis that receiving an impression is a transaction in nature, there is now no good inference to the conclusion drawn by Sellars and Davidson, that the idea of receiving an impression must be foreign to the logical space in which concepts such as that of answerability function . . . In receiving impressions, a subject can be open to the way things manifestly are.[28]

Rational Freedom

McDowell says that "responsiveness to reasons" is a good gloss on one notion of freedom. But, he continues, there may be philosophical puzzlement about how such responsiveness fits into the natural world. Humean compatibilists like Davidson, Dennett, and myself, people who want to dissolve rather than solve the problem of freedom and determinism, think that such puzzlement should disappear once we see that the tools we use to apply and change our norms are often different from those we use to predict what will happen next. So we do not see the need to do what McDowell calls "looking for a conception of our nature that includes a capacity to resonate to the structure of the space of reasons."[29]

But for McDowell the notions of "rational freedom," "openness to the world" and "answerability to the world" stand or fall together. So does the notion of "spontaneity," in Kant's sense of "the spontaneity of the understanding." So also does that of "empirical content." McDowell thinks that Davidson does not see that a merely causal account of our responses to the non-human threatens our empirical judgments with "emptiness," in the sense of contentlessness: "if we are to avert the threat of emptiness, we need to see intuitions as standing in rational relations to what we should think."[30]

On McDowell's understanding of "content," some uses of words to classify visible and tangible things—such as "witch" and "Boche" and "phlogiston"— turn out not to have empirical content. They are pseudo-concepts. As we learn more and more about the world, the fewer pseudo-concepts we have and the more real, contentful, empirical concepts. As we make intellectual progress, we become more and more open to the world. The world manages

to fill our beliefs up with more and more empirical content, and thus, so to
speak, to tell us more and more about itself.[31]

Davidson, Sellars, and Brandom have no use for this contrast between uses
of words which have content and uses which do not. As good inferentialists
and pan-relationalists, they think that all a concept needs to have content is
for the word to function as a node in a pattern of inferences. All the words
ever systematically bandied about, by superstitious cavemen as well as by sophisticated physicists, are on a par as far as content or lack of content goes.
Whereas McDowell wants to revive a version of Russell's idea that non-
referring singular terms are only pseudo-singular terms, Davidson, Sellars,
and Brandom all want to claim that any singular term that has a use is as
good a singular term as any other.

Just because the notion of "rational freedom" is, as McDowell uses it, so
interlocked with other notions which I have no use for—notions like answerability and content—I have no use for it. So I construe "rational freedom" as
that funny thing McDowell thinks we would not have if Davidson were right
that there is "a merely causal, not rational, linkage between thinking and independent reality." I find it hard to associate this sense of the term "free"
with the only one Hume was interested in: the sense in which you are not
free if there is a gun at your child's head or if you are under hypnosis—the
one we invoke when ascribing moral responsibility. I also find it hard to associate it with Hegel's claim that history is the story of increasing freedom.
It seems to me a specifically Kantian sense of the term "freedom"—one
which we could discard if we were willing to abandon the Kantian dichotomy
between kinds of intelligibility, and to talk instead about techniques of
problem-solving.

So much for the three McDowellian notions that I have used as pegs on
which to hang my account of McDowell's solution to his problem—the
problem of how to avoid both bald naturalism and the view, common to Sellars, Davidson, and Brandom, that the notion of "perceptual experience" can
simply be discarded.

I think that this solution is brilliantly original and completely successful.
McDowell is just the philosopher you want if you fear losing your grip on
the notion of "perceptual experience." He does a splendid job of reconciling
common turns of speech such as "a glimpse of the world" and "openness to
the world" and "answerability to the world" with a repudiation of the confu-

sion between causation and justification embodied in the Myth of the Given. His conception of "second nature" is just what is needed for this job of reconciliation. He has rehabilitated empiricism.

But, of course, I do not *want* such a reconciliation or such a rehabilitation. I think that most of the common turns of speech which McDowell invokes should be discarded rather than given philosophical backup. I see nothing worth saving in empiricism. I think that saving the notion of answerability to the world saves an intuition which clashes with Dewey's romantic polytheism. It retains the figure of "the world" as a non-human authority to whom we owe some sort of respect.

In his discussion of my views in *Mind and World,* McDowell quotes me as saying that "there seems no obvious reason why the progress of the language-game we are playing should have anything in particular to do with the way the rest of the world is." He rebuts this by saying that "It is the whole point of the idea of norms of inquiry that following them ought to improve our chances of being right about 'the way the world is.'"[32]

I think that this view of the function of norms of inquiry will lead one back to the distinction between scheme and world, and to the notion that the progress of inquiry consists in an increasingly tight "fit" with the world. McDowell, who accepts Davidson's critique of the scheme-content distinction, denies this. "The world as I invoke it here," he says, "is not the world that is well lost, as Rorty sees [it] . . . It is the perfectly ordinary world in which there are rocks, snow is white, and so forth . . . It is that ordinary world on which our thinking bears in a way that Rorty's separation of viewpoints leaves looking mysterious, precisely because it separates relatedness to the world from the normative surroundings that are needed to make sense of the idea of bearing—rational bearing—on anything." My own thinking, McDowell says, makes this problem urgent, so my "refusal to address them can only be an act of will, a deliberate plugging of the ears."[33]

I, of course, think that McDowell has been seduced by an empiricist siren song, and that my deafness to that song is an example of hard-won intellectual virtue, rather than the result of a perverse act of will. But I also think that that there is very little neutral ground for the two of us to stand on while we debate our disagreements. In particular, I do not think that more rigorous formulation of the issue is going to help. For I simply cannot believe that anything important hangs on saying, with McDowell, that we should lose our

Kantian freedom unless perceptual appearances were distinct from judgments, rather than saying, with Brandom, that Kantian freedom consists
simply in being able to withhold an "is-claim" and make a "looks-claim"
instead.

Cracker-barrel pragmatists like me always ask, as William James did, "what
difference to practice is that funny little difference in theory supposed to
make?" So I find myself asking how that nice, clean-cut disagreement between
Brandom and McDowell about the nature of looks could possibly tie in with
the politicocultural hopes that led Kant and Hegel to write their books. One
lesson we should have learned from the revolt against medieval scholasticism
is that when philosophers start quarreling about whether there is a third thing
intermediate between two other things (Aquinas's *materia signata*, for example, an intermediary between prime matter and substantial form), they
have traded cultural significance for professional rigor.

So my inclination is to turn away from nice, precise formulations of the
issue and to start talking in fuzzy, world-historical-cum-psychoanalytic terms
about the need to bring mankind to full maturity by discarding the image of
the fierce father-figure. When I succumb to this inclination, I start using the
kind of rhetoric I was using on Tuesday and on Thursday.* This leads me to
seek out the passages in McDowell in which he offers his own version of world
history. The most pregnant of these is his remark that "our philosophical anxieties are due to the intelligible grip on our thinking of a modern naturalism" and his suggestion that we "work at loosening that grip."[34]

I read this passage in McDowell as echoing similar passages in Gadamer
and in Charles Taylor—two other philosophers who think that Aristotle
grasped something important, something we began to lose our grip on when
corpuscularian mechanics made Aristotelianism seem obsolete. I also read
it in the light of McDowell's remark to me, in correspondence, that a "Darwinian tone" pervades a lot of my writing. McDowell expands on this point
by saying that my suspicion of pre-Darwinian ways of talking "reflects a precisely *non*-pragmatist favoring of Darwinian vocabulary, as the only linguistic apparatus that we can genuinely see as permitting us to describe
reality."

* Rorty is referring to Lecture 1 and Lecture 7 in this volume.

I indignantly* deny thinking that Darwin describes reality, or even just us human beings, better than anybody else. But his way of describing human beings, when supplemented (as Dewey and Dennett supplement it) by a story about cultural evolution, does give us a useful gimmick to prevent people over-dramatizing dichotomies, and thereby generating philosophical problems. By pressing an analogy between growing a new organ and developing a new vocabulary, between stories about how the elephant got his trunk and stories about how the West got particle physics, we neo-Darwinians hope to fill out the self-image sketched by the Romantic poets and partially filled in by Nietzsche and James.

In this image, our attitude toward the non-human is, as Heidegger lamented, one of Baconian mastery rather than one of respect. When we adopt that attitude, artistic and political judgments, rather than scientific and perceptual ones, become the focus of philosophers' attention. We get philosophers like Nietzsche, Ortega y Gasset, and Heidegger, rather than philosophers like Moore, Carnap, and Austin. This seems to me a great improvement.†

---

* In *TP* "indignantly" has been replaced by "stoutly." See p. 152.
† This last paragraph has been deleted from *TP*, p. 152.

Epilogue

EDUARDO MENDIETA

It is unfortunate and remarkable that these lectures have not been published together in English until now. Together they constitute Rorty's most comprehensive presentation of his own version of pragmatism, how he saw his relationship to classical pragmatism and contemporary neo-pragmatism, and how he sees the relationship between contemporary analytical philosophy and his catholic version of continental philosophy. Rorty conceived these lectures as the coherent articulation of his own philosophical views on where we have arrived after having taken the pragmatic turn in the philosophy of language. They develop and present a careful argument about how pragmatism is a form of both romantic polytheism and Enlightenment anti-authoritarianism in epistemology and ethics. The titles he gave to his lectures, their eventual published titles, whether in English or another language, and their retitling when some were republished in Rorty's *Philosophical Papers* weave a narrative about how Rorty saw the evolution and unfolding of his own version of pragmatism. They constitute an indispensable source for a deeper and broader understanding of Rorty's take on the distinctive philosophical tradition of American pragmatism, which he did so much to revive and make relevant to our contemporary U.S. culture and politics.

Richard Rorty delivered the Ferrater Mora Lectures at the University of Girona between June 25 and June 29, 1996. The lectures were given to fulfill, in part, the duties of the Ferrater Mora Chair of Contemporary Thought, which is a distinguished visiting chair established in 1989 "with the basic objective of organizing contemporary thinking courses led by eminent thinkers with internationally renowned prestige. It is a chair of thought—and not strictly philosophy—because it is open to the interdisciplinary teaching of personalities from different fields, including philosophy, science and arts, formal, experimental, historical and human. It is also a chair of contemporary thought in a very strict sense, because invited professors set out the main lines of their own thinking. From its creation to this day, the Chair has regular teaching periods every year: during the month of November and during the month of June. The first lecture was led by Professor Josep Ferrater Mora in November 1989."[1]

The chair was established at the University of Girona to honor Josep Ferrater Mora (1912–1991), who along with Miguel de Unamuno, José Ortega y Gasset, and Javier Zubiri, was one of Spain's most important philosophers of the twentieth century. Ferrater Mora lived in exile in France, Cuba, and Chile during the Franco dictatorship. In 1949, he settled in New York, where he taught at Bryn Mawr College until his retirement in 1981. He is the author of over thirty-five books, including the famous four-volume *Dictionary of Philosophy*, still considered by many as the best single-authored dictionary of philosophy. His work dealt with every major area of philosophy: ontology, history of philosophy, metaphysics, anthropology, the philosophy of history and culture, epistemology, logic, philosophy of science, and ethics.[2] He also wrote several novels and directed movies.

Some of the thinkers that have delivered Ferrater Mora Lectures include: Quentin Skinner, Judith Butler, Allen Buchanan, Boaventura de Sousa Santos, Lluís Duch, Jane Goodall, John Searle, Daniel Dennett, Giorgio Agamben, Jordi Savall, Zygmunt Bauman, John Urry, Agnès Varda, Peter Sloterdijk, Rafael Moneo, Josep Fontana, Gianni Vattimo, Joseph Stiglitz, Ernst Tugendhat, Michael Nyman, Agnes Heller, Seyla Benhabib, Peter Singer, Edgar Morin, Donald Davidson, Karl-Otto Apel, Noam Chomsky, and Eric Hobsbawn, to name only a handful of the distinguished lecturers.

Rorty's lectures were to be delivered over five days, two each day, the first in the morning and the second in the afternoon. Rorty chose "Anti-Authoritarianism in Epistemology and Ethics" as the title for the whole series. In a letter from January 23, 1996, to Josep-Maria Terricabras, who was the director of the Ferrater Mora Chair, Rorty writes that the ten lectures can be "labeled as follows":

1. Is *knowing* the most distinctively human capacity?
2. Knowledge from a Darwinian point of view
3. Pragmatism as romantic utilitarianism

4. The linguistification of pragmatism
5. A world of relations without substances
6. Cartesian skepticism and Cartesian dualism
7. Two misleading Kantian distinctions: justification vs. truth and sentiment vs. obligation
8. The anti-Kantian revolt in ethics
9. Brandom's neo-Wittgensteinian philosophy of language
10. McDowell on the relation between reason and nature.[3]

The flyer promoting the lectures has the same list of titles, and in addition, it announces that Robert Brandom, John McDowell, and Bjørn Ramberg are confirmed as participants. The lectures were first published in Catalan in 1998 and in Spanish in 2000,[4] but they were not published together in English, the language in which they were written, until now. In a headnote to each lecture, I have stated where, or whether, it has appeared in English. I have also annotated the differences among the lecture manuscript, the Spanish translation, and the English publication. The manuscript of the lectures, it must be noted, is remarkably finished, as if ready for the printers. It reads sequentially, coherently, developing slowly but surely its argument. When I first read the lectures in Spanish, I wondered why Rorty's most detailed and synthetic explication of his philosophy in its most developed and up-to-date presentation should not be in English. The manuscript I edited had handwritten corrections made by Rorty (whose hand I knew well from my work with his other manuscripts), many of which were included in the Spanish translation but sometimes not the published English versions of some of the lectures. I have incorporated Rorty's corrections and noted where the printed and manuscript versions diverge. Many sections of the manuscript were deleted when Rorty published them in English. I have flagged those deletions in my editorial notes.

Many of the lectures were published in English in at least two venues—first in an edited volume by a colleague, or as a journal article, and later in his *Philosophical Papers*. I have triangulated the differences among the manuscript, the Spanish publication, and the English publication by following, where available, the version in his *Philosophical Papers,* volumes 3 and 4, which I took to be the latest and most authoritative version.

A critical point of reference for appreciating the importance of the Ferrater Mora Lectures is another set of talks Rorty gave in 1993 at the Institut für die Wissenschaften vom Menschen (IWM) in Vienna and Paris which were published in German as *Hoffnung statt Erkenntnis: Eine Einführung in die pragmatische Philosophie* and in French as *L'Espoir au lie de savoir: Introduction au pragmatisme*.[5] The table of contents lists the three lectures as:

1. Wahrheit ohne Realitätsentsprechung
2. Eine Welt ohne Substanz oder Wesen
3. Ethik ohne allgemeine *Pflichten*

These lectures were published six years later in Rorty's *Philosophy and Social Hope*, part II, "Hope in Place of Knowledge: A Version of Pragmatism."[6] There the titles of the lectures, differently numbered, are:

2. Truth without Correspondence to Reality
3. A World without Substances or Essences
4. Ethics without Principles

It is to be noted that the themes of these three lectures converge with the themes in the first, third, fourth, and seventh Ferrater Mora lectures (Lectures 1, 3 & 4, and 7 in this volume). In fact, the third Vienna lecture is the same as the seventh Ferrater Mora lecture (Lecture 7). The theme of the second Vienna lecture is taken up in the fifth Ferrater Mora lecture (Lecture 5), which deals with what Rorty calls "pan-relationalism." In the preface to *Philosophy and Social Hope*, Rorty writes that he had wanted to expand and revise the Vienna and Paris lectures, but decided to publish them as he delivered them. These lectures offered what Rorty called "a fairly simple, albeit sketchy, outline of my own version of pragmatism. This version makes no pretence of being faithful to the thoughts of James or Dewey (much less Peirce, whom I barely mentioned). Rather, it offers my own, sometimes idiosyncratic, restatements of Jamesian and Deweyan themes." Rorty notes that the themes signaled in the titles of the lectures result from his conviction that James's and Dewey's principal accomplishments were of a critical and negative nature. They showed us to how dispense, how to "slough off," a lot of the baggage we inherited from the Platonic tradition. James and Dewey, according to Rorty, taught us to think "without" a lot of ideas that led us into blind alleys or subordinated us to an authority other than the authority of our social practices and vocabularies. As Rorty explains: "The title 'Hope in Place of Knowledge' is a way of suggesting that Plato and Aristotle were wrong in thinking that humankind's most distinctive and praiseworthy capacity is to know things as they really are—to penetrate behind appearance to reality. That claim saddles us with the unfortunate appearance-reality distinction and with metaphysics: a distinction, and a discipline, which pragmatism shows us how to do without . . . My candidate for the most distinctive and praiseworthy human capacity is our ability to trust and to cooperate with other people, and in particular to work together so as to improve the future."[7]

This is also a key theme of the Ferrater Mora Lectures, but now developed further, more fully, with incursions and engagements with several of the contemporary key thinkers with whom Rorty had frequent and intense dialogues: Brandom, Habermas, McDowell, and Williams. In these lectures, however, Rorty gives a different tonality to his earlier version of pragmatism. Now, if we are to nurture and develop our capacity to "trust" and "cooperate" with each other so as to improve the future, then we have to advance the Enlightenment and Reformation tasks of demystifying the authority of the God, Church, and even the idea of "human nature" as designed and dictated by an omnipotent and inscrutable creator. This is what pragmatism, as a form of both polytheism and romanticism, enables us to do, namely to embrace anti-authoritarianism in epistemology and ethics. This means thinking of truth as justification within a community of discourse and practices, and ethics as loyalty and sensitivity to the suffering of others. It could be said that the title Rorty gave to his Ferrater Mora Lectures, "Anti-Authoritarianism in Epistemology and Ethics," could be glossed as "Epistemology and Ethics without Non-human Authorities and without Universality." Rorty's version of pragmatism, then, is to see pragmatism as a form of extending, continuing, and "achieving the Enlightenment" as Brandom puts it in his Foreword to this volume.

Another important point of reference is Rorty's introduction to *Philosophie und die Zukunft: Essays*, a collection of his essays translated into German in 2000 and dedicated to Jürgen Habermas. There, Rorty writes: "Instead of metaphors of approximation to something that is not us, we should use metaphors of expansion of our becoming, metaphors of making ourselves more capable and better. As Newton replaced Aristotle, and Einstein Newton, we became more capable and better human beings, beings that could link more things, synthesize more data, register more phenomena, undertake and carry out more projects of self-transformation. To the extent that the religion of love has replaced the religion of the law, we have become beings with a greater capacity for sympathy. We are less inclined to exclude, to prohibit, and to ban, and more inclined to accept, to include the poor, or at least to be more tolerant."[8] There is a recurrent theme, then, between the Vienna and Paris lectures and the Ferrater Mora Lectures, which is a hallmark of Rorty's overall thinking, and that is the imperative to change our vocabularies. In the passage quoted just above, Rorty talks about the contrast between metaphors of approximation and unveiling, on the one hand, and expansion and inclusion, on the other. In the Ferrater Mora Lectures, Rorty uses the language of the contrast between metaphors of depth and height, or elevation, and those of breath and extent, between metaphors of verticality and of horizontality.

Anti-authoritarianism in epistemology and ethics is what we get when we let pragmatism carry forward the unfinished project of the Enlightenment, when we let the vocabularies of pragmatism help us slough off metaphors of depth and altitude for metaphors of expansion and inclusion, when we stop looking to and talking to a silent authority and start looking around us and talking to each other in more expansive and inspirational vocabularies. Anti-authoritarianism is what we get when all we have is the horizontality of human linguistic and social practices. Like no other text in Rorty's oeuvre, these lectures give us the most eloquent and elaborate articulation of his version of Enlightenment pragmatism.

The question, nonetheless, must be asked: why didn't Rorty publish these lectures together? A quick look at Rorty's itinerary in the 1990s may give us a clue.[9] The 1990s, arguably, were some of Rorty's busiest and most productive years. In 1991, he published volumes 1 and 2 of his philosophical papers: *Objectivity, Relativism and Truth* and *Essays on Heidegger and Others*. As I have noted, in 1993 he delivered a series of three lectures in Vienna and Paris, which appeared in German (as *Hoffnung statt Erkenntnis: Eine Einführung in die pragmatische Philosophie*) and French (*L'Espoir au lie de savoir: Introduction au pragmatisme*), later included in his 1999 collection *Philosophy and Social Hope*, which also gathered lectures intended for a general audience and occasional essays from the period 1989–1997. In 1993, Rorty also delivered the Oxford Amnesty Lecture, now included in volume 3 of his *Philosophical Papers*. In 1996 Rorty delivered these Ferrater Mora Lectures at the University of Girona, some of which appeared in 1998 in the third volume of his *Philosophical Papers, Truth and Progress,* and the fourth volume, *Philosophy as Cultural Politics.* In 1997 he delivered the William E. Massey Lectures in the History of American Civilization, which were published in 1998 as *Achieving Our Country: Leftist Thought in Twentieth Century America,* a book that continues to receive much attention. In the same year, he also delivered the Spinoza Lectures at the University of Amsterdam, which appeared under the title *Truth, Politics, and "Postmodernism."*[10] In 1998 he retired from the University of Virginia and moved to Stanford University, where he was Professor of Comparative Literature until 2005, when he retired for a second time. In 2000, he published a collection of his essays in German under the title *Philosophie und die Zukunft: Essays.*[11] In that same year, Robert B. Brandom's edited volume *Rorty and His Critics* appeared, with twelve essays by prominent philosophers and responses to each by Rorty. In 2001 Matthew Festenstein and Simon Thompson's edited volume *Richard Rorty: Critical Dialogues* was published, containing ten essays by critics, with responses by Rorty to each. Rorty's responses in these two latter volumes alone constituted a small book.

Rorty was, needless to say, extremely busy during these years. It could also be said that after *Contingency, Irony, and Solidarity* and *Achieving Our Country,* Rorty became preoccupied with political issues.[12] He began to write more frequently for the popular media, for newspapers, and for leftist journals and magazines. Against the background of the shift in the political mood of the nation, Rorty seems to have felt the pressing need to engage more directly with political issues and address citizens, rather than professional philosophers. An overview of the bibliography of Rorty's publications from the 1990s reveals a growing number of publications in popular media, although he continued to write and publish his professional philosophical papers.[13] In the turmoil and backlash occasioned by his critical stance toward what he called the "academic left," and his call for a return to "class politics," the urgency or even relevance of publishing a book with the title *Pragmatism as Anti-Authoritarianism* may have appeared moot, or less urgent. And, yet, against Rorty's own deferral to the inertia of books left in drawers to the criticism of mice, these lectures were his "final, mature version and vision of his path-breaking pragmatism."[14]

NOTES
INDEX

Notes

Foreword

1. J. L. Austin warned us that pretty much all philosophers' speech acts include both "the bit where you say it and the bit where you take it back." In this spirit, it should be acknowledged that it is not quite right to call this book "long-lost." Soon after Rorty wrote it, it was published in both Catalan and Spanish. What is true is that the volume has not, like his other books, ever been made available in the English in which he wrote it. Rorty did mine it for essays that were published elsewhere in English. What was lost—besides what remained unpublished in any form in English—was the unity of the book, the significance of reading it all together. He wrote the ten chapters that make up the body of this work to be presented to a single audience, in sequence, and as a unified whole, as his 1996 Ferrata Mora Lectures at the University of Girona, under the title "Anti-Authoritarianism in Epistemology and Ethics." It should also be noted that it was not technically his *last* book—even putting aside mere collections of essays. As he was preparing this book for publication, Rorty was working furiously on his next set of lectures, addressing quite a different topic, for quite a different audience. The result was subsequently published the next year as his last proper book, *Achieving Our Country: Leftist Thought in Twentieth-Century America* (Cambridge, MA: Harvard University Press, 1997). Rorty always planned to publish *Pragmatism as Anti-Authoritarianism* in English, but the press of circumstance in the busy last decade of his life pushed that project onto the back burner, where it languished. So his intent and aspiration has remained unfulfilled until now.

2. Jean-Jacques Rousseau, *The Social Contract,* 1762, Book I, section 8.

3. "Intellectual Autobiography," in *The Philosophy of Richard Rorty,* ed. Randall E. Auxier and Lewis Edwin Hahn, Library of Living Philosophers, 32 (Chicago: Open Court Publishing, 2007), 13.

4. With characteristic modesty and honesty, in the same essay Rorty offers a similar assessment of his earlier anthology *The Linguistic Turn* (Chicago: University of Chicago Press, 1967, rev. ed. 1992). In his substantial introduction, he pitches

202 Notes to Pages xxv–24

the book as addressing the urgent metaphilosophical question "What does it mean to say that philosophy is, or should become, the analysis of language?" In his assessment forty years later he says, "People stopped making that claim just about the time I published my collection, so *The Linguistic Turn* is now a quaint historical artifact . . . I learned quite a bit from . . . trying to adjudicate the issues between 'ideal language philosophy' (Carnap, Quine) and 'ordinary language philosophy' (Austin, Wittgenstein). These two terms were, however, dropping out of use just about the time *The Linguistic Turn* was published" (12).

5. Here again we are reminded of the extent to which Rorty uses specifically Kantian conceptual raw materials in both the earlier and the later forms of his criticism of Enlightenment epistemology. The arguments of *PMN* turn to a substantial extent on the Kantian distinction between norms and causes, the *quid juris* and the *quid facti*. (It is because he failed to separate these, Kant teaches us, that "the celebrated Mr. Locke" fails to produce a real epistemology, substituting for it "a mere physiology of the Understanding.") I mentioned above that Rorty depends on distinguishing the causal role of reality as constraining us via the consequences of our doings (good) from its normative role as authority (bad). According to the story I have told here, at the heart of *Pragmatism as Anti-Authoritarianism* is the application of this insight of Kant into the normative character of intentionality generally, as it applies specifically to Enlightenment epistemology's master-concept, *representation*.

1. Pragmatism and Religion

1. See Michael Williams, *Unnatural Doubts* (Oxford: Blackwell, 1991), 116: "we can characterize foundationalism as the view that our beliefs, simply in virtue of certain elements in their contents, stand in *natural epistemological relations* and thus fall into *natural epistemological kinds.*"

2. Pragmatists can, of course, make a distinction between hope and knowledge in cases where knowledge of causal mechanisms is available. The quack hopes, but the medical scientist knows, that the pills will cure. But in other cases, such as marriage, the distinction often cannot usefully be drawn. Does the groom know, or merely hope, that he is marrying the right person? Either description will explain his actions equally well.

2. Pragmatism as Romantic Polytheism

Full bibliographical references have been added to the endnotes. Ed.

1. René Berthelot, *Un romantisme utilitaire: Etude sur le mouvement pragmatiste*, vol. 1 (Paris: F. Alcan, 1911), vol. 1, 62–63.

2. Berthelot also looked back behind Darwin and Spencer to Hume, whom he regarded as "la transition entre la psychologie utilitaire et intellectualiste d'Helvétius

et la psychologie vitaliste de l'instinct que nous rencontrons chez les Ecossais," and to Lamarck who was "la transition entre cette conception vitaliste de la biologie et ce qu'on peut appeler l'utilitarisme mécanique de Darwin" (Berthelot, *Un romantisme utilitaire*, vol. 1, 85).

3. Berthelot, *Un romantisme utilitaire*, vol. 1, 128.

4. Friedrich Nietzsche, *The Gay Science*, section 354.

5. M. H. Abrams, *The Mirror and the Lamp* (New York: Oxford University Press, 1953), 334–335.

6. Abrams, *The Mirror and the Lamp*, quoting a letter to Bulwer-Lytton, 333.

7. Abrams, *The Mirror and the Lamp*, 335.

8. William James, *Varieties of Religious Experience* (Cambridge, MA: Harvard University Press, 1985), 384.

9. John Dewey, "A Common Faith," in Dewey, *Later Works, 1925–1953*, vol. 9: *1933–1934*, ed. Jo Ann Boydston (Carbondale: Southern Illinois University Press, 1986), 36.

10. See my "Religious Faith, Intellectual Responsibility, and Romance," in *The Cambridge Companion to William James*, ed. Ruth-Anna Putnam, 84–102 (Cambridge: Cambridge University Press, 1997).

11. Alan Ryan, *John Dewey and the High Tide of American Liberalism* (New York: Norton, 1995), 102.

12. John Dewey, "Christianity and Democracy" (March 27, 1892), in Dewey, *Early Works, 1882–1898*, vol. 4: *1893–1894*, ed. Jo Ann Boydston (Carbondale: Southern Illinois University Press, 1971), 6–7.

13. John Dewey, "Maeterlinck's Philosophy of Life," in Dewey, *The Middle Works, 1899–1924*, vol. 6: *1910–1911*, ed. Jo Ann Boydston, 123–135 (Carbondale: Southern Illinois University Press, 1978), 135. Dewey says that Emerson, Whitman, and Maeterlinck are the only three to have grasped this fact about democracy.

14. Nietzsche, *The Gay Science*, section 143. "Der Monotheismus ... diese starre Konsequenz der Lehre von einem Normalmenschen—also der Glaube an einem Normalgott, neben dem es nur noch falsche Luegengoetter gibt—war vielleicht die groessste Gefahr der bisherigen Menschheit."

15. John Dewey, *Reconstruction in Philosophy*, in Dewey, *The Middle Works, 1899–1924*, vol. 12: *1920*, ed. Jo Ann Boydston (Carbondale: Southern Illinois University Press, 1982), 186.

16. See Dewey, "A Common Faith," 36. See also Dewey, "Poetry and Philosophy" (1890), in Dewey, *Early Works, 1882–1898*, vol. 3: *1889–1892*, ed. Jo Ann Boydston, 110–124 (Carbondale: Southern Illinois University Press, 1969). In the latter Dewey says that "the source of regret which expires from Arnold's lines is his consciousness of a twofold isolation of man—his isolation from nature, his isolation from fellow-man" (115).

17. The passage cited is in John Dewey, "Creative Democracy—The Task Before Us" (1939), in Dewey, *Later Works, 1925–1953*, vol. 14: *1939–1941*, ed. Jo Ann Boydston (Carbondale: Southern Illinois University Press, 1988), 229. Dewey says "I state briefly the democratic faith in the formal terms of a philosophic position."

18. John Dewey, "Christianity and Democracy," 5.

19. Dewey, *Reconstruction in Philosophy*, 201.

20. Ryan, *John Dewey and the High Tide of American Liberalism*, 274.

21. Ryan, *John Dewey and the High Tide of American Liberalism*, 102.

22. Ryan, *John Dewey and the High Tide of American Liberalism*, 361.

3 & 4. Universality and Truth

The endnotes have incorporated the editorial apparatus in Rorty, "Universality and Truth," in *Rorty and His Critics*, ed. Robert Brandom, 1–30 (Malden, MA: Blackwell, 2000) (hereafter *RHC*). Ed.

1. This paper was prepared for presentation to a colloquium held at Cerisy-la-Salle in 1993, and a revised version was read at the University of Girona in 1996. A shortened version was published in French as "Les assertions expriment-elles des prétentions à une validité universelle?" in *La Modernité en Questions: de Richard Rorty á Jürgen Habermas*, ed. Françoise Gaillard, Jacques Poulain, and Richard Shusterman (Paris: Editions de Cerf, 1993). Another, also shortened, version, appeared as "Sind Aussagen universelle Geltungsansprüche?" *Deutsche Zeitschrift für Philosophie* 42, no. 6 (1994): 975–988. This is the first appearance of the English original of the full text.

2. Nietzsche is the paradigm irrationalist because he had no interest whatever in democracy, and because he stoutly resisted all three premises. James is thought to be more confused than vicious because, although committed to democracy, he was not willing to affirm two of the premises: he admitted that all human beings desire truth, but he thought the claim that truth is correspondence to reality unintelligible, and he toyed with the claim that, since reality is malleable, truth is Many. Habermas sets his face firmly against the latter idea, even though he agrees with James that we have to give up the correspondence theory of truth. So Habermas is condemned as an irrationalist only by die-hards who claim that doubts about truth as correspondence are doubts about the existence, or at least the unity, of Truth. Straussians, and even analytic philosophers such as Searle, claim that you need all three premises: to give up any of them is to put yourself on a slippery slope, to risk ending up agreeing with Nietzsche.

3. Readers of my paper "Solidarity or Objectivity?" will recognize this line of argument as a variant on my earlier claim that we need to restate our intellectual ambitions in terms of our relations to other human beings, rather than in terms of

our relation to non-human reality. As I say below, that claim is one with which Apel and Habermas are inclined to agree, even though they think my way of carrying through on this effort goes too far.

4. The relevance of the sublime to the political is, of course, a point of dispute between Lacanians like Žižek and their opponents. It would take more than a footnote to deal with their arguments. I have tried to offer some preliminary backup for my claim of irrelevance in the pages of my *Contingency, Irony and Solidarity* (Cambridge: Cambridge University Press, 1989), at which I discuss the difference between the private pursuit of sublimity and the public search for a beautiful reconciliation of conflicting interests. In the present context, perhaps it is enough to remark that I agree with Habermas that Foucault's exaltation of a "sublime," inexpressible, impossible kind of freedom—a kind which was *not* constituted by power—made it impossible for him to recognize the achievements of liberal reformers and thus to engage in serious political reflection on the possibilities open to welfare-state democracies. See Jürgen Habermas, *The Philosophical Discourse of Modernity*, trans. Frederick G. Lawrence (Cambridge, MA: MIT Press, 1987), 290–291.

5. If you linguistify reason by saying, with Sellars and Davidson, that there are no non-linguistic beliefs and desires, you automatically socialize it. Sellars and Davidson would heartily agree with Habermas that "There is no pure reason that might don linguistic clothing only in the second place. Reason is by its very nature incarnated in contexts of communicative action and in structures of the lifeworld" (Habermas, *Philosophical Discourse of Modernity*, 322).

6. Habermas, *Philosophical Discourse*, 322–323.

7. I replied to Putnam's criticism of my view in Hilary Putnam, "Why Reason Can't Be Naturalized," in *Philosophical Papers*, vol. 3: *Realism and Reason*, 229–247 (Cambridge: Cambridge University Press, 1983) in my "Solidarity or Objectivity," reprinted in my *Philosophical Papers*, vol. 1: *Objectivity, Relativism and Truth* (Cambridge: Cambridge University Press, 1991), and have replied to Putnam's further criticisms of this view in Putnam, *Realism with a Human Face* (Cambridge, MA: Harvard University Press, 1990) in Rorty, "Putnam and Relativist Menace," *Journal of Philosophy* 90, no. 9 (1993): 443–461.

8. Habermas, *Philosophical Discourse*, 311. At page 312 Habermas claims that most philosophy of language outside the Austin-Searle "speech-act" tradition, and in particular Donald Davidson's "truth-condition semantics," embodies the typically logocentric "fixation on the fact-mirroring function of language." I think that there is an important strain in recent philosophy of language which is not guilty of this charge, and that Davidson's later work is a good example of freedom from this fixation. See, for example, Davidson's doctrine of "triangulation" in his "The Structure and Content of Truth," a doctrine which helps explain why fact-stating and communicating cannot be separated. I discuss this doctrine

below. (In my view, accepting Davidson's point makes it unnecessary to postulate what Habermas calls "'worlds' analogous to the world of facts . . . for legitimately regulated interpersonal relationships and for attributable subjective experiences" (Habermas, *Philosophical Discourse*, 313). But this disagreement is a side-issue which does not need to be explored further in the present context.)

9. Habermas, *Philosophical Discourse*, 296.

10. As I read Dewey, he would sympathize with Castoriadis's emphasis on imagination, rather than reason, as the engine of moral progress.

11. Consider Habermas's criticism of Castoriadis: "one cannot see how this *demiurgic setting-in-action* of historical truths could be transposed into the *revolutionary project* proper to the practice of consciously acting, autonomous, self-realizing individuals" (Habermas, *Philosophical Discourse*, 318). My reaction to this comment is that the history of the United States of America shows how this transposition can be achieved. Apel and Habermas tend to think of the American Revolution as firmly grounded in the sort of universal-validity-claiming principles of which they approve, and which Jefferson spelled out in the Declaration of Independence. See Karl-Otto Apel, "Zuruck zur Normalität?" in *Zerstörung des moralischen Selbstbewusstseins, Chance oder Gefährdung?: praktische Philosophie in Deutschland nach dem Nationalsozialismus*, ed. Forum für Philosophie Bad Homburg (Frankfurt am Main: Suhrkamp, 1988), 117). I should rejoin that the Founding Fathers were just the sort of demiurges whom Castoriadis has in mind when he talks about "the institution of the social imaginary." What we now think of as "the American people," a community of "consciously acting, autonomous, self-realizing individuals" devoted to those principles, slowly came into existence in the course of the (very gradual—ask any African-American) process of living up to the Founders' imaginations. So when Habermas goes on to criticize Castoriadis for acknowledging "no reason for revolutionizing reified society except the existentialist resolve 'because we will it,'" and asks "who this 'we' of the radical willing might be," I think it would be fair to answer that in 1776 the relevant "we" was not the American people but Jefferson and his some of his equally imaginative friends. When Habermas says that "Castoriadis ends where Simmel began: in *Lebensphilosophie*," I can only say that I am happy to join Castoriadis there.

12. See, on this point, the opening pages of my "Pragmatism, Davidson and Truth," in *Philosophical Papers*, vol. 1: *Objectivity, Relativism and Truth*. What I there call the "endorsing" and the "disquotational" uses of the "true" can easily be paraphrased in terms which do not include "true."

13. Being a coherentist in this sense does not necessarily mean having a coherence theory of truth. Davidson's repudiation of the latter label for his view, a label he had previously accepted, is a corollary of his claim that there can be no definition of the term "true-in-L" for variable L. Davidson's present view, with which I have come to agree, is that "We should not say that truth is correspon-

dence, coherence, warranted assertibility, ideally justified assertibility, what is accepted in the conversation of the right people, what science will end up maintaining, what explains the convergence on single theories in science, or the success of our ordinary beliefs. To the extent that realism and antirealism depend on one or another of these views of truth we should refuse to endorse either." Donald Davidson, "The Structure and Content of Truth," *Journal of Philosophy* 87, no. 6 (1990): 279–328, 309.

14. Davidson too thinks that there is more to be said, but the sort of thing he wants to say is, as far as I can see, irrelevant to politics. In what follows I draw upon Davidson, but I postpone discussion of the claim, at p. 326 of "The Structure and Content of Truth," that "the conceptual underpinning of interpretation is a theory of truth," in a sense of "theory of truth" in which there is one such theory per language. This claim seems to me distinct from the claim, which I invoke below, that "the ultimate source of both objectivity and communication" is what Davidson calls "triangulation." I am not sure why, apart from respect for the memory of Tarski, a theory that codifies the results of such triangulation should be described as a theory of *truth*, rather than of the behavior of a certain group of human beings.

15. Putnam has sometimes repudiated this thesis of convergence (see Putnam, *Realism with a Human Face*, 171, on Bernard Williams), but (as I argue in my "Putnam and the Relativist Menace"), I do not think that he can reconcile this repudiation with his notion of "ideal assertibility." As I see it, the only sense in which Truth is One is that, if the process of developing new theories and new vocabularies is choked off, and there is an agreement on the aims to be fulfilled by a belief—that is, on the needs to be fulfilled by the actions dictated by that belief—then a consensus will develop about which of a finite list of candidates is to be adopted. This sociological generalization, which is subject to lots of obvious qualifications, should not be confused with a metaphysical principle. The trouble with the idea of convergence at the end of inquiry, as many critics (notably Michael Williams) have pointed out, is that it is hard to imagine a time at which it would seem desirable to cease developing new theories and new vocabularies. As Davidson has remarked, Putnam's "naturalistic fallacy" argument applies as much to his "ideal acceptability" theory of truth as to any other theory of truth.

16. "Communicative reason stretches across the entire spectrum of validity claims: the claims to propositional truth, subjective, sincerity and normative rightness." Jürgen Habermas, *Between Facts and Norms*, trans. William Rehg (Cambridge, MA: MIT Press, 1996), 5.

17. Habermas, *Between Facts and Norms*, 6.

18. Habermas, *Between Facts and Norms*, 8.

19. Habermas, *Between Facts and Norms*, 8.

20. Habermas, *Between Facts and Norms*, 15.

21. For Quinean and David Lewis–like reasons, I should prefer the term "practices" to "conventions," but I shall treat the two as synonymous here.

22. Habermas, *Between Facts and Norms*, 16.

23. I am not sure whether, when I do this, Apel and Habermas would still view me as *arguing*, or as having abandoned argument and fallen back on strategic sensitivity training.

24. In *RHC* this note starts differently: "Duelists used to say some people were not *satisfaktionsfähig*: one did not have to accept if challenged by such people." Ed. The Austrian *Burschenschaften* decided that people of Jewish blood, even though they were university students or held the Emperor's commission, were not *satisfaktionsfähig*. So one did not have to accept if these people challenged you to a duel. We need some notion which is the analogue of *nicht satisfaktionsfähig* for requests for justification, invitations to participate in dialogue. Joachim Schulte has suggested *nicht rechtfertigungsempfänglich* to me, which sounds about right. Whatever the right term is, my point is that the sort of exclusivist bigot I have in mind does not see his or her claim as requiring justification to the wrong sort of people. But the bigot is not the only person who needs some such notion as *Rechtfertigungsempfänglichkeit*. None of us take all audiences seriously; we all reject requests for justification from some audiences as a waste of time. (Consider the physician refusing to justify her procedure to Christian Scientists, or to Chinese physicians who rely on acupuncture and moxibustion.) The big difference between us and the bigot, as I say below, is that he thinks such non-discursive matters as racial descent matter in this context, whereas we think only beliefs and desires matter.

25. The bigot may not know how to do this, but then the local conventions which Habermas and I share suggest that we philosophers should step in and help him out—help him construct meanings for these terms which will build in his exclusivist view, just as Habermas's and my inclusivist view is built into our use of those terms.

26. The point of talking about universal validity rather than about truth seems to be to avoid the question of whether ethical and aesthetic judgments have a truth-value. Doubt that they do arises only among representationalists, people who think that there has to be an object to "make" true judgments true. Non-representationalists like Davidson and I, and even quasi-representationalists like Putnam, are perfectly content to think that "Love is better than hate" is as good a candidate for truth-value as "Energy always equals mass times the square of the speed of light."

27. Albrecht Wellmer, *Endgames: The Irreconcilable Nature of Modernity: Essays and Lectures*, trans. David Midgley (Cambridge, MA: MIT Press, 1998), 150.

28. Wellmer, *Endgames*, 151.

29. Wellmer, *Endgames*, 142.

30. Consider a lawyer saying to his clients, the officers of a multi-national corporation, "My brief relies, I'm afraid, on a funny little kink in the *Code Napoleon*.

So though we clearly have a winning case in France, the Ivory Coast, and Louisiana, I can't do anything for you in the courts of, for example, Britain, Germany, Ghana, or Massachusetts." His clients consult another, better, lawyer who says "I can transcend *that;* I've got an argument that will work in the courts of every country except Japan and Brunei."

31. This rhetorical question might be answered by saying: it is important in mathematics. There we say not only that all the Euclidean triangles so far drawn have interior angles which sum to 180 degrees, but that this is the case for all possible triangles. But, as Wittgenstein reminds us in *Remarks on the Foundations of Mathematics,* the cash-value of this claim to have surveyed the realm of possibility is just that one will not try to justify certain claims to certain people: you don't discuss Euclidean geometry with people who keep on trying to square the circle and double the cube. Once, with Quine and the later Wittgenstein, we drop the analytic-synthetic and language-fact distinctions, we cannot be as comfortable with the distinction between "all possible *X*'s" and "all *X*'s envisaged so far" as we once were.

32. Wellmer, *Endgames,* 138.

33. Wellmer, *Endgames,* 137–138.

34. See Rorty, "Is Truth a Goal of Inquiry? Donald Davidson vs. Crispin Wright," in *Philosophical Papers,* vol. 3: *Truth and Progress,* 19–42 (Cambridge: Cambridge University Press, 1998).

35. This metaphor of being nudged toward truths by objects sounds less plausible in ethics and aesthetics than in physics. That is why representationalists are often "anti-realists" in respect to the former, and why they often reserve the notion of truth-making for elementary particles, which seem more plausible candidates for nudgers than do moral or aesthetic values.

36. Wellmer, *Endgames,* 148.

37. This is the point made in Donald Davidson, "On the Very Idea of a Conceptual Scheme" (1974), in Davidson, *Inquiries into Truth and Interpretation,* 2nd ed. (Oxford: Clarendon, 2001).

38. Wellmer, *Endgames,* 150.

39. Wellmer, *Endgames,* 152.

40. Wellmer, *Endgames,* 152.

41. Wellmer, *Endgames,* 152.

42. I develop this point at some length in "Putnam and the Relativist Menace." There I argue that Putnam and I both have the same idea of what counts as a good argument—namely, one which would satisfy an audience of wet liberals like ourselves—and that my view, though unlike his in being explicitly ethnocentric, is no more "relativistic" than his.

43. I tend to agree with Vincent Descombes (in the final chapter of his *The Barometer of Modern Reason: On the Philosophies of Current Events,* trans. Stephen Adam Schwartz [New York: Oxford University Press, 1993]) that Weber's distinction

is an invidious and self-serving use of the term "rational." But I should admit that if Chomsky, Kohlberg, and the rest survive current criticism, their claims would suggest that Weber had a point.

44. It is perhaps worth remarking that one of the presuppositions of communication which Habermas mentions—the ascription of identical meanings to expressions—is endangered by Davidson's argument in "A Nice Derangement of Epitaphs" that linguistic competence can be had without such ascription, that holistic strategies of interpretation dictated by the principle of charity render this ascription unnecessary. Davidson's argument that there is no such thing as language-mastery in the sense of the internalization of a set of conventions about what means what chimes with recent "connectionist" criticism of MIT "cognitivism" and thus of Chomsky's universalism. Perhaps what Habermas means by "ascription of identical meanings" is simply what Davidson means by "being charitable," but if so then, since charity is not optional, neither is such ascription. It is automatic, and nobody could be convicted of failing to abide by it. So it cannot form the basis for a charge of performative self-contradiction. Donald Davidson, "A Nice Derangement of Epitaphs" (1986), in Davidson, *Truth, Language, and History* (Oxford: Clarendon, 2005).

45. The "MIT" notion, associated with Chomsky and Fodor, of "communicative competence" is gradually being displaced, within the field of artificial intelligence, by the "connectionist" view favored by those who see the brain as containing no hard-wired flow-charts of the sort constructed by "cognitivist" programmers. Connectionists urge that the only biologically universal structures to be found in the brain are ones which cannot be described in terms of flow-charts labeled with the names of "natural kinds" of things and words. So the notion of "communicative competence," as something common to all human linguistic communities, drops out in favor of the notion of "enough neural connections to permit the organism to be programmed into a language-user."

46. Davidson, "The Structure and Content of Truth," 325.

47. Jürgen Habermas, *Postmetaphysical Thinking: Philosophical Essays,* trans. William Mark Hohengarten (Cambridge, MA: MIT Press, 1992), 50.

48. Habermas, *Postmetaphysical Thinking,* 116–117.

49. Michael Kelly, "MacIntyre, Habermas and Philosophical Ethics," in *Hermeneutics and Critical Theory in Ethics and Politics,* ed. Michael Kelly (Cambridge, MA: MIT Press, 1990).

50. Habermas, *Postmetaphysical Thinking,* 117.

51. Habermas, *Postmetaphysical Thinking,* 47.

52. Habermas, *Postmetaphysical Thinking,* 103.

53. Habermas, *Postmetaphysical Thinking,* 89–90.

54. Habermas, *Postmetaphysical Thinking,* 116.

55. Habermas, *Postmetaphysical Thinking,* 117.

56. Habermas, *Postmetaphysical Thinking*, 138.

57. Habermas, *Postmetaphysical Thinking*, 138.

58. These last three quotations are from Habermas, *Postmetaphysical Thinking*, 138–139. The passage from Putnam is from his essay "Why Reason Can't Be Naturalized," in Putnam, *Reason, Truth and History* (Cambridge: Cambridge University Press, 1981), 228.

59. Habermas, *Postmetaphysical Thinking*, 138.

60. One might try to justify this rule by deriving it from the rule that reason alone should have force. If that means "argument alone should have force," then you have to find some sense in which arguments based on the authority of the Christian Scriptures are not really arguments. But does the grammar of concepts like "reason" really tell you that reason gets distorted when you invoke the authority of the Bible? If so, does it also get distorted by a *Bildungsroman* which arouses the reader's pity and sympathy by telling her what it's like to find out, to your horror, that you can only love members of your own sex?

61. Habermas, *The Philosophical Discourse of Modernity*, 296.

62. Consider Vasari on the artistic movement that began with Giotto as an analogue of Hegel on the inclusivist movements which started when Greek philosophy joined up with Christian egalitarianism. Modern art has trained us to see the former movement as optional, but not something we should want to give up now that we have got it. I take post-Nietzschean philosophy to have helped us see that the latter movement was optional, even though not something we have any reason to give up. "Optional" here contrasts with "destined," in a wide sense of "destined" which covers Habermas's notion about the universalistic tendency of phylogenetic development.

63. See Habermas, *Moral Consciousness and Communicative Action*, trans. Christian Lenhardt and Shierry Weber Nicholson (Cambridge, MA: MIT Press, 1990), 206: "In contrast to the neo-Aristotelian position, discourse ethics is emphatically opposed to going back to a stage of philosophical thought before Kant." The context makes clear that Habermas means that it would be wrong to give up on the morality-prudence distinction which Kant made and Aristotle did not.

64. Dewey could of course have accepted Goodman's distinction between nomological necessity and universal generalizations which are merely accidental, but that is because Goodman makes nomologicality not a feature of the universe but of the coherence of our descriptive vocabulary. (See, on this point, Davidson's comment on Goodman: Donald Davidson, "Emeroses by Other Names," *Journal of Philosophy* 63, no. 24 [1966]: 778–780.) Nomological necessity holds of things under descriptions, not, as for Aristotle, of things *kath' auto*.

65. Habermas, *Moral Consciousness and Communicative Action*, 118.

66. Baier describes Hume as "the woman's moral philosopher" because his treatment of morals facilitates her suggestion that we replace "obligation" by

"appropriate trust" as the basic moral notion. In "Human Rights, Rationality and Sentimentality," reprinted in Rorty, *Truth and Progress*, 167–185, I discuss Baier's suggestion in connection with my claim (reiterated in this paper) that we should try to create, rather than to presuppose, universality.

67. Another aspect of these two differing stories about maturation is the different attitudes they encourage to the quarrel between Socrates and the Sophists, and more generally to the distinction between *argument* and the modes of persuasion which I have described as "educative" in the previous section. Apel says that one of the many things wrong with the sort of view common to Gadamer, Rorty, and Derrida is these men's insouciance about the "Unterschied zwischen dem *argumentativen Diskurs* und, anderseits, dem *"Diskurs"* im Sinne von *Verhandlungen, Propaganda,* oder auch von *poetischer Fiktion* nicht mehr zu erkennen bzw. anzuerkennen vermoegen." Karl-Otto Apel, *Diskurs und Verantwortung: das Problem des Übergangs zur postkonventionellen Moral* (Frankfurt am Main: Suhrkamp, 1988), 353n. Apel goes on to say that that attitude marks "the end of philosophy." It seems to me that it marks a stage in the further maturation of philosophy—a stage away from the power-worship involved in the idea that there is a power called "reason" which will come to your aid if you follow Socrates's example and make your definitions and premises explicit. As a Deweyan tells the story, the idea of philosophy as a *strenge Wissenschaft,* as a search for knowledge, is itself a symptom of immaturity; the Sophists were not wholly in the wrong. The reciprocal accusations of immaturity to which Apel and I tempt one another can easily seem cheap and empty, but they do express heartfelt convictions on both sides, convictions about what utopia looks like, and hence about what progress toward utopia requires.

5. Pan-Relationalism

Full bibliographical references have been added to the endnotes. Ed.

1. It is useful to think of this Whiteheadian criticism of Aristotle (a criticism found in other early twentieth-century philosophers—e.g., Peirce and Russell—who tried to formulate a non-subject-predicate logic) as paralleling Derrida's criticism of logocentrism. Derrida's picture of words as nodes in an infinitely flexible web of relationships to other words is obviously reminiscent of Whitehead's account, in his *Process and Reality,* of actual occasions as constituted by relations to all other actual occasions. My hunch is that the twentieth century will be seen, by historians of philosophy, as the period in which a kind of neo-Leibnizian pan-relationalism was developed in various different idioms—a pan-relationalism which restates Leibniz's idea that each monad is nothing but all the other monads seen from a certain perspective, each substance nothing but its relations to all the other substances.

2. See Peirce's review of Fraser's edition of Berkeley: Charles S. Peirce, [Fraser's *The Works of George Berkeley*], *North American Review* 113 (1871): 449–472;

reprinted in *Collected Papers of Charles Sanders Peirce*, vol. 8: *Reviews, Correspondence, and Bibliography*, ed. A. W. Burks (Cambridge, MA: Harvard University Press, 1958), especially pp. 33–34 (section 8.33). See also vol. 6: *Scientific Metaphysics*, ed. Charles Hartshorne and Paul Weiss, p. 328 (section 6.482).

3. The properties usually called "non-relational" (e.g., "red," as opposed to "on the left-hand side") are treated by psychological nominalists as properties signified by predicates which are, for some purpose or another, being treated as primitive. But the primitiveness of a predicate is not intrinsic to the predicate; it is relative to a way of teaching, or otherwise exhibiting, a use of the predicate. The putative non-relationality of a property signified by a predicate is relative to a certain way of describing a certain range of objects having the predicate. It is not an intrinsic feature of the property. One way of putting the lesson taught by both Saussure and Wittgenstein is to say that no predicate is intrinsically primitive. One way of putting the corollary drawn by Derrida is that every predicate denotes a property—that there is no point in trying to distinguish between referring and non-referring predicates (except, again, for some particular practical purpose, as when one uses "but there are no witches" as an abbreviation for all the reasons it is unprofitable to conduct witch-hunts).

For a clear and strong statement of the contrasting, anti-nominalist, anti-pragmatist view, see John Searle, *The Rediscovery of the Mind* (Cambridge, MA: MIT Press, 1992), 211. The contrast which Searle draws there between intrinsic features of the world such as molecules and observer-relative features such as being a nice day for a picnic is, for pragmatists, merely a preference for the human purposes served by physicists over those served by picnickers.

4. On the fundamental importance of this latter Wittgensteinian point, see Barry Allen, *Truth in Philosophy* (Cambridge, MA: Harvard University Press, 1993).

5. For examples of the sort of glorification of elementary particles which I have in mind, see the passage from Searle, *Rediscovery of the Mind*, 211; and also David Lewis, "Putnam's Paradox," *Australasian Journal of Philosophy* 62, no. 3 (1983): 221–236. I discuss Lewis's article briefly at pp. 7ff. of my *Philosophical Papers*, vol. 1: *Objectivity, Relativism and Truth* (Cambridge: Cambridge University Press, 1991).

6. This is certainly its appeal to Bernard Williams. See *Ethics and the Limits of Philosophy* (Cambridge, MA: Harvard University Press, 1986), ch. 8, "Knowledge, Science, Convergence"; and my criticism of Williams in "Is Natural Science a Natural Kind?" included in my *Philosophical Papers*, vol. 1: *Objectivity, Relativism and Truth*, 46–62.

7. As I have said elsewhere, I think that Derrida is importantly right in seeing Heideggerian renunciation as just one more twist on the attempt to affiliate oneself with power.

8. The best account of the contrast between propositions which are candidates and those which are not is William James's discussion of the difference between

"live" and "dead" intellectual options in his famous essay "The Will to Believe" (1896), in *The Will to Believe, and Other Essays in Popular Philosophy* (New York: Longmans, Green, 1897).

9. This analogy should not be construed as an "aesthetic" theory of the nature of philosophy, any more than as a "philosophical" theory of the nature of painting. Pragmatists do not have much use for Kant's distinctions between the cognitive, the moral, and the aesthetic. I am not trying to say that philosophy is less "cognitive" than had been thought, but merely to point to the difference between situations in which there is sufficient agreement about ends to make possible fruitful argument about alternative means to those ends, and situations in which there is not. But this difference is of course not sharp. A continuous spectrum runs between unquestioning devotion to common ends and inability to understand how one's interlocutor could be so crazy as not to share one's own ends.

10. See Derrida's discussion of the need to talk about language and of the need to guard against its becoming one more buzzword in Jacques Derrida, *De la grammatologie* (Paris: Minuit, 1967), 15.

11. I have tried to make this point at some length at pp. 257–266 of my *Philosophy and the Mirror of Nature* (Princeton, NJ: Princeton University Press, 1979).

12. See Wilfrid Sellars, *Science and Metaphysics* (London: Routledge, 1969); and Donald Davidson, "Rational Animals," in *Actions and Events: Perspectives on the Philosophy of Donald Davidson*, ed. Ernest LePore, 473–480 (Oxford: Blackwell, 1985).

13. John Dewey, *Reconstruction in Philosophy*, in Dewey, *The Middle Works, 1899–1924*, vol. 12: *1920*, ed. Jo Ann Boydston (Carbondale: Southern Illinois University Press, 1982), 94.

14. See Manfred Frank, *What Is Neostructuralism?* (Minneapolis: University of Minnesota Press, 1989), 217: "the *linguistic turn* consists in the transferal of the philosophical paradigm of consciousness onto that of the sign." Frank's book is very valuable in giving a sense of the continuity between Herder and Humboldt's eighteenth-century view of language and the view common to Derrida and Wittgenstein. In particular, Frank's comparison of Herder's claim that "Our reason is formed only *through fictions*" with Nietzsche's more famous claim that language is "a mobile army of metaphors, metonymies, anthropomorphisms" (in Frank, *What Is Neostructuralism*, 129) makes one realize that anti-essentialism is at least as old as the suggestion that there is no Adamic language, and that different languages, including our own, serve different social needs. Reading Frank leads one to wonder whether, if Hegel had followed Herder's lead, and thus had been led to talk more about social needs and less about Absolute Knowledge, Western philosophy might not have saved itself a century of nervous shuffling.

6. Against Depth

Full bibliographical references have been added to the endnotes. Ed.

1. Bernard Williams, *Shame and Necessity* (Berkeley: University of California Press, 1993), 163.
2. Hilary Putnam, *Renewing Philosophy* (Cambridge, MA: Harvard University Press, 1992), 187.
3. Thomas Nagel, *The View from Nowhere* (New York: Oxford University Press, 1986), 105–106.
4. Nagel, *The View from Nowhere*, 9.
5. Nagel, *The View from Nowhere*, 11–12.
6. Nagel, *The View from Nowhere*, 11.
7. Nagel, *The View from Nowhere*, 11–12.
8. Nagel, *The View from Nowhere*, 24.
9. Nagel, *The View from Nowhere*, 107.
10. Nagel, *The View from Nowhere*, 107.
11. Nagel, *The View from Nowhere*, 109.
12. Dennett does not think he is quite as much a pragmatist as I claim he is. See my "Holism, Intentionality, and the Ambition of Transcendence," in *Dennett and His Critics: Demystifying Mind*, ed. Bo Dahlbom, 184–202 (Oxford: Blackwell, 1993); and Dennett's reply in the same volume.
13. Daniel Dennett, *Consciousness Explained* (Boston: Little Brown, 1991), 399–400.
14. Dennett, *Consciousness Explained*, 381.
15. Thomas Metzinger, ed., *Conscious Experience* (Paderborn: Schöningh, 1995), 27. Compare Metzinger's claim that "the subject of consciousness has been accepted even by the best analytical thinkers as a serious and promising area of theory formation" (26). But note that Dennett's "Multiple Drafts" theory cannot count as a theory formed to solve the problem in question, because it offers itself as an alternative to the existence of quality rather than as an explanation of them.
16. Peter Bieri, "Why Is Consciousness Puzzling?" in *Conscious Experience*, ed. Metzinger, 54.
17. Daniel Dennett, *Elbow Room: The Varieties of Free Will Worth Wanting* (Cambridge, MA: MIT Press, 1984).
18. Nagel, *The View from Nowhere*, 6.
19. In his article "The Myth of the Subjective" Davidson criticizes Fodor by saying that "it is instructive to find the effort to make psychology scientific turning into a search for internal propositional states that can be detected and identified apart from relations to the rest of the world, much as earlier philosophers sought for something 'given in experience' which contained no necessary

clue to what was going on outside. The motive is similar in the two cases: it is thought that a sound footing, whether for knowledge or for psychology, requires something inner in the sense of being nonrelational." Donald Davidson, "The Myth of the Subjective" (1988), in *Philosophical Essays*, vol. 3: *Subjective, Intersubjective, Objective* (Oxford: Clarendon, 2001), 51.

20. Barry Stroud, *The Significance of Philosophical Scepticism* (Oxford: Clarendon Press, 1984), 30.

21. Stroud, *The Significance of Philosophical Scepticism*, 35.

22. Stroud, *The Significance of Philosophical Scepticism*, 43.

23. Michael Williams, *Unnatural Doubts: Epistemological Realism and the Basis of Scepticism* (Cambridge, MA: Blackwell, 1991; Princeton: Princeton University Press, 1996), 35.

24. Williams, *Unnatural Doubts*, xx.

25. Williams, *Unnatural Doubts*, 35.

26. Williams, *Unnatural Doubts*, 37.

27. Williams, *Unnatural Doubts*, 35.

28. Williams, *Unnatural Doubts*, 35.

29. Williams, *Unnatural Doubts*, 354.

30. Williams, *Unnatural Doubts*, 12.

31. Williams, *Unnatural Doubts*, 91.

32. Williams, *Unnatural Doubts*, 91.

33. Williams, *Unnatural Doubts*, 119.

34. Williams, *Unnatural Doubts*, 116.

35. Williams, *Unnatural Doubts*, 119.

36. Williams, *Unnatural Doubts*, 134.

37. Stroud, *The Significance of Philosophical Skepticism*, 13.

38. See Williams, *Unnatural Doubts*, 117.

39. Williams, *Unnatural Doubts*, 121.

40. Bieri, "Why Is Consciousness Puzzling?" gives "Why is there anything at all rather than nothing?" as an example of an "idle metaphysical question" (55) which contrasts with the non-idle and proper question about the origin of consciousness. I would urge that the former question can be given a context, a job, and a certain urgency just as easily as the latter. For an example of a language-game in which it acquires all these, see Heidegger's *Was ist Metaphysik?*

41. Hilary Putnam, "The Question of Realism" in Putnam, *Words and Life* (Cambridge, MA: Harvard University Press, 1994), 299, quoted in James Conant, "Introduction," in Putnam, *Words and Life*, xxix.

42. Conant, "Introduction," xxv.

43. Conant, "Introduction," xxvi.

44. Conant, "Introduction," xxx–xxxi.

7. Ethics without Universal Obligations

Full bibliographical references have been added to the endnotes in accordance with Rorty, *Philosophy and Social Hope*, 72–90 (New York: Penguin, 1999) (hereafter *PSH*). The Girona lecture manuscript has additional citations, however, which I have retained here, noting when they have been deleted from *PSH* and what material has been affected. Ed.

1. John Dewey, *Human Nature and Conduct*, in Dewey, *The Middle Works, 1899–1924* vol. 14: *1922*, ed. Jo Ann Boydston (Carbondale: Southern Illinois University Press, 1983), 224.

2. Dewey, *Human Nature and Conduct*, 56–57.

3. Dewey, *Human Nature and Conduct*, 168.

4. Dewey, *Human Nature and Conduct*, 169.

5. Dewey, *Human Nature and Conduct*, 164. Annette Baier quotes Nietzsche's remark that "a bad smell of sado-masochism, the reek of blood and torture, lingers on the categorical imperative." Annette Baier, *Moral Prejudices* (Cambridge, MA: Harvard University Press, 1993), 277. I think that Dewey would have agreed with Nietzsche on this point, and also would have agreed with Baier when she says, "If we are to avoid the deficiencies of the mind and the perversity of heart which this Kantian tradition incorporates, then it is time that we stopped paying deferential lip service to Immanuel Kant or, indeed, to any other preachers of the piety that consists in reverence for the faith of our patriarchal fathers" (267).

This reference to Baier's citation from Nietzsche and the comparison with Dewey are missing from *PSH*. See p. 89. Ed.

6. Annette Baier, "Knowing Our Mind in the Animal World," in Baier, *Postures of the Mind* (Minneapolis: University of Minnesota Press, 1985),147.

7. Baier, "Doing without Moral Theory," in Baier, *Postures of the Mind*, 232.

8. Baier, "Doing without Moral Theory," 236.

9. Baier, "Theory and Reflective Practices," in Baier, *Postures of the Mind*, 208.

10. Dewey, *Human Nature and Conduct*, 95.

11. Dewey, *Human Nature and Conduct*, 96.

12. Dewey, *Human Nature and Conduct*, 96.

13. See Donald Davidson, "Paradoxes of Irrationality," in *Philosophical Essays on Freud*, ed. Richard Wollheim and James Hopkins (Cambridge: Cambridge University Press, 1982). Davidson's view of Freud is expanded and developed by Marcia Cavell in *The Psychoanalytic Mind: From Freud to Philosophy* (Cambridge, MA: Harvard University Press, 1993). See also Michael Walzer, *Thick and Thin: Moral Argument at Home and Abroad* (Notre Dame, IN: University of Notre Dame Press, 1994), ch. 5, "The Divided Self"; and especially Walzer's suggestion that "thick, divided selves are the characteristic products of, and in turn require, a thick, differentiated and pluralist society" (101)—a suggestion which Dewey would have heartily endorsed.

At p. 89 Walzer offers an instructive and invidious comparison between the philosopher's and the psychoanalyst's approach to division within the self.

The references to chapter 5 of Walzer's *Thick and Thin* are not included in *PSH*. See p. 89. Ed.

14. Baier, "Secular Faith," in Baier, *Postures of the Mind*, 293.

15. Here I draw upon Daniel Dennett's very enlightening account of the self as a "center of narrative gravity" in his *Consciousness Explained* (Boston: Little, Brown, 1991). I have attempted to develop the anti-essentialism of the second of these lectures in an article on Dennett, in which I suggest that what goes for selves goes for objects in general, and that a pragmatist should think of all objects as centers of descriptive gravity. See my "Holism, Intentionality, and the Ambition of Transcendence," in *Dennett and His Critics: Demystifying Mind*, ed. Bo Dahlbom, 184–202 (Oxford: Blackwell, 1993).

In *PSH* Rorty refers to the essay as it appeared under a different title: Richard Rorty, "Daniel Dennett on Intrinsicality," in *Philosophical Papers*, vol. 3: *Truth and Progress*, 98–121 (Cambridge: Cambridge University Press, 1998). Ed.

16. As I see it, the notion of a "universal validity claim," as used by Habermas and Apel, is just the claim to such a medal, and is thus dispensable. Although I entirely agree with Habermas about the desirability of substituting what he calls "communicative reason" for "subject-centered reason," I think of his insistence on universality, and his dislike for what he calls "contextualism" and "relativism," as leftovers from metaphysics: leftovers from a period of philosophical thought in which it seemed that an appeal to the universal was the only alternative to immersion in the contingent status quo. I have tried to develop this criticism of Habermas in my "Sind Aussagen universelle Geltungsansprüche?" forthcoming in *Deutsche Zeitschrift für Philosophie*.

This last sentence is not in *PSH*. The reference is to Rorty, "Sind Aussagen universelle Geltungsansprüche?" *Deutsche Zeitschrift für Philosophie* 42, no. 6 (1994): 975–988; see also Lectures 2 and 3 in this volume. Ed.

17. See Ronald Dworkin, *Taking Rights Seriously* (Cambridge, MA: Harvard University Press, 1978). For criticism of the tradition Dworkin praises, see Mary Ann Glendon, *Rights Talk: The Impoverishment of Political Discourse* (New York: Free Press, 1991).

In *PSH*, this endnote has been deleted. See p. 89. Ed.

18. This is a point which I emphasize in Rorty, "Human Rights, Rationality, and Sentimentality," in *On Human Rights: The Oxford Amnesty Lectures 1993*, ed. Stephen Shute and Susan Hurley (New York: Basic Books, 1993). That paper offers a more extended version of the view of human rights which I am summarizing here.

In *PSH*, Rorty added a reference to the republication of this essay in his "Human Rights, Rationality, and Sentimentality," in *Philosophical Papers*, vol. 3: *Truth and Progress*, 167–185 (Cambridge: Cambridge University Press, 1998). Ed.

19. Here again I agree with Habermas about the linguistic character of rationality, but try to use this doctrine to show that we need not think in universalist terms. Habermas's universalism, of course, forbids him to adopt the view of human rights I am offering here. The view that I am offering in these lectures is anti-universalistic, in the sense that it discourages attempts to formulate generalizations which cover all possible forms of human existence. Hope for a presently unimaginably better human future is hope that no generalization we can presently formulate will be adequate to cover that future.

20. John Dewey, *Reconstruction in Philosophy,* in Dewey, *The Middle Works, 1899–1924,* vol. 12: *1920,* ed. Jo Ann Boydston (Carbondale: Southern Illinois University Press, 1982), 179: "When the consciousness of science is fully impregnated with the consciousness of human value, the greatest dualism which now weighs humanity down, the split between the material, the mechanical, the scientific and the moral and ideal will be destroyed." I view the work of post-Kuhnian philosophers, historians, and sociologists of science as having helped with this task of fuller impregnation. See, for example, Steven Shapin and Simon Schaffer, *Leviathan and the Air-Pump* (Princeton: Princeton University Press, 1985); and Bruno Latour, *We Have Never Been Modern* (Cambridge, MA: Harvard University Press, 1993). Latour's book argues for a thesis which Dewey would have heartily endorsed: that the distinction between the "found" realm of nature and the "made" realm of society is thoroughly misleading. This endnote was deleted in *PSH*. Ed.

21. Hilary Putnam, *The Many Faces of Realism* (La Salle, IL: Open Court, 1987), 70. I explore the differences between my version of pragmatism and Putnam's in Richard Rorty, "Putnam and the Relativist Menace," *Journal of Philosophy* 90, no. 9 (1993): 443–461. This endnote was deleted in *PSH*. Ed.

8. Justice as a Larger Loyalty

Full bibliographical references have been added to the endnotes in accordance with Rorty, "Justice as a Larger Loyalty," in *Philosophical Papers,* vol. 4: *Philosophy as Cultural Politics,* 42–55 (Cambridge: Cambridge University Press, 2007) (hereafter *PCP*). The Girona lecture manuscript has additional citations, however, which I have retained here, noting when they have been deleted from *PCP* and what material has been affected. Ed.

1. Donald Fites, the CEO of the Caterpillar tractor company, explained his company's policy of relocation abroad by saying that "as a human being, I think what is going on is positive. I don't think it is realistic for 250 Americans to control so much of the world's GNP." (Quoted in Edward Luttwak, *The Endangered American Dream* (New York: Simon and Schuster, 1993), 184.)

2. Michael Walzer, *Thick and Thin: Moral Argument at Home and Abroad* (Notre Dame, IN: Notre Dame University Press, 1994), 4.

3. Baier's picture is quite close to that sketched by Wilfrid Sellars and Robert Brandom in their quasi-Hegelian accounts of moral progress as the expansion of the circle of beings who count as "us." See Annette Baier, *Moral Prejudices: Essays on Ethics* (Cambridge, MA: Harvard University Press, 1994).

4. John Rawls, *Political Liberalism* (New York: Columbia University Press, 1993), 14n15.

5. This sort of debate runs through a lot of contemporary philosophy. Compare, for example, Walzer's contrast between starting thin and starting thick with that between the Platonic-Chomskian notion that we start with meanings and descend to use, and the Wittgensteinian-Davidsonian notion that we start with use and then skim off meaning as needed for lexicographical or philosophical purposes.

6. John Rawls, "The Law of Peoples," in *On Human Rights: The Oxford Amnesty Lectures, 1993*, ed. Stephen Shute and Susan Hurley, 41–82 (New York: Basic Books, 1993), 44. I am not sure why Rawls thinks historicism undesirable, and there are passages, both early and recent, in which he seems to throw in his lot with the historicists. (See the passage quoted in note 11 below from his recent "Reply to Habermas.") Some years ago I argued for the plausibility of an historicist interpretation of the metaphilosophy of Rawls's *A Theory of Justice* in my "The Priority of Democracy to Philosophy," reprinted in my *Philosophical Papers*, vol. 1: *Objectivity, Relativism and Truth*, 175–196 (Cambridge: Cambridge University Press, 1991).

7. Rawls, "The Law of Peoples," 81.

8. Rawls, "The Law of Peoples," 61.

In *PCP*, endnotes 7–8 have been combined as footnote 7. Ed.

9. Rawls, "The Law of Peoples," 63.

10. Rawls, "The Law of Peoples," 62.

11. All quotations in this paragraph are from Jürgen Habermas, *Justification and Application: Remarks on Discourse Ethics*, trans. Ciaran P. Cronin (Cambridge, MA: MIT Press, 1993; originally published in German in 1991), 95. Habermas is here commenting on Rawls's use of "reasonable" in writings earlier than "The Law of Peoples." The latter appeared subsequent to Habermas's book.

When I wrote the present paper, the exchange between Rawls and Habermas published in the *Journal of Philosophy* (1995) had not yet appeared. This exchange rarely occasionally touches on the question of historicism vs. universalism. But one passage in which this question emerges explicitly is in Rawls, "Reply to Habermas": "Justice as fairness is substantive . . . in the sense that it springs from and belongs to the tradition of liberal thought and the larger community of political culture of democratic societies. It fails then to be properly formal and truly universal, and thus to be part of the quasi-transcendental presuppositions (as Habermas sometimes says) established by the theory of communicative action" (179). Jürgen Habermas, "Reconciliation through the Public Use of Reason: Remarks on John Rawls's Political Liberalism," and John Rawls, "Political Liberalism: Reply to Habermas," both in *Journal of Philosophy* 92, no. 3 (1995).

12. Habermas, *Justification and Application*, 95–96.

13. Rawls, "The Law of Peoples," 46.

14. My own view is that we do not need, either in epistemology or in moral philosophy, the notion of universal validity. I argue for this in Richard Rorty, "Sind Aussagen universelle Geltungsansprüche?" *Deutsche Zeitschrift für Philosophie* 42, no. 6 (1994): 975–988. Habermas and Apel find my view paradoxical, and likely to produce performative self-contradiction.
See Lectures 3 & 4 in this volume. Ed.

15. Rawls, "The Law of Peoples," 46.

16. Both quotations are from Rawls, "The Law of Peoples," 45.

17. I quote here from Rawls's summary of Scanlon's view; Rawls, *Political Liberalism*, 49n2.

18. Walzer thinks it is a good idea for people to have lots of different moral identities: "thick, divided selves are the characteristic products of, and in turn require, a thick, differentiated, and pluralist society" (Walzer, *Thick and Thin*, 101).

19. Note that in Rawls's semi-technical sense an overlapping consensus is not the result of discovering that various comprehensive views already share common doctrines, but rather something that might never have emerged had the proponents of these views not started trying to cooperate.

20. Davidson has, I think, demonstrated that any two beings that use language to communicate with one another necessarily share an enormous number of beliefs and desires. He has thereby shown the incoherence of the idea that people can live in separate worlds created by differences in culture or status or fortune. There is always an immense overlap—an immense reserve army of common beliefs and desires to be drawn on at need. But this immense overlap does not, of course, prevent accusations of craziness or diabolical wickedness. For only a tiny amount of non-overlap about certain particularly touchy subjects (the border between two territories, the name of the One True God) may lead to such accusations, and eventually to violence.

21. I owe this line of thought about how to reconcile Habermas and Baier to Mary Rorty.

22. This notion of "the better argument" is central to Habermas's and Apel's understanding of rationality. I criticize it in the article cited above in note 14.
See Lectures 3 & 4 in this volume. Ed.

23. For a claim that such a theory of truth is essential to "the Western Rationalist Tradition," see John Searle, "Rationality and Realism: What Difference Does It Make?" *Daedelus* 122, no. 4 (Fall 1992): 55–84. See also my reply to Searle

in Rorty, "Does Academic Freedom Have Philosophical Presuppositions?" *Academe* 80, no. 6 (November–December 1994): 52–63. I argue there that we should be better off without the notion of "getting something right," and that writers such as Dewey and Davidson have shown us how to keep the benefits of Western rationalism without the philosophical hang-ups caused by the attempt to explicate this notion.

In *PCP*, Rorty changed the reference to the version republished under a different title: Richard Rorty, "John Searle on Realism and Relativism," *Philosophical Papers*, vol. 3: *Truth and Progress*, 63–83 (Cambridge: Cambridge University Press, 1998). Ed.

9. Is There Anything Worth Saving in Empiricism?

The in-text citations of the original manuscript have been turned into endnotes, and full bibliographical references added, as well as references to citations that have since appeared in print. Ed.

1. Wilfrid Sellars, "Empiricism and the Philosophy of Mind," sec. 29.

This essay, first published in 1956, was first reprinted in Sellars, *Science, Perception and Reality* (London: Routledge, 1963). It was reprinted as a book: Sellars, *Empiricism and the Philosophy of Mind* (Cambridge, MA: Harvard University Press, 1997), which includes an introduction by Richard Rorty and a commentary by Robert Brandom. Ed.

2. Sellars, "Empiricism and the Philosophy of Mind," sec. 50.

3. Robert Brandom, *Making It Explicit* (Cambridge, MA: Harvard University Press, 1994), 276 (emphasis added).

4. Brandom, *Making It Explicit*, 23. See also 77, 629.

5. Donald Davidson, "A Coherence Theory of Truth and Knowledge," in Ernst Lepore, ed., *Truth and Interpretation: Perspectives on the Philosophy of Donald Davidson*, 307–319 (Oxford: Blackwell, 1986), 314. Ed.

6. Davidson, "A Coherence Theory of Truth and Knowledge," 317.

7. See Davidson's remark that we do not "understand the notion of truth, as applied to language, independent of the notion of translation (Davidson, "On the Very Idea of a Conceptual Scheme," in *Inquiries into Truth and Interpretation*, (Oxford: Oxford University Press, 1984), 194). Compare Sellars's claim that "semantical statements of the Tarski-Carnap variety do not assert relations between linguistic and extra-linguistic items" (Wilfrid Sellars, *Science and Metaphysics* [London: Routledge and Kegan Paul, 1968], 82), but rather relate linguistic items with whose use we are familiar, elements of a language we already know, with other linguistic items. (See also Sellars, "Empiricism and the Philosophy of Mind," sec. 31.)

8. Brandom, *Making It Explicit*, 152–153.

9. Donald Davidson, "The Myth of the Subjective," in Michael Krausz, ed. *Relativism: Interpretation and Confrontation*, 159–172 (Notre Dame, IN: Notre Dame University Press, 1989), 165–666.

10. Brandom, *Making It Explicit*, 495–496.

11. Brandom, *Making It Explicit*, 515.

12. Brandom, *Making It Explicit*, 594–595.

13. Brandom, *Making It Explicit*, 594.

14. Brandom, *Making It Explicit*, 600.

15. Brandom, *Making It Explicit*, 600.

16. Brandom, *Making It Explicit*, 601; emphasis added.

17. Brandom, *Making It Explicit*, 331.

18. Brandom's essay later appeared as "Vocabularies of Pragmatism: Synthesizing Naturalism and Historicism" in Robert B. Brandom, ed., *Rorty and His Critics* (Malden, MA: Blackwell, 2000), 156–183, with a response by Richard Rorty, 183–189. "Vocabularies of Pragmatism" was reprinted in Robert Brandom, *Perspectives on Pragmatism: Classical, Recent, & Contemporary*, 116–157 (Cambridge, MA: Harvard University Press, 2011). Ed.

19. Brandom, "Vocabularies of Pragmatism," *Perspectives on Pragmatism*, 125.

10. McDowell's Version of Empiricism

The in-text citations of the original manuscript have been turned into endnotes, and full bibliographical references added, as well as references to citations that have since appeared in print. Ed.

1. John McDowell, *Mind and World*, with a new introduction by the author (Cambridge, MA: Harvard University Press, 1996), xi–xii.

2. This, of course, is the point at which people begin to quarrel about whether to be "realists" about artistic, moral and political judgments. The recent prevalence of utterly pointless quarrels about when and where there is "a fact of the matter"—quarrels whose participants have never been able to say what difference in practice would be made by the victory of one side or the other—seems to me to give us good reason to banish the term "fact of the matter" from philosophy. I fear that if "world-directedness" becomes popular it will encourage people to prolong these tedious controversies about "realism."

3. McDowell, *Mind and World*, xii.

4. McDowell, *Mind and World*, xii.

5. McDowell, *Mind and World*, 68.

6. McDowell, *Mind and World*, xii.

7. McDowell, *Mind and World*, xv.

8. McDowell, *Mind and World*, xvi.

9. McDowell, *Mind and World*, xvii.

10. McDowell, *Mind and World,* 142n17. In this footnote McDowell is criticizing me rather than Sellars and Davidson. But what he says goes for them if they are interpreted as I interpret them, as saying that renouncing empiricism will leave us in Wittgensteinian peace and Humean good spirits—able to walk away from the traditional epistemological problematic with a good conscience.

11. McDowell, *Mind and World,* 86.

12. McDowell, *Mind and World,* 143.

13. McDowell, *Mind and World,* xxiii.

14. McDowell, *Mind and World,* xxiii.

15. McDowell, *Mind and World,* xvi.

16. McDowell, *Mind and World,* xvii.

17. McDowell, *Mind and World,* xix.

18. For criticism of Davidson on this point, see Rorty, "Davidson's Mental-Physical Distinction," in Lewis Hahn, ed., *The Philosophy of Donald Davidson,* 575–594 (La Salle, IL: Open Court, 1999).

19. McDowell, *Mind and World,* 72.

20. McDowell, *Mind and World,* 108.

21. Another way of putting this point is to say that intelligibility is cheap: you can get it just by training people to talk in a certain way. That a view is intuitive, or a phrase intelligible, shows very little about the utility of either. By way of contrast, consider McDowell's claim that "the sheer intelligibility of the idea [of openness to facts] is enough" for his purposes (of finding a middle way between bald naturalism and the renunciation of empiricism) (McDowell, *Mind and World,* 113). He thinks that the idea of our being open to facts has an advantage in "intelligibility" over that of "the fact itself impressing itself on a perceiver." But any greater plausibility of metaphors of transparency over metaphors of impression is entirely a function of the rhetoric to which one has previously been exposed.

In *TP* "exposed" has been changed to "charmed." See p. 145, footnote 18. Ed.

22. McDowell, *Mind and World,* xix.

23. McDowell, *Mind and World,* xx.

24. McDowell, *Mind and World,* 84.

25. McDowell, *Mind and World,* p. 111.

26. John McDowell, "Knowledge and the Internal," *Philosophy and Phenomenological Research* 55, no. 4, (December 1995): 877–893, 887.

27. McDowell, *Mind and World,* xx.

28. McDowell, *Mind and World,* xx.

29. McDowell, *Mind and World,* 109.

30. McDowell, *Mind and World,* 68.

31. Davidsonians like me explicate Kant's slogan "concepts without intuitions are empty" as "linguistic behavior which is not interpreted, eventually, by reference to its causal interaction with the speaker's environment is not interpretable

at all." So we drop the metaphors of fullness and emptiness in favor of metaphors of causal relatedness and lack of causal relatedness.

32. McDowell, *Mind and World*, 151.

33. McDowell, *Mind and World*, 151. In *TP* Rorty incorrectly cites p. 51. The page reference has been corrected. Ed.

34. McDowell, *Mind and World*, 177.

Epilogue

1. Information on the Ferrata Mora Chair can be found at: https://www.catedraferratermora.cat/catedra/historia/en/.

2. For a good overview and sampling of Ferrater Mora's philosophical work, see José Ferrater Mora, *Three Spanish Philosophers: Unamuno, Ortega y Gasset, Ferrater Mora*, edited and with an introduction by J. M. Terricabras (Albany: SUNY Press, 2003).

3. This is the same list of titles announced on the website of the Ferrater Mora Chair. See: https://www.catedraferratermora.cat/llicons/en/rorty/

4. In Catalan they appeared as Richard Rorty, *El pragmatisme, una versió. Anti-autoritarisme en ètica i epistemologia* (Vic: Eumo Editorial, 1998) and in Spanish as Richard Rorty, *El pragmatismo, una versión. Antiautoritarismo en ética y epistemología* (Barcelona: Editorial Ariel, 2000). Both versions were translated by Joan Vergés Gifra.

5. Richard Rorty, *Hoffnung statt Erkenntnis: Eine Einführung in die pragmatische Philosophie*, trans. Joachim Schulte (Wien: Passagen Verlag, 1994), and *L'Espoir au lie de savoir: Introduction au pragmatisme*, trans. Claudia Cowan and Jacques Poulain (Paris: Albin Michel, 1995).

6. Richard Rorty, *Philosophy and Social Hope* (New York: Penguin Books, 1999), 23–90.

7. Rorty, *Philosophy and Social Hope*, xiii.

8. Richard Rorty, *Philosophie und die Zukunft: Essays* (Frankfurt am Main: Fischer Taschenbuch Verlag, 2000), 7–8. My translation.

9. For further discussion of Rorty's intellectual itinerary, see my "Richard Rorty's Intellectual Biography," in *Handbuch Richard Rorty*, ed. Marti Müller (Springer, forthcoming).

10. Richard Rorty, *Truth, Politics, and "Post-Modernism"* (Assen: Van Gorcum, 1997).

11. This book has a preface that should be translated so that we can understand how Rorty's work on epistemology and ethics relates to his work on political philosophy.

12. See Christopher J. Voparil, *Richard Rorty: Politics and Vision* (Lanham, MD: Rowman and Littlefield, 2006), as well as his introduction to *The Rorty Reader*

(Oxford: Wiley-Blackwell, 2010), an anthology he co-edited with Richard J. Bernstein.

13. See Richard Rorty, *Take Care of Freedom and Truth Will Take Care of Itself: Interview with Richard Rorty,* edited and with an introduction by Eduardo Mendieta (Stanford: Stanford University Press, 2006), 161–205.

14. See the Foreword by Robert B. Brandom in this volume, page vii.

Index